James Walter White

Flora of the Bristol Coal-Field

Part 1

James Walter White

Flora of the Bristol Coal-Field
Part 1

ISBN/EAN: 9783743325913

Manufactured in Europe, USA, Canada, Australia, Japa

Cover: Foto ©ninafisch / pixelio.de

Manufactured and distributed by brebook publishing software (www.brebook.com)

James Walter White

Flora of the Bristol Coal-Field

FLORA

OF THE

BRISTOL COAL-FIELD.

EDITED (FOR THE BRISTOL NATURALISTS' SOCIETY) BY

JAMES WALTER WHITE,

Hon. Secretary of the Botanical Section.

"*Rerum cognoscere causas.*"—VIRGIL.

PART I.

THALAMIFLORÆ.

BRISTOL:
JAMES FAWN & SON.
PRINTED BY E. AUSTIN & SON, CHRONICLE OFFICE, CLIFTON.
MDCCCLXXXI.

INTRODUCTION.

SEVEN years have elapsed since the Botanical Section resolved to commence the compilation of a local Flora. At that time our knowledge of the plants of the district was very imperfect; but in view of the fact that the publication could only be issued by annual instalments spread over a lengthened period, it was not considered wise to defer the beginning, lest perchance the end might never be attained. Thus, under many adverse conditions, the work was undertaken and carried through; gathering, as it advanced year by year, increased solidity and completeness, in proportion to the growing extent and accuracy of our own information.

Knowing this, the reader will need no explanation of what is plainly perceptible; namely, that the later portions of the "Flora" are distinctly superior to the earlier ones, both in knowledge of the occurrence of individual species, and in fulness of detail concerning their distribution.

"Additions" to parts previously published preface each of the last four numbers, and show how rapid has been our progress towards an exact acquaintance with Bristol botany. The sum of the species given in regular sequence is 986. Besides these, seventeen are recorded in the additions, making in all the large total of 1,003 species treated as inhabitants of the Bristol Coal-field. It may eventually be found that two or three of these have been included on insufficient grounds. On the other hand, in a district so extensive, and, in some portions, so imperfectly explored, we may anticipate that a few plants still remain to be discovered, as well as many additional facts to be recorded regarding the distribution of those already met with.

Our meagre botanical literature has been made use of to its full extent, as follows: two or three local references in the works of Hudson and Ray; a few pamphlets and manuscripts; some notices of Bristol plants, published chiefly in the *Phytologist;* and Swete's "Flora Bristoliensis," issued in 1854. Of the MS., a catalogue of Somersetshire plants by W. Sole, in the possession of Mr. T. B. Flower, is the most important. The notices in periodicals were mostly written by Mr. Flower, whose acquaintance with Bristol botany covers a period of half a century. He supplied a very large number of the localities given in Swete's "Flora," and to him we also are much indebted for many interesting and valuable communications. Withering's "Arrangement" contains many references to the vicinity of Bristol, but they are little to be relied on, and we have not thought it advisable to quote them, unless when confirmed by recent observation.

The Herbarium of the late Miss Powell, which is housed in the Bristol Museum, and that of the late Dr. Stephens, now the property of our Society, are excellent collections of local plants, made by trustworthy botanists. In them we have found specimens of great value, often corroborating book records which, in the absence of confirmation, might have been deemed unreliable and worthless; and in some instances furnishing examples of plants that cannot now be found, and may since have become extinct. These collections also possess the additional interest that they supplied a considerable proportion of the localities mentioned by Swete, who, as his pages show, relied almost entirely upon the three botanists we have named. It is only to be regretted that many of Dr. Stephens' specimens lack essential particulars of date or place of collection, without which such witnesses can render little service.

The Rev. R. P. Murray has very liberally furnished us with notes taken from his researches among the plants of Somersetshire; and we are very grateful to several other naturalists outside our ranks who have cheerfully contributed their labour.

Our chief aim in the construction of this "Flora," undoubtedly has been to use such care and precision as should engender confidence in its accuracy on the part of those who may have occasion to consult it. It is accordingly the Editor's intention to at once begin revising the earlier Parts, with a view to the preparation of a second edition. To that end we now venture to address a request to the friends who have already favoured us, as well as to our own members, that they will aid in making the work as complete and accurate as possible. The correction of any errors which may exist, the confirmation of stations resting on old or doubtful authority, and additional plants or stations from any part of the district, will all be very gladly received, especially when accompanied by specimens. Supported by such aid, we may not unreasonably expect to lay before the Society in our next effort a thoroughly worthy account of the botanical wealth of Bristol.

June, 1886.

EXPLANATORY NOTE.

IN introducing to the reader the first instalment of the new local Flora which has been undertaken by the Bristol Naturalists' Society, a few words from the President may serve to explain both the origin of the work and the method in which it is proposed to carry it out.

The want of a published Flora embracing the whole of the district known as the Bristol Coal-field, with its wide diversity of hill and dale, wood, river, and marsh, and its great variety of geological formation, has been long felt by the local botanist; and our Society had not been many years in existence before this want found expression in a series of resolutions, which were submitted by Mr. Leipner, the Honorary Secretary, and which pledged the members to undertake the registration of all objects of natural history found within a specified area, with a view to publication. These resolutions were adopted by the Society so long ago as the year 1864, but, although considerable progress has been made in other departments of natural history, it was not until about two years since that any systematic attempt was made to collect materials for a Phanerogamic Flora. In the spring of 1879 a programme of weekly excursions was organised by the Botanical Section of the Society, with the definite object of acquiring such a knowledge of the Botany of the district as might justify the publication of a Flora. These excursions have been continued in each succeeding year, and have been useful in keeping up a general interest in the work; although, necessarily, the chief labour has fallen upon a very few individuals. To the Honorary Secretary of the Botanical Section, who edits the publication, the Society is especially indebted.

The area chosen by the Society for the botanical, as for the other fields of research and registration, is that adopted by the late Mr. William Sanders in his geological "Map of the Bristol Coal-fields and country adjacent." It extends to different distances in different directions. In a northerly and north-easterly direction it includes Berkeley, Dursley, and Wotton-under-Edge; south-eastward, it takes in Bath; southward, Shepton Mallet and Wells; while in a south-westerly direction it reaches as far as Huntspill, which is twenty-four miles distant from Bristol. Altogether, it comprises (roughly) about 700 square miles.

A work embracing so large an area, and the preparation of which has extended over so short a time, must necessarily be incomplete, especially in its earlier portions. It is believed, however, that it will be found to be accurate.

It is intended that a portion of the work shall be published with each annual Part of the Proceedings of the Society until it is complete. The instalment now presented contains Thalamiflorals; the second will contain Calyciflorals; the third, Corolliflorals; the fourth, Apetalous Plants; and the fifth and last, Endogens, Gymnosperms, and Vascular Cryptogams.

The arrangement and nomenclature used are almost entirely those adopted by Professor Babington in the seventh edition of his "Manual of British Botany."

Although bound up with the Proceedings, the Flora will be paged independently, with a view to the ultimate collection of the several parts into a single volume.

The help of botanists residing within the district is solicited, that the work may be as complete as possible. Information of omissions in any published part will be gladly received by the Editor, and will be recorded in a supplementary list.

Certain abbreviations used in the Flora require explanation. The capital letters G. and S. indicate the counties of Gloucester and Somerset respectively. The Roman numerals denote the months in which the plants have been found in flower.

June, 1881.

PHANEROGAMIA.

Class 1. *DICOTYLEDONES.*
Div. 1. *THALAMIFLORÆ.*

RANUNCULACEÆ.

CLEMATIS, *L.*

1. **C. Vitalba,** *L. Old Man's Beard, Traveller's Joy,* "because of its decking and adorning the ways and hedges where people travel," *Gerarde*, p. 886.

    Native; frequent throughout the district, though mostly on calcareous soil. It appears to prefer submaritime situations. VII.—IX.

THALICTRUM, *L.*

2. **T. minus,** *L. β. (T. montanum, Wallr.)*

    Native; on limestone rocks, very local. Grows plentifully on the Cheddar Cliffs. It occurs also in the vicinity of Clifton, where we believe it to be native. Here, however, it shows no inclination to spread and become plentiful, a few plants only having been observed at any time. It was first recorded in the Bristol habitat by Sole about 1786, and has been gathered there by Mr. T. B. Flower, who possesses Sole's manuscript containing his record. Mr. G. H. K. Thwaites also found it many years ago, as did Mr. C. B. Dunn in 1875. Two plants were known to exist in 1880. VI.—VII.

3. **T. minus,** *L.* γ. *(T. flexuosum, Bernh.)*
   Native; at Cheddar, where it has undoubtedly been found. This view is in accordance with that of Dr. Boswell-Syme expressed in E. B., ed. 3 This is one of the many segregates into which the Linnæan *minus* has been divided. Their history and recognition form one of the most difficult studies afforded by our Flora to the critical botanist.

   (*T. saxatile, Schleich.*, has been reported from Cheddar, but probably in error, as is now thought by Professor Babington.)

4. **T. flavum,** *L.* *Common Meadow-Rue.*
   Native; in wet places, not common.
   G. Baptist Mills. Stapleton.
   S. In plenty by the Avon, opposite Cook's Folly. Long Ashton, Yatton, and the marshes in the Cheddar Valley. VII. VIII.

ANEMONE, *L.*

5. **A. nemorosa,** *L.* *Wood Anemone.*
   Native; in woods and thickets; common, but much more abundant in some localities than in others. III.—V.

ADONIS, *L.*

6. **A. autumnalis,** *L.* *Pheasants' Eye.*
   Alien or colonist; as a weed on cultivated land. Is only of casual occurrence, not being permanently established in this district.
   G. Near the old quarry (now filled up), Durdham Down, July, 1855. Specimen in the Stephens' Herbarium from Baptist Mills, no date.
   S. Wookey, "one plant yearly for some time," *Miss Livett.* VII.

RANUNCULUS, *L.*

7. R. tricophyllus, *Chaix.*
Native; in ponds and ditches, frequent. The rare form with floating leaves grows in a pond by the roadside near Charfield, G. V. VI.

8. R. Drouetii, *F. Schultz.*
Native; in marsh ditches, rare.
G. Sea Mills.
S. Between Portbury and Weston-in-Gordano. V. VI.

9. R. heterophyllus, *Fries.*
Native; in ponds and streams, rare.
G. Chipping Sodbury. Shirehampton. New Passage.
V. VI.

10. R. Baudotii, *Godr.*
Native; in ponds and ditches of brackish water near the estuaries, frequent. V.—VIII.
β. *(R. confusus, Godr.)* Differs so slightly from *R. Baudotii* that it cannot be separated from it except by the length of the stamens.
G. Shirehampton marshes, and ditches east of New Passage. V.—VIII.

11. R. peltatus, *Fries.*
Native; rare and local. The typical plant *(a. vulgaris, Syme's E. B.)* grows in a pool near Yate Station, G.
V.—IX.

12. R. floribundus, *Bab.*
Native; more general than the last.
G. Near Chipping Sodbury, Shirehampton, Westbury.
S. Portbury. V.—IX.

13. R. penicellatus, *Hiern.*
A plant which grows in running water, and is abundant in the stream at Cheddar, S., near the mills, must be

placed here. Floating leaves are absent, and those submersed are long with flaccid segments. It is probably *R. pseudofluitans*, Hiern., which may be identical with *R. peltatus, c. penicellatus* of the Lon. Cat., ed. 7. Another plant with still longer leaf segments is no doubt *d. elongatus* of the same Catalogue. It grows in the river Avon. True *R. fluitans* is not found in the district. V.—VIII.

14. R. circinatus, *Sibth*.
Native; in marsh ditches. locally common.
G. Shirehampton. Stapleton.
S. Very plentiful in the "rhines" throughout the marshlands, extending from Yatton and Weston-super-Mare to Draycot, Highbridge, and Wells. VII.—IX.

15. R. Lenormandi, *Shultz*.
Native; in shallow pools or on mud, rare.
G. Bitton. Shirehampton. VI.—VIII.

16. R. hederaceus, *L.*
Native; in like situations to those of the last species, but more common.
G. Bitton. Hook's Mills. Mangotsfield, near the railway station. Stapleton. Stoke Bishop, extremely local.
S. Ashton Park. Between Abbot's Leigh and Portbury.
VI.—IX.

17. R. sceleratus, *L.*
Native; by and in ditches and ponds, not uncommon.
G. Berkeley. Charfield. Hook's Mills. Lawrence-Weston. New Passage. Shirehampton. Thornbury.
S. Draycot. Kewstoke. Long Ashton. Portbury. Yatton. Wookey. VI.—IX.

18. R. Flammula, *L. Lesser Spearwort.*
Native; in swampy places, frequent. It varies greatly in size, habit. and shape of the leaves.

G. Berwick Wood. Filton Meads. Mangotsfield. Stapleton. Yate.

S. Abbot's Leigh. Ashton. Bedminster. Clevedon. Failand. Horrington. Yatton. VI.—VIII.

19. R. Lingua, *L.*
Native; rare and local.

S. In some spots on the moors, as near Clevedon, Walton-in-Gordano, and Yatton. VI.—VII.

20. R. Ficaria, *L.* *Lesser Celandine; Pilewort.*
Native; very common.

In the herbarium of the Bristol Naturalists' Society there are specimens of an abnormal form of this species, possessing 13 to 18 petals, and 5 sepals. These were gathered at Shirehampton in March, 1868, by the Rev. W. W. Spicer. IV.—V.

21. R. auricomus, *L.*
Native; in woods and shady places, generally distributed.
IV. V.

22. R. acris, *L.* *Meadow Crowfoot; Buttercup.*
Native; in meadows and pastures, very common.

The variation, *a. Steveni*, grows on the sand hills at Weston-super-Mare, and probably elsewhere in the district. VI. VII.

23. R. repens, *L.* *Creeping Crowfoot.*
Native; in moist places, common.

The primary stem in this species, especially in damp situations, is much more robust, and produces much larger flowers than the flowering shoots thrown up by the runners towards autumn. V.—VIII.

24. R. bulbosus, *L.* *Bulbous Crowfoot; Buttercup.*
Native; in pastures, &c., common.

A flower of this Buttercup has been observed in which the gynæceum was entirely absent. V.

25. **R. hirsutus,** *Curt.*
>   Native; on cultivated land, rare.
>   G. Lawrence-Weston. Stapleton.
>   S. Weston-super-Mare.
>   (*R. parvulus*, L., is a small few-flowered form.)   VI.—X.

26. **R. parviflorus,** *L.*
>   Native; in dry places, rare.
>   G. Baptist Mills. Henbury. Kingsweston. Lawrence-Weston.
>   S. Bedminster Down, near the three plantations.   V. VI.

27. **R. arvensis,** L.
>   Colonist, though apparently native; only on cultivated land, not very common, but very generally distributed.
>   VI.

CALTHA, *L.*

28. **C. palustris,** *L.* *Marsh Marigold.*
>   Native; in marshes and on ditch banks, common.
>   β. (*C. Guerangerii, Bor.*)
>   Rare; at Stapleton, G., and Wells, S., whence a good specimen was forwarded by *Miss Livett*, in April, 1880.
>   III.—V.

HELLEBORUS, *L.*

29. **H. viridis,** *L.* *Green Hellebore.*
>   Native, or denizen; in stony thickets, and old orchards in many places.
>   G. The cherry orchard near Westbury. Henbury Combe.
>   S. The Roman intrenchment in Leigh Wood. In a stony field at Failand. Bourton. Sandford. Wellesley, near Wells.   III. IV.

30. **H. fœtidus,** *L.* *Stinking Hellebore.*
>   Native; in woods, rather rare.
>   G. Stapleton Wood.

S. Brockley Combe. Cleeve Combe. Goblin Glen. Churchill. Near Ham Green. Kingswood, near Yatton. Frequent about Bath. III. IV.

AQUILEGIA, *L.*

31. A. vulgaris, *L. Columbine.*

Native; in woods and on bushy hills, preferring the limestone; frequent.

G. Durdham Down, in plenty. Westridge Wood, near Wotton-under-Edge.

S. Gurney Slade. King's Wood, near Yatton. Leigh Wood, opposite the Black Rock. Long Ashton, introduced on the G. W. Railway embankment. Portbury. Weston-in-Gordano. V. VI.

ACONITUM, *L.*

32. A. Napellus, *L. Monkshood.*

Alien; on river banks and in damp hedges, very rare.

S. A few plants by water in the corner of a copse near Failand Farm, these seemed to have escaped from garden refuse which had been cast near by. On the bank of a stream near Wells, apparently native, *Miss Livett.* Lane in Bourton leading to the Combe, *Miss Winter.* VI. VII.

DELPHINIUM, *L.*

33. D. Ajacis, *Gay. Larkspur.*

Alien or colonist. In a sandy field near Kewstoke, S. *T. F. Perkins!* The only record. VI. VII.

BERBERIDACEÆ.
BERBERIS, *L.*

34. B. vulgaris, *L. Barberry.*

Native, or denizen; in hedges and thickets. Usually it has been planted where found in this district.

S. Long Ashton. Castle Hill, Clevedon. V. VI.

(*Epimedium alpinum, L.*, was found in Leigh Wood many years ago by Dr. Rogers and Dr. Stephens. It was probably an escape, and there is now no sufficient reason for regarding the plant as a Bristol species.)

NYMPHÆACEÆ.
NYMPHÆA, *L.*

35. N. alba, *L.*   *White Water-Lily.*
  Native; in rivers and ponds, frequent.
   G. Pool near the railway at Dursley. Henbury. Redland. Shirehampton.
   S. Pools near Highbridge. Tickenham Moor.   VII.

NUPHAR, *Sm.*

36. N. lutea, *Sm.*   *Yellow Water-Lily.*
  Native; in rivers, ponds, and boggy ditches, frequent.
   G. In the river Avon near Hanham. Henbury. In the river Frome near Stapleton.   VII.

PAPAVERACEÆ.
PAPAVER, *L.*

37. P. Argemone, *L.*
  Colonist; in cornfields, very rare.
   G. Cornfields near Fishponds.   VI. VII.

38. P. hybridum, *L.*
  Colonist; in cornfields, very rare.
   S. Cornfields at Burnham, *Mr. T. B. Flower.* VI. VII.

39. P. Rhæas, *L.* *Red Poppy.*
  Colonist; on and about cultivated land, very common.
                                                    VI. VII.

40. P. dubium, *L.*
  Colonist; in waste and stony fields, and dry places, frequent. We have failed to distinguish *P. Lecoqii, Lamotte.*

G. Ashley. Near Combe Glen. Mangotsfield. Stapleton.
S. Clevedon. Dundry. Easton. Knowle. South Stoke. Twerton. Uphill. Very abundant about Weston-super-Mare during the summer of 1880, being then more common than *P. Rhœas*. VI. VII.

MECONOPSIS, *Vig.*

41. M. cambrica, *Vig. Welsh Poppy.*
Native; on the Cheddar Cliffs, S. Now scarce. VI.

GLAUCIUM, *Tourn.*

42. G. luteum, *Scop. Horned Poppy.*
Native; on the sandy shores of the Bristol Channel, from New Passage, G., to Burnham, S., but nowhere abundant.
VI.—VIII.

CHELIDONIUM, *L.*

43. C. majus, *L. Common Celandine.*
Denizen; on garden walls, and about farm buildings, rather common. Remarkably luxuriant plants have been observed by a cow yard at Kingsweston, G. It seems as if this plant cannot exist without a good supply of nitrogenous food. Always flourishing where there is house refuse or drainage from farm or cottage, it is most rarely or never to be seen in the open country. V.—VIII.

FUMARIACEÆ.

CORYDALIS, *Cand.*

(*C. solida*, Hook, is reported from near Wells, S., by *Miss Livett*. As an alien, not even naturalized in any part of the country, it must be excluded from our list.)

44. C. lutea, *DC. Yellow Fumitory.*
Alien; naturalized on walls, and about old gardens, frequent.

FUMARIACEÆ.

G. Filton. Henbury. Redland.
S. Brislington. Clevedon. Kewstoke. Long Ashton. Loxton. Milton. Norton. South Brent. Old walls under Dolbery Camp. Common on walls at Wells. Weston-in-Gordano. V.—VIII.

45. C. claviculata, *DC.*
Native; very rare,
S. St. Stephen's Hill, near Temple Cloud. *Mr. T. B. Flower.* VI. VII.

FUMARIA, L.

46. F. confusa, *Jord.*
Colonist; on cultivated land, rare.
G. Cornfields near Fishponds.
S. Wells. VI.—IX.

47. F. officinalis, *L.*
Colonist; on arable land, and as a garden weed, common.
VI.—IX.

CRUCIFERÆ.

CHEIRANTHUS, L.

48. C. Cheiri, *L. Wallflower.*
Alien, or denizen; on walls and rocks, rather common.
In great abundance on St. Vincent's Rocks, which are never so attractive as when in the early summer they teem with the fragrance of this beautiful Crucifer. V.

NASTURTIUM, R. Br.

49. N. officinale, *R. Br. Water Cress.*
Native; in ditches and running water. Very common, and very variable in size and appearance. VI. VII.

50. N. sylvestre, *R. Br.*
Native; on a river bank, very rare.
G. Bank of the Avon at Crew's Hole. VI. VIII.

CRUCIFERÆ.

51. N. palustre, *DC.*   *N. terrestre, Sm.*
  Native ; on river banks, and in wet places, very rare.
  G.   Frome Glen, near Stapleton.
  S.   On a peaty moor north of Shapwick.   VII. – IX.

BARBAREA, *R. Br.*

52. B. vulgaris, *R. Br.*
  Native ; in damp places, common.
  A plant differing widely from the type was gathered in the marsh by Stapleton Bridge, June, 1880. Its uppermost leaves were pinnatifid, with a toothed terminal lobe, pedicels and pods long, the latter spreading erect patent.   V.—VII.

53. B. præcox, *R. Br.*
  Colonist ; in dry and rocky places, frequent.
  G.   Conham. Montpelier. St. Vincent's Rocks. Stapleton.
  S.   Brislington. South Stoke. Clevedon.   V. VI.

ARABIS, *L.*

54. A. hirsuta, *R. Br.*
  Native.   Frequent on the limestone about Clifton, and on old walls in many places.   VI. VII.

55. A. stricta, *Huds.*
  Native ; on the limestone on both sides of the Avon at Clifton, and at Penpole Point. The only British habitat. This great rarity is to be found in many spots within its limited area, mostly upon the living rock, but sometimes amid débris from the quarries, and in turf. Unfortunately its situations are nearly always easy of access, and we are not aware that the plant has ever shewn a preference for the precipitous portions of the cliffs. Exposed as it is, therefore, to the ravages of plant collectors and thoughtless strangers, it behoves every botanist to do all that in him lies to guard it from destruction.   IV. V.

There is an interesting remark in "The British Herbal," by John Hill, M.D., pub. 1756. The author, when writing of the "Daisy-leaved Ladysmock, *Cardamine pumila bellidis folio*," says, "It is common on the mountains in Wales, whence the winds seem to have blown some of its seeds to Bristol; the plant some years being very frequent on St. Vincent's Rock." There is no doubt that Dr. Hill had in mind the *Arabis stricta*, but what other Crucifer he confounded with it is not apparent.

(*A. perfoliata*, *Lam.*, has but a slight claim to be considered a Bristol plant. On the authority of Withering in Turner and Dillwyn's Botanist's Guide it was once to be found on St. Vincent's Rocks, but has certainly not been seen there for very many years.)

CARDAMINE, *L.*

56. C. pratensis, *L.* *Cuckoo-flower.*
Native; in moist meadows, marshes, and on ditchbanks, very common. The flowers are occasionally double (Bishport, S., May, 1880), and in damp seasons some plants develop buds on the leaves, and small bulbs at the base of the stem, as supplementary means of propagation. IV. V.

57. C. impatiens, *L.*
Native; in but one habitat. Abundant on the Pennant at Stapleton, G.; chiefly on the right bank of the river Frome, near the mills. VII.

58. C. flexuosa, *With.* (*C. sylvatica*, *Link.*)
Native; in damp and shady places, common.
Rootstock shortly creeping. Radical leaves few. Biennial or perennial. IV. V.

CRUCIFERÆ.

59. C. hirsuta, *L.*
  Native; on walls, banks, &c., very common.
  Rootstock none. Annual. Stamens usually four. III. IV.

HESPERIS, *L.*

60. H. matronalis, *L.* *Dame's Violet.*
  Alien. A favourite plant in old cottage gardens, and occurs usually as an escape from cultivation.
  S. Formerly at Long Ashton, and at St. Anne's Wood, Brislington. Prior Park Woods, 1869. V. VI.

SISYMBRIUM, *L.*

61. S. officinale, *Scop.*
  Native; by roadsides, and in waste places everywhere.
  VI. VII.

62. S. Sophia, *L.*
  Native. "Undoubtedly gathered at Burnham, S., in 1869." *Miss Livett.* VI. VIII.

63. S. thalianum, *Gaud.*
  Native; on walls, banks, and cultivated ground, rather common.
  G. Baptist Mills. Frenchay. Plentiful about Stapleton. St. George's.
  S. Clevedon. Ham Green. Pill. Luxuriant in arable fields bordering St. Anne's Wood, Brislington. IV. V.

ALLIARIA, *Adans.*

64. A. officinalis, *Andrzj.* *Garlic Hedge Mustard.*
  Native; on hedgebanks, very common. V. VI.

ERYSIMUM, *L.*

65. E. cheiranthoides, *L.* *Worm-seed.*
  Native, or colonist. On cultivated or waste ground, and on peat soil in the south of the district; rare.
  G. Kingsdown, *Mr. Rootsey's List*, 1828. On walls at St. George's. Stapleton.

S. Bishport. Easton. Brislington. Uphill. In some plenty on Worlebury Hill, near Weston-super-Mare, 1880. Yatton. Near Shapwick.

BRASSICA, *L.*

66. **B. campestris,** *L. Swede.*

β. *B. Rapa, L. Turnip.*

Colonist; on borders of fields and cultivated land, and on river banks. Rather common. VII.

"I am unable to distinguish any constant difference between this plant and *B. Napus*, except that the radical leaves are hispid in *B. campestris* and glabrous in *B. Napus*. Sometimes the hairs on the radical leaves are very few, and confined to the midrib." *Dr. Boswell-Syme.*

(*B. Napus, L. Rape or Cole Seed.* An escape from cultivation. Perhaps not distinguishable from the last. "Whole plant very glaucous, and quite smooth." *Dr. Boswell-Syme.*)

SINAPIS, *L.*

67. **S. nigra,** *L. Black Mustard.*

Native; on river banks and in waste places. Frequent, especially on the banks of the Avon. VI. VIII.

68. **S. arvensis,** *L. The Common Charlock.*

Native, or colonist. In cornfields, and about arable land generally. Very common. V.—IX.

69. **S. alba,** *L. White Mustard.*

Native, or colonist; not so common about Bristol as *S. nigra*, but occurs frequently on cultivated land. VII.

DIPLOTAXIS, *DC.*

70. **D. tenuifolia,** *DC.*

Denizen; on old walls and buildings in Bristol and the vicinity, rare.

CRUCIFERÆ. 19

 G. Horfield. Hotwells. St. Philip's Marsh. Shirehampton.
 S. Totterdown. Knowle.   VII.—IX.

71. D. muralis, *DC.*
 Native, or colonist; abundant about Bristol, Weston-super-Mare, Clevedon, and elsewhere, preferring the coast. This plant is now much more plentiful than it was formerly, and has within a few years greatly extended its area in the West of England. We have both forms or varieties, but the plants are chiefly annual. Occasionally, however, may be noticed a fine biennial or perennial β. *Babingtonii,* probably sometimes mistaken for the last species, but always to be distinguished by the length of the pedicels, and shape of the leaves.
                 VI. VIII.

ALYSSUM, *L.*

72. A. maritimum, *L.*
 Alien; naturalized on rocks and in waste places near the sea. An escape from cultivation.
 S. Anchor Head Rocks, Weston-super-Mare. Clevedon.
                 VIII. IX.

DRABA, *L.*

73. D. muralis, *L.*
 Native; in one spot, very rare.
 G. In and about an old quarry at Henbury, where it was discovered by *Miss Powell* about 1846. Still growing there in 1879, but sparingly.   IV. V.

74. D. verna, *L. Common Whitlow-grass.*
 Native; on walls, banks, and dry rocky places, as on Durdham Down, Bristol; common.   III. IV.

COCHLEARIA, *L.*

75. C. officinalis, *L. Scurvy-grass.*
 Native; in submaritime situations, and on limestone rocks; very local.

S. Very luxuriant at Weston-super-Mare, in and about the wood, and at Birnbeck. Brean Down. Abundant on the Cheddar Cliffs. V. VI.

76. C. danica, *L.*

Native; on the shores of the Bristol Channel. Has been observed at New Passage, G., and at Weston-super-Mare, S. It may probably be gathered at many other places on the coast, but will not be found inland.

IV.—VI.

77. C. anglica, *L.*

Native. Very plentiful on the muddy banks of the New Cut and Avon, at and below Bristol. The Bristol plant differs from that figured in E. B. The pods are shorter and broader, with turgid valves, very much constricted at the replum. We have never found the leaves to be cordate, nor have we seen any specimen which might be thought intermediate in any degree between this species and *C. officinalis*. V. VI.

ARMORACIA, *Rupp.*

78. A. rusticana, *Rupp.* Horse-radish.

Alien; though in some spots it has the appearance of a native. Wherever planted it establishes itself tenaciously, and is sometimes found in deserted garden plots, the sole survivor of ancient cultivation. Frequent about Bristol. V. VI.

79. A. amphibia, *Koch.*

Native; by water, rare and local. Reported only from Shirehampton, G., and from both banks of the Avon above Bristol. VI.—VIII.

CAMELINA, *L.*

80. C. sativa, *L.*

Alien; not naturalized, occurring rarely in arable fields.

VII.

THLASPI, *L.*

81. T. arvense, *L. Penny Cress.*
Colonist; on cultivated land and near farm buildings, very rare.
G. Cornfields about Horfield, sparingly, but has been gathered in many seasons.
S. Eastwood, Brislington. *Dr. H. O. Stephens.*
VI.—VIII.

82. T. perfoliatum, *L.*
This plant has been reported from St. Vincent's Rocks by *Mr. Salisbury*, and from Montpelier and Ashley, G., by *Dr. H. O. Stephens*, many years ago. We fear it is now lost.

83. T. alpestre, *L.*
Native; on limestone hills, very rare and local.
S. Dry pasture near Sidcot. *Mr. W. B. Waterfall.* On débris from the mines on Mendip, not far from Cheddar. *Mr. T. B. Flower.* Between Shipham and Rowberrow, near Axbridge. *Rev. R. P. Murray, in J. of B.*, 1881, *p.* 174.
VI. VII.

HUTCHINSIA, *R. Br.*

84. H. petræa, *R. Br.*
Native; on limestone rocks about Bristol, and also upon walls, very local.
G. St. Vincent's Rocks. Durdham Down. Grows sparingly and of small size only at these habitats, but is very plentiful and luxuriant on walls at Westbury. Blaize Castle.
IV. V.

(*Teesdalia nudicaulis, R. Br.*, is recorded in the Phytologist as having been seen at Cheddar, S., but we possess no confirmation of the record.)

LEPIDIUM, *L.*

85. L. Draba, *L.*
Alien; introduced with seed.

G. Cornfields at Stapleton! *Herb. Dr. H. O. Stephens.* Plentiful in St. Philip's Marsh, where it has existed for many years. In the *Stephens Herbarium* Dr. S. notes his fear or belief that the plant had been built out of St. Philip's Marsh, thus making it clear that he had known it there prior to 1846, the date of the memorandum. Roadside at Patchway, June, 1881. V. VI.

86. **L. campestre,** *R. Br.*
Native; by roadsides and on cultivated land, frequent.
G. Bank of Avon. Berkeley.
S. Henley. Long Ashton. Abundant in cornfields near Portbury. Weston-super-Mare. VI. VII.

87. **L. Smithii,** *Hook.*
Native; in one spot, perhaps now extinct. On the roadside leading from Shirehampton to the Lighthouse; *Mr. T. B. Flower.* Seen there also by the late *Miss Powell,* of Henbury. As a casual upon refuse from a straw-paper mill at Henley, near Wells; *Miss Livett.*
VI. VII.

88. **L. ruderale,** *L.*
Alien; on quays about Bristol, and near the shore of the estuaries, rare.
G. Crew's Hole. Kingsweston. Rather plentiful at St. Philip's Marsh. On the quays at Cumberland Basin.
S. Clevedon. Rownham Ferry. V. VI.

(*L. sativum, L.,* is frequently found in the neighbourhood of gardens, and on rubbish heaps.)

89. **L. latifolium,** *L.*
Native.
S. Near the Axe, between Brean Down and Brean. *Mr. T. B. Flower.* VII. VIII.

CAPSELLA, *Vent.*

90. **C. Bursa-pastoris,** *DC.* *Shepherd's Purse.*

Native. An extremely common weed, found everywhere by roadsides and in waste places.   III.—X.

SENEBIERA, *Pers.*

91. S. Coronopus, *Poiret.*
Native; on damp pasture and waste land; common.
VI. IX.

92. S. didyma, *Pers.*
Probably introduced with ballast about Bristol. Now frequent.
G. Sea Mills, abundant. Westbury-on-Trym.
S. Burnham. Weston-super-Mare.   VII. IX.

(*Isatis tinctoria*, *L.* " Formerly cultivated about Keynsham, S., where I have occasionally found it." *Mr. T. B. Flower* in Swete's Fl. Brist.)

CAKILE, *Gaert.*

93. C. maritima, *Scop.*
Native; on the sandy coast of the Channel, between Clevedon and Burnham; plentiful in some places.
VI.—VIII.

CRAMBE, *L.*

94. C. maritima, *L.* *Sea-Kale.*
Native; on the coast, perhaps now extinct.
S. Burnham. *Mr. T. B. Flower.*

RAPHANUS, *L.*

95. R. Raphanistrum, *L.*
Colonist; in cornfields, &c.; frequent. Sometimes with lilac flowers.   VI. VII.

" The repetition of a generic name with the addition of ' istrum ' or ' astrum ' applied to a species, indicates that it is a useless or contemptible member of that genus, or bears a false resemblance to the species which comprise it." *Syme's E. B.*

96. R. maritimus, *Sm.*   *Sea Radish.*
  Native; near the coast; very rare.
  S.   Portishead.   *Rev. W. W. Spicer!*   Sandy fields, near Brean.   *Miss M. W. Mayow, Mr. T. B. Flower.*
  VI.—VIII.

RESEDACEÆ.
RESEDA, *L.*

97. R. lutea, *L.*
  Native, or Colonist.   Scarce about Bristol.
  G.   Combe Hill.   Henbury.   Shirehampton.
  S.   Pill.   Portbury.   Sandford.   Walton-in-Gordano.
  VI.—VIII.

98. R. suffruticulosa, *L.*
  Alien, or Colonist.   Very rare.
  S.   Anchor-Head rocks, Weston-super-Mare!   It was found some years ago at Wells, by *Miss Livett.*
  VII.—VIII.

99. R. Luteola, *L.*   *Dyer's Weed.   Weld.*
  Native; on the rubble about the limestone quarries at Bristol, and elsewhere.   Locally common.   VII.—VIII.

CISTACEÆ.
HELIANTHEMUM, *Gaert.*

100. H. vulgare, *Gaert.*   *Common Rock-Rose.*
  Native; on dry, rocky banks and hilly places, especially about Clifton, where a white-flowered variety has been observed.   VII.—IX.

101. H. polifolium, *Pers.*
  Native.
  S.   On Brean Down.   There is but one other habitat in Britain.   This great rarity continues to grow plentifully, chiefly on declivities facing the south-west, where there are plants of huge size, and apparently of great age.
  VII.—VIII.

(*H. canum, Dun.* Reported in error from Penpole Point, G. The plant was *H. vulgare.*)

(*H. ledifolium, Willd.* "Brean Down, Somerset," *Hudson*. An error. It is generally supposed that *Hudson* mistook *H. polifolium* for it.)

VIOLACEÆ.
VIOLA, *L.*

102. V. palustris, *L. Marsh Violet.*
Native.
S. Recorded from "Mendip Marsh, near the Minories," from whence we have seen a specimen collected by *Miss M. W. Mayow.* "Bog near the 'Castle of Comfort,' Mendip," *Herb. Dr. H. O. Stephens.* IV.—VI.

103. V. odorata, *L. Sweet Violet.*
Native. Plentifully distributed throughout the district. The type *violacea* is very much less frequent in the vicinity of Bristol than the var. *alba*. This has been accounted for by supposing that the blue violets have nearly all been dug up and transplanted into gardens, or hawked for sale in the streets, a fate which yearly befalls thousands of our ferns and spring flowers, not merely in this district, but in the neighbourhood of all large towns. In this genus the ordinary spring flowers do not generally ripen seed; later in the season minute apetalous flowers, which never expand, and are self-fertilized, develope seed in abundance. The leaves do not attain their full development until the fruit ripens; thus specimens of this species and of *V. hirta* when in fruit present an appearance very different from that of others gathered when the spring flowers are expanded. Both states should be represented in the herbarium. III. IV.

104. V. hirta, *L. Hairy Violet.*
Native; on shady banks and in rocky woods, frequent.
G. Bitton. Clifton Down. Shirehampton.
S. Brockley Combe. Cheddar. Clevedon. Congresbury. Easton. Frequent about Failand and in Leigh Wood.

If the var. β. *calcarea, Bab.*, is nothing more than a small state of this plant, we have it in Leigh Wood, where in some stony spots very tiny specimens may be found. As in the last species the leaves continue growing after the flowers fade, sometimes attaining very large dimensions. III.—V.

105. V. sylvatica, *Fries.*
Native.
a. *V. Reichenbachiana, Bor.*
On shady banks and in woods; not common, but to be found in many places. Near Bristol, it may be gathered in the wood at Combe Glen, and in hollow lanes about Failand.

β. *V. Riviniana, R.*
A more robust plant, and much more plentiful than var. a. Very abundant about Bristol, and not confined to shady places. Makes a great show in open parts of Leigh Wood and at Cheddar. A dwarf form — *V. flavicornis, Forst.*—is met with frequently. It grows chiefly on downs and dry turfy places. IV. V.

106. V. canina, *L.*
Native; on heaths and sandy ground; rare.
G. Kingsweston.
S. Burnham sand-hills. Leigh Down.
We have not seen β. *V. lactea, Sm.*, which, however, should be found amid the heath and bog of the southern portion of the district. IV. V.

107. **V. tricolor,** *L. Heartsease, Pansy.*
Native, or colonist; on cultivated ground. The large-flowered type is very rare, and usually found singly, but β. *arrensis* is everywhere common. V.—IX.

DROSERACEÆ.
DROSERA, *L. Sundew.*

108. **D. rotundifolia,** *L.*
Native; only on the peaty moors in Somersetshire, from Wedmore to Wells. VII. VIII.

109. **D. intermedia,** *Hayne.*
Native; with the last species. VII. VIII.

110. **D. anglica,** *Huds.*
Native. The only specimens we have are in the Stephens Herbarium, from Wedmore, S. VII. VIII.

POLYGALACEÆ.
POLYGALA, *L. Milkwort.*

111. **P. vulgaris,** *L.*
Native; on dry banks, heaths, and commons; common. The most frequent form at Clifton is *P. oxyptera, R.*
β. *P. depressa, Wend.* is chiefly to be found on damp heaths and moors, as on Yate Common, G. VI.—VIII.

112. **P. calcarea,** *F. Sch.*
Native; on the Mendips, very rare.
Sandford Hill, S. *Mr. W. B. Waterfall, "fide Mr. T. R. A. Briggs."* V.

CARYOPHYLLACEÆ.
DIANTHUS, *L.*

(One plant of *D. Armeria, L.,* was seen on a wall at West Town, S., July 20, 1880.)

113. D. cæsius, *Sm.* *Cheddar Pink.*
Native; on the Cheddar Cliffs, still plentiful.
Mr. T. B. Flower says that many years ago there was a large patch of this pink on St. Vincent's Rocks, near the Observatory. No doubt it had been planted there, and we believe it has now disappeared. VI. VII.

SAPONARIA, *L.*

114. S. officinalis, *L.* *Soapwort.*
Native; on the bank of the Avon, near Hanham, G., now scarce. Abundant on a sand-bank between Brean and Burnham, S., and also on hedge-banks at Burnham. Wells, S., not seen since 1878, *Miss Livett.* With double flowers in the Somersetshire habitats, and, no doubt, introduced there. VIII.

SILENE, *L.*

115. S. anglica, *L.*
Native, or colonist. Recorded only from Yatton, S., and very scarce even there. VI.—X.

116. S. inflata, *Sm.* *Bladder Campion.*
Native; in fields and by waysides, rather common. The hairy variety *(S. puberula, Jord.)* is often met with; it differs but little from the type. VI.—VIII.

117. S. maritima, *With.* *Sea Bladder Campion.*
Native; on the Channel shore only, rather rare.
S. Clevedon. Weston-super-Mare. Brean Down.
VI.—VIII.

LYCHNIS, *L.*

118. L. Flos-cuculi, *L.* *Ragged Robin.*
Native; in ditches and swamps, frequent. Rarely with white flowers. V. VI.

CARYOPHYLLACEÆ.

119. L. vespertina, *Sibth.*
Colonist; in borders of grass-fields, and under hedges, generally distributed. VI.—IX.

120. L. diurna, *Sibth. Red Campion.*
Native; on banks and in moist, shady places, very common. Staminiferous plants are far more abundant than those bearing pistils. The variety with white flowers is rare, but some luxuriant plants of it have been observed in a damp wood bordering the lane between Leigh and Failand Farm, S. V. VI.

121. L. Githago, *Scop. Corn-Cockle.*
Colonist; on arable land, not common.
G. Shirehampton. Stapleton.
S. Failand. Nailsea. Yatton. VI.—VIII.

SAGINA, L.

122. S. procumbens, *L.*
Native: in waste places, by footpaths, and on turf; very common. V.—IX.

123. S. apetala, *L.*
Native; on walls and in dry places; very common.
V.—IX.

124. S. ciliata, *Fr.*
Native. We have this species reported only from Stapleton and Clifton, G. There is little doubt, however, that it will be found in other localities when its distinctness from the last is better understood. V.—VI.

125. S. maritima, *Don.*
Native; only on the coast from Weston-super-Mare to Burnham; rather rare. V.—IX.

126. S. nodosa, *E. Meyer. Knotted Spurrey.*
Native; in sandy and peaty places, locally plentiful.

S. On the peat towards the southern limit of the district. Kewstoke Sands, Sands between Weston-super-Mare and Brean Down, and Burnham Sands. In the maritime localities the plant is very glandular-hairy, *(S. glandulosa, Bess.)*. VII. VIII.

HONKENEJA, *Ehrh.*

127. H. peploides, *Ehrh.*
Native; abundant on the sandy shore of the Bristol Channel, from Clevedon to Burnham, S. VI.—IX.

ALSINE, *Wahl.*

128. A. verna, *Jacq.*
Native; on the Mendip Hills, rare.
Mendip Hills below Banwell, abundant, 1846, *Mr. T. B. Flower.* Mendip Marsh, at the Minories, 1866! *Miss M. W. Mayow.* Specimens in the Stephens Herbarium are marked "near the 'Castle of Comfort,' Mendip Hills." V. IX.

(*A. tenuifolia, Wahl.* We cannot retain this plant in the Bristol Flora. There is little doubt that it was found at Clifton half a century ago, but the circumstances are unknown, and no specimens are extant. It is included in Mr. Rootsey's list of Bristol Plants, pub. 1828, with the habitat "Foot of St. Vincent's Rocks." "In the chink of a wall near Cornwallis Grove, Clifton, *Miss M. Atwood.*" *Swete, Fl.* 14.)

ARENARIA, *L.*

129. A. trinervis, *L.*
Native; in damp and shady places, common. V. VI.

130. A. serpyllifolia, *L.*
Native; on walls, banks, and in dry spots throughout the district. Very common. VI.—VIII.

STELLARIA, *L.*

131. S. media, *Vill. Chickweed.*
Native; a common weed in all kinds of situations, and very variable in habit and luxuriance.
δ. *S. umbrosa, Opitz. S. grandiflora, Woods.*
G. This well-marked variety is frequent about Charfield and Sodbury.
S. Bishport, Englishcombe, and Winscombe. III.—IX.

132. S. Holostea, *L.*
Native; everywhere on hedgebanks. IV.—VI.

133. S. glauca, *With.*
Native; only on the peat towards the southern limit of the district, rare. V. VII.

134. S. graminea, *L.*
Native; in dry, heathy, and bushy places, frequent.
G. Bank of Avon. Berkeley. Clifton Down. Mangotsfield. Glen Frome, near Stapleton. Westbury-on-Trym.
S. Leigh Wood. Yatton. Wells. V.—VIII.

135. S. uliginosa, *Murr.*
Native; in wet and swampy places, common. V. VI.

MALACHIUM, *Fries.*

136. M. aquaticum, *Fr.*
Native; on ditchbanks, rare. Swete's remark, " Common throughout the district," is inexplicable.
G. By the river Frome, near Stapleton.
S. Knowle, *Miss Livett.* St. Anne's Wood, Brislington.
VII. VIII.

CERASTIUM, *L.*

137. C. glomeratum, *Thuil.*
Native; on banks, walls, and railway ballast. Common.
IV.—IX.

CARYOPHYLLACEÆ.

138. C. triviale, *Link.*
    Native; on wall-tops, banks, and in pasture land. More common than the last.   IV.—IX.

139. C. semidecandrum, *L.*
    Native; in dry places, rather rare.
    G.   St. Vincent's Rocks. Durdham Down. Stapleton. Brandon Hill.
    S.   Clevedon. Cheddar.   IV. V.

140. C. pumilum, *Curt.*
    Native; on rocks about Clifton, local. St. Vincent's Rocks. Clifton Down. Rocks near the Sea Wall. The Stephens Herbarium possesses a good series of specimens from St. Vincent's Rocks, and some interesting letters from Prof. Babington with reference to this plant. IV. V.

141. C. tetrandrum, *Curt.*
    Native.
    G.   St. Vincent's Rocks, Durdham Down, and Brandon Hill, Bristol. Sea Mills. Dr. H. O. Stephens submitted a Clifton specimen to Prof. Babington, who pronounced it to be his *C. atrovirens*, " with shorter footstalks than usual."
    S.   Elevated rocks at Cheddar.   V. VII.

MOENCHIA, *Ehrh.*

142. M. erecta, *Sm.*
    Native. There are specimens in Dr. Stephens' Herbarium marked " Keynsham " and " Brandon Hill," no date. The authority is undoubted, otherwise we might hesitate to include this plant in our Flora, in the absence of additional records.   V. VI.

LEPIGONUM, *Fries.*

143. L. rubrum, *Fr.*
    Native; in sandy and heathy places, rare. It grows in several spots on the common near Mangotsfield, G.   VI.—IX.

144. **L. marinum,** *Wahl.*
   Native. Abundant about the estuaries in muddy and marshy situations. VI.—IX.
   It is probable that other forms of *Lepigonum* are to be found in the district, but at present our records are confined to the species mentioned.

SPERGULA, *L.*

145. **S. arvensis,** *L.*
   Native; on cultivated land, rather rare.
   G. Horfield. Stapleton.
   S. Fields near the coast between Clevedon and Portishead. Yatton.

SCLERANTHUS, *L.*

146. **S. annuus,** *L.*
   Native; on dry sandy ground, very rare.
   G. It still lingers on Brandon Hill, half-a-dozen specimens having been seen this season (June 10, 1881). We wish that all the plants formerly stationed at this spot had been able to battle as successfully against the adverse environment.
   S. On the railway near Yatton Station! *Mr. W. E. Green.*

MALVACEÆ.
MALVA, *L.*

147. **M. moschata,** *L.* *Musk Mallow.*
   Native; in waste places and by roadsides, frequent.
   G. Very plentiful about the railway between Clifton and Avonmouth, and at Stapleton.
   S. Clevedon. Leigh. Milton. Yatton. VII. VIII.

148. **M. sylvestris,** *L.* *Common Mallow.*
   Native; very common everywhere. VI.—IX.

149. M. rotundifolia, *L.* *Dwarf Mallow.*
Native; in dry waste places, frequent.
G. Plentiful on a pebbly beach between the New Passage and Avonmouth. Shirehampton. Stapleton.
S. Brislington. Clevedon. Easton. Knowle. Strode. Long Ashton. VI.—IX.

ALTHÆA, *L.*

150. A. officinalis, *L.* *Marsh Mallow.*
Native; in marsh ditches near tidal waters; very rare.
G. In ditches near the rifle-range at Avonmouth, now scarce.
S. Portishead. VIII. IX.

151. A. hirsuta, *L.*
Alien. Grows sparingly on Pur Down, G., where it was discovered a few years ago by *Mr. W. E. Green.* VI.

LAVATERA, *L.*

152. L. arborea, *L.*
Native, or denizen. Occurs generally as an escape from gardens, but is doubtfully wild at one or two stations on the coast.
S. Clevedon. St. Thomas's Head. Woodspring, at the mouth of the river Wick; perhaps now extinct. Weston-super-Mare. VII.—IX.

TILIACEÆ.
TILIA, *L.*

153. T. intermedia, *DC.* *Common Lime-tree.*
In plantations, parks, and hedgerows, with no claim to be indigenous in the district. VII.

154. T. parvifolia, *Ehrh.*
Native. Truly wild in Leigh Wood, S., where it is abundant. VIII.

HYPERICACEÆ.
HYPERICUM, *L.*

155. H. calycinum, *L.*
Alien. Naturalized in Leigh Wood, in the railway cutting at Bourton, and at Clevedon, S. VII.—IX.

156. H. Androsæmum, *L. Tutsan.*
Native; in woods, frequent.
G. Haw Wood, Henbury. Frome Glen, Stapleton.
S. King's Wood, Yatton. Leigh Wood. Clevedon. Portishead. Wookey. VII. VIII.
(*H. elatum, Ait.*, has escaped from cultivation at Max, S., and at Worle, S.)
(*H. hircinum, L.* With the last at Max, S., " unquestionably planted," *Mr. W. B. Waterfall.*)

157. H. tetrapterum, *Fr. H. quadrangulum, Sm.*
Native; banks of ditches and streams, common. VII.

158. H. perforatum, *L.*
Native; in woods and on dry banks, common. VII. VIII.

159. H. dubium, *Leers.*
Native: in moist places, very rare.
G. Stapleton.
S. Leigh Wood. Yatton. VII.

160. H. humifusum, *L.*
Native; in many woods, and on shady banks, rather common. VII.

161. H. hirsutum, *L.*
Native; in woods, frequent.
G. Very plentiful in woods about Berkeley.
S. Leigh Wood. Walton-in-Gordano. Wells. Yatton.
VII. VIII.

162. H. montanum, *L.*
Native. In bushy places on limestone; local, but frequent about Bristol.

G. Conham. St. Vincent's Rocks, and in the Great Quarry, Clifton.

S. Failand. Leigh Wood. Walton-in-Gordano. Weston-super-Mare. VII. VIII.

163. **H. pulchrum,** *L.*
Native. The most common *Hypericum* in the district.
VI. VII.

ACERACEÆ.

ACER, *L.*

164. **A. campestre,** *L.* *Maple.*
Native; at least in Leigh Wood, S., where are many trees of good size. Common in hedgerows. V. VI.

165. **A. Pseudo-platanus,** *L.* *Sycamore.*
Alien; in woods, hedges, and plantations, common.
V. VI.

GERANIACEÆ.

GERANIUM, *L.*

166. **G. phæum,** *L.*
Alien; established in one or two spots, very rare.
G. Sea Mills, sparingly, from 1868 to the present time.
S. Stockwood, and on the banks of the stream at Long Ashton. *Swete, Fl.* 19. Probably extinct in both these habitats. V. VI.

(*G. striatum, L.* will be found as an escape from cultivation in many places, notably at Bourton Combe, S.)

167. **G. pratense,** *L.*
Native. This beautiful Geranium is frequent in moist

pastures, and especially by the sides of rivers, throughout the district. In the near vicinity of Bristol it is very scarce, as might be expected; the existence of so attractive a wild-flower being incompatible with the extension of a large city.

G. Bitton. Ashley Hill. Chipping Sodbury. Filton. Tortworth.

S. Ashton. Brockley. Draycot. Kewstoke. Keynsham. Pensford. Wells. VI.—VIII.

168. G. sanguineum, *L.*
Native; on dry limestone banks, very rare.
G. Plentiful about St. Vincent's Rocks, Clifton.
S. Walton-by-Clevedon. *Mr. W. E. Green.* VII.

169. G. pyrenaicum, *L.*
Alien, or denizen in this district. Very rare.
S. Plentiful in a cultivated field near Abbot's Leigh, 1878. Clevedon. Wells. In a churchyard at Wells. Hedgebanks at Englishcombe, May, 1881.

VI. VII.

170. G. molle, *L.*
Native; in waste places and dry spots, very common. The variety with white flowers at Weston-super-Mare, 1880. IV.—VIII.

171. G. rotundifolium, *L.*
Native; on and under old walls and in hedgebanks, locally common.
G. Hanham. St. Vincent's Rocks. Sea Mills. Shirehampton. Stapleton.
S. Abundant under the walls of Ashton Park, by the road to Abbot's Leigh. Clevedon. Portbury. Yatton. By the Kennet and Avon Canal, near Combe Hay.

VI. VII.

GERANIACEÆ.

172. G. pusillum, L.

Native; on gravelly soil. Very rare, or, perhaps, sometimes overlooked.

G. Combe Hill. Crew's Hole. Shirehampton.
S. Bedminster. VI.—VIII.

173. G. dissectum, L.

Native; in pastures and waste places. Very common.

VI.—VIII.

174. G. columbinum, L.

Native; in thickets and dry pastures, and on banks, frequent.

G. St. Vincent's Rocks, and bank of Avon. Stapleton.
S. Plentiful at Cheddar, where on the dry turfy slopes may be seen minute specimens of great beauty, bearing but one flower on the summit of a tiny stem. Clevedon. Wells. Weston-super-Mare. Yatton.

VI. VII.

175. G. lucidum, L.

Native. Singularly common about Bristol, considering how very seldom it is met with in some districts. Grows chiefly on walls and in rocky places. Common also at Bath, Wells, Weston-super-Mare, and Yatton, S.

V. VIII.

176. G. robertianum, L. *Herb-Robert.*

Native; on hedgebanks, and in waste shady places, very common.

The variety with white flowers at Claverham, S. *Miss Winter.* V.—VIII.

ERODIUM, L'Hérit.

177. E. cicutarium, Sm.

Native; in dry places, common. Varies very greatly in size and appearance; large coast specimens are sometimes mistaken for the next species. VI. VIII.

178. E. moschatum, *Sm.*
   Native; only near tidal waters, very rare.
   G.   Bank of Avon. Penpole Point.
   S.   Weston-super-Mare. VI. VII.

179. E. maritimum, *Sm.*
   Native; on elevated pastures, local.
   G.   Penpole Point, perhaps now extinct.
   S.   Roman entrenchment in Leigh Wood; small plants amongst the turf. Court Hill near Clevedon. Very luxuriant on the hills about Goblin Combe. Dolbery Camp, and frequent on other eminences in that neighbourhood. VI.—IX.

OXALIDACEÆ.

OXALIS, *L.*

180. O. Acetosella, *L.* *Wood Sorrel.*
   Native; in woods and moist shady places, frequent. The flowers are rarely pink or purplish.
   G.   Abundant by the river Trym below Westbury.
   S.   Cheddar. Failand. Leigh Wood. Wells. Yatton. V.

LINACEÆ.

LINUM, *L.*

181. L. angustifolium, *Huds.*
   At present reported only from Wookey, S., by *Miss Livett*, but is likely to be found elsewhere. VII.

182. **L. usitatissimum,** *L.* *Common Flax.*
   Alien. Is met with in many spots, but scarce about Bristol, and perhaps not permanent anywhere. VII.
183. **L. catharticum,** *L.*
   . Native. Very common on dry turfy banks and elevated pastures. VI.—VIII.

FLORA

OF THE

BRISTOL COAL-FIELD.

EDITED (FOR THE BRISTOL NATURALISTS' SOCIETY) BY

JAMES WALTER WHITE,

Hon. Secretary of the Botanical Section.

"*Rerum cognoscere causas.*"—VIRGIL.

PART II.
CALYCIFLORÆ.

BRISTOL:
JAMES FAWN & SON.

PRINTED BY E. AUSTIN & SON, CHRONICLE OFFICE, CLIFTON.

MDCCCLXXXII.

PHANEROGAMIA.

Class 1. *DICOTYLEDONES.*
Div. 2. *CALYCIFLORÆ.*

CELASTRACEÆ.
EUONYMUS, L.

184. **E. europæus,** *L. Spindle-tree.*
Native; common in hedges and woods.
G. Abundant about Charlton, Patchway, Sea Mills, Shirehampton, and Wotton-under-Edge.
S. Also abundant at Brislington, St. Anne's Wood, Wells, and Winscombe. V. VI.

RHAMNACEÆ.
RHAMNUS, L.

185. **R. catharticus,** *L. Buckthorn.*
Native; in hedges and woods, rather rare.
G. Ashley. Filton. Horfield. Shirehampton. Westbury.
S. Cadbury Hill. Clevedon, on Walton Castle Hill. Hutton. Ken. Leigh Wood. Pensford. Sidcot. Ebbor Rocks, near Wells.
It happens rather curiously that with us this shrub is of solitary habit. We have not in a single instance found two plants growing together. V.—VII.

D

186. R. Frangula, *L.* *Black Alder.*
  Native; in copses and wet thickets, rare.
  G. Crew's Hole. Horfield. "Copse between Horfield and Stapleton." *Herb. Dr. H. O. Stephens.*
  S. Max Mills, Winscombe.

LEGUMINOSÆ.

ULEX, *L.*

187. U. europæus, *L.* *Furze. Gorse.*
  Native; on downs and commons, very common.   I.—VI.

188. U. Gallii, *Planch.* *Planchon's Furze.*
  Native; on heaths and downs, locally common.
  G. Bank of Avon below Bristol. Clifton and Durdham Downs. Yate Common.
  S. Clevedon. Leigh Down. Weston-super-Mare.
                                      VIII.—XI.

We have not met with *U. eu-nanus* in the district.

GENISTA, *L.*

189. G. tinctoria, *L.* *Dyer's Weed.*
  Native; in damp meadows and pastures, frequent.
  G. Filton Meads. Abundant in meadows about Charlton and Patchway. Wick. "Fields behind Stoke House, Stapleton." *Herb. Dr. H. O. Stephens.*
  S. In marshy fields west of Dundry Hill. Easton, near Wells. Winscombe. Barrow Hill, near Buckland Dinham. Great Elm.   VI.—VIII.

190. G. anglica, *L.* *Needle Whin.*
  Native; on a boggy common. Very rare.
  G. Yate Common.   V. VI.

SAROTHAMNUS, *Wimm.*

191. S. scoparius, *Koch.* *Broom.*
Native; on dry heathy and rocky banks, locally common. The habitats nearest to Bristol are at Cook's Folly Wood and bank of Avon underneath; and at Crew's Hole, St. George's. V. VI.

ONONIS, *L.*

192. O. arvensis, *L.*
Native; on banks, commons, and barren pastures, common. We have gathered the spinous form at Kewstoke, S.
VI.—IX.

193. O. campestris, *Koch.*
Native; chiefly in submaritime situations, and sometimes abundant.
G. By the Avon near Avonmouth, and by the Severn between Avonmouth and Berkeley.
S. Kewstoke. Knowle. Nailsea. VI.—IX.

MEDICAGO, *L.*

194. M. sativa, *L.* *Lucerne.*
Alien. Established here and there on dry banks, and by roadsides.
G. Clifton Down, here for many years. Westbury.
S. Burnham. Kewstoke Sands. Weston-super-Mare.
VI.—VIII.

195. M. lupulina, *L.*
Native; in pastures and waste places, very common.
V.—VIII.

196. M. maculata, *Sibth.*
Native; in pastures and by roadsides, scarce about Bristol.
G. Bank of Avon at Cumberland Basin, and at Sea Mills. Stapleton. The habitat at Sea Mills has been

recorded by very many botanists. It extends about half-a-mile along the river bank.

S. Brean Down. Clevedon. Wells. Weston-super-Mare.   V.—VIII.

197. M. minima, *Lam.*
Native. Recorded by *Dr. H. O. Stephens* as found on Brandon Hill and St. Vincent's Rocks. A specimen from the latter place, bearing Dr. Stephens' name, but not dated, is in the Society's herbarium. We hope this rare little plant may not be extinct, but many years have passed since it was last seen.   V.

198. M. denticulata, *Willd.*
Casual in this district, having been introduced within the last decade. It grows freely about Cumberland Basin and the riverside adjacent.   V.—VIII.

MELILOTUS, *L.*

199. M. officinalis, *Willd.* *Common Melilot.*
Native; on dry banks and by roadsides, frequent.
G. Bank of Avon below Bristol.
S. Bedminster. Bourton. Brislington. Burnham. Bank of Avon below Bristol. Uphill. Wells. Weston-super-Mare. Yatton.   VI.—VIII.

200. M. alba, *Lam.*
Casual; in waste places, very rare.
G. Ashley. *Mr. W. E. Green.* Kingswood Hill. *Dr. A. C. Hassé.*
S. Ashton Vale Colliery, one plant, 1880. *Mr. T. F. Perkins.* Burnham. *Miss Winter.*   VII. VIII.

TRIFOLIUM, *L.*

201. T. pratense, *L.* *Purple Clover.*
Native; in fields and pastures, very common. White-flowered plants have been noted at Dundry and Clevedon.   V.—IX.

LEGUMINOSÆ. 45

202. T. medium, *L.*
Native; in elevated pastures and bushy places, frequent.
G. Cook's Folly Wood. Durdham Down. Stinchcombe Hill.
S. Bank of Avon. Bishport. Clevedon. Under Crook's

CORRECTION.

No. 203. Trifolium ochroleucum has been inserted in error, and must be struck out.

. . . . . by roadsides where it has escaped from cultivation. Rare.
G. Westbury.
S. Clevedon. Weston-super-Mare. VI. VII.

205. T. arvense, *L.* *Hare's-foot Trefoil.*
Native; chiefly on the sandy shores of the Channel, where it is very plentiful.
G. Conham. Hanham. "Holly Gess" coalpit.
S. Brislington. Burnham. Kewstoke. Walton, by Clevedon. Wells. Weston-super-Mare. VI.—VIII.

206. T. striatum, *L.*
Native; in dry pastures and sandy places, rather rare.
G. On the sandy heath near Mangotsfield Station. Penpole Point. Trooper's Hill, Crew's Hole. *Herb. Dr. H. O. Stephens.* We have found only *T. scabrum* on Durdham and Clifton Downs.
S. Burnham. Kewstoke; plentiful both on the sands and among the turf along the ridge from Sand Point to Woodspring. VI.—VIII.

207. T. scabrum, *L.*
Native; in dry, gravelly, and rocky pastures, and in sand. Not uncommon.

G. Brandon Hill. Clifton and Durdham Downs. Penpole Point.

S. Clevedon. Kewstoke sands, abundantly. VI.—VIII.

208. T. maritimum, *Huds*.

Native; in sub-maritime pasture land, rare.

G. Sea Mills. The plant grows in a meadow very plentifully, and also by the river side in great luxuriance. One specimen gathered here July 4, 1880, bore 241 heads of flowers averaging 40 in each head, or a total of 9640 individual flowers.

S. Clevedon. *Mr. W. E. Green.* Specimen in *Herb. Dr. H. O. Stephens,* from " Burnham, Somerset, *W. R. Crotch,*" no date. Weston-super-Mare. VI. VII.

209. T. subterraneum, L.

Native; in dry places, very rare.

G. "St. Vincent's Rock." *Shiercliff's Bristol and Hotwell Guide for* 1789. Brandon Hill, and Hanham. *Swete Fl.* p. 22.

S. Clevedon. *Mr. W. E. Green.* Keynsham! *Herb. Dr. H. O. Stephens.* V. VI.

210. T. repens, L. *White, or Dutch Clover.*

Native; very common everywhere. In wet seasons frequently with foliaceous petals, and subject to monstrous growths. The rose-pink variety has been found at Clevedon by *Mr. W. E. Green.* V. IX.

211. T. hybridum, L.

Alien. It has been introduced with seed, and is now of frequent occurrence. Sometimes it is viviparous.

S. Abbots' Leigh. Ashton. Clevedon. Nailsea. Radstock. VI.—VIII.

212. T. fragiferum, L.

Native; in pastures near salt water and elsewhere, frequent.

This is a tiny and inconspicuous plant, easily overlooked, and may still grow where it was found by Mr. Thwaites, the exact locality being unknown. We therefore hesitate to exclude it from our list, although we have never met with anyone who had seen it in the Bristol district. In a list of plants published in 1789, it is said to have grown on St. Vincent's Rocks.

LOTUS. *L.*

217. L. corniculatus, *L.*
Native; very common in dry pastures.
β. *villosus*, *Ser*.
S. Wells. *Miss Livett.*
δ. *L. tenuis*, *Sm.*
G. Ashley. Damory Bridge. Dyrham.
S. Abundant near the Avon under Leigh Wood, and on the other side of the river also. Brean Sands. Easton.
VI.—VIII.

218. L. major, *Scop.*
Native. Frequent, especially in marshy spots.
G. Berkeley. Kingswood. Thornbury. Mangotsfield.
S. Abbots' Leigh. Bishport. Portbury. Portishead. Winscombe. Wookey. Yatton. VII. VIII.

(*L. angustissimus*, *L.* We agree with Mr. Flower in believing that this species was never found in the locality recorded for it in *Swete's Fl. Brist.* Lotus *tenuis*, *Sm.* must have been mistaken for it.)

ANTHYLLIS, *L.*

219. A. vulneraria, *L. Lady's Fingers.*
Native; in dry, hilly pastures, rather local.
G. Clifton and Durdham Downs. Kingswood.
S. Bank of Avon. Axbridge. Great Elm. Clevedon. Milton. South Stoke. Weston-super-Mare. VI.—VIII.

LEGUMINOSÆ. 47

G. Dyrham. Horfield. Sea Mills. St. Philip's Marsh. By the Severn between New Passage and Berkeley.
S. Burnham sands. Easton. Kingston Seymour. Abundant at Woodspring, and on the sands S.W. of Weston-super-Mare. VII. VIII.

(*T. resupinatum, L.* This alien formerly grew abundantly in a meadow below Shirehampton, G., but as commonly happens, the station did not prove to be permanent. *Mr. Flower* says he has several times fruitlessly searched for it when in company with *Prof. Babington*. There is a specimen in the herbarium B. N. S. not labelled, but stated to be from "Shirehampton, *E. H. Swete*," no date.)

213. T. procumbens, *L.*
Native; in dry places, common.
G. Plentiful by the Avon under Durdham Down. Ashley. Mangotsfield.
S. Brean Down. Clevedon. Draycot. Ken. Kewstoke Sands. Wells. Weston-super-Mare. VI. VII.

214. T. minus, *Sm.*
Native; in pastures and dry places, very common.
V.—VIII.

215. T. filiforme, *L.*
Native; in dry places, rather rare.
G. Clifton Down. Durdham Down. Brandon Hill, *Sw. Fl.*
S. Clevedon. Portishead. Weston-super-Mare.
V.—VIII.

FALCATULA, *Brot.*

216. F. ornithopodioides, *Bab.*
"Lamplighter's Hall. *Mr. G. H. K. Thwaites.*" *Swete, Fl.* p. 23.

ASTRAGALUS, *L.*

220. A. glycyphyllos, *L.*
Native, in thickets, rare.
G. On Henbury Hill!
S. Egford, *Miss Livett.* Portishead, *Rev. W. W. Spicer!* and *Herb. Dr. H. O. Stephens.* On the eastern border of the district, near Buckland Dinham. *Dr. H. F. Parsons.* VI. VII.

VICIA, *L.*

221. V. hirsuta, *Koch.*
Native; in hedges and waste spots, common.
G. Dry banks in Glen Frome. Kingsweston. Mangotsfield. Nibley. Plentiful near Sea Mills.
S. Knowle. Portishead. Yatton. Weston-super-Mare.
VI.—VIII.

222. V. tetrasperma, *Moench.*
Native; in grassy and bushy places, not so frequent as the last species.
G. Charfield. Between Sea Mills and Shirehampton.
S. Leigh Down. Portbury. Weston-super-Mare. Yatton. VI.—VIII.

223. V. sylvatica, *L.*
Native; in woods and thickets, local.
S. Abundant for about half a mile along the bank of the Avon, opposite Sea Mills. Clevedon. Hutton. Portbury. Portishead. Stockwood, *Herb. Dr. H. O. Stephens.* Weston-in-Gordano. Between Norton St. Philip and Wellow, on oolite; and in Asham Wood between Nunney and Downhead, on limestone. *Dr. H. F. Parsons.* VII. VIII.

224. V. Orobus, *DC.*
Abundant in an open pasture by Tining's Farm, near Cheddar, and is also to be found nearer Cheddar. "The

plant is now extinct in the old locality (Emborrow Ponds) mentioned in the Bot. Guide." *Rev. R. P. Murray.*

225. **V. Cracca,** *L.*
Native; in hedges and waste grassy places, very common. One of the most beautiful ornaments of our country lanes.   VI.—VIII.

226. **V. bithynica,** *L.*
Native; in bushy and hilly places, rare.
G. Shirehampton. *Swete, Fl.,* p. 24. Swete also records this plant, on the authority of Mr. T. B. Flower, as growing in the Green Valley, Clifton, and on St. Vincent's Rocks. This is a mistake, as Mr. Flower gathered *Lathyrus macrorrhizus,* and the *Vicia* has never been found at the stations named.
S. Abundant at Cleeve. Also abundant on the side of a hill between Keynsham and Pensford, and on another hill to the north of Pensford. *Mr. T. B. Flower.* "Stockwood, near Brislington." *Herb. Dr. H. O. Stephens.* Easton and Yarley. *Miss Livett.* VII. VIII.

227. **V. sepium,** *L. Bush Vetch.*
Native; on hedgebanks and among bushes. Very common. With pure white flowers at Combe Hay, S., near the canal.   VI.—VIII.

228. **V. sativa,** *Sm. Cultivated Vetch.*
Occurs casually on the borders of fields, but only as an escape from cultivation.   V. VI.

229. **V. angustifolia,** *Roth. Wild Vetch.*
Native; on dry banks and in pastures, common.
G. Crew's Hole. Frome Glen. Kingsweston.
S. Bishport. Clevedon. Easton. Kewstoke.
Var. *Bobartii, Forst.*
G. On débris from the quarry at Damory Bridge. V. VI.

230. V. lathyroides, *L.*

Native; on the sandy shores of the Channel, very local.

S. Plentiful on Kewstoke sands, whence first reported to us by the *Rev. W. H. Painter.* Brean Down. *Dr. St. Brody.* Burnham. *Miss Livett.*

This tiny vetch flowers and passes away very quickly. The open valves of the fruit and withered stems alone remain at the middle of June.   V. VI.

LATHYRUS, *L.*

231. L. Aphaca, *L.*

Native; in cultivated ground and waste places, very rare and not often stationary in its localities.

G. Henbury. Westbury. *Swete, Fl.,* p. 25. Horfield. *Mr. T. B. Flower.*

S. Bedminster. *Mr. T. B. Flower.* Yarley, where it has been known for thirty years by *Miss M. W. Mayow.*
     V.—VII.

232. L. Nissolia, *L.*

Native; in grass, or among bushes, very rare.

G. In plenty on a railway embankment at Ashley. *Mr. W. E. Green.* Berwick. Henbury. *Swete, Fl.,* p. 25. It still grows plentifully at the spot in Shirehampton Marshes first recorded by *Mr. Flower,* but this habitat is not easy to find.

S. Easton and Yarley, sparingly. *Miss Livett.* Stockwood. *Mr. G. Thwaites, in Swete, Fl.,* p. 25.   VI.

(*L. hirsutus, L.* " On the sides of two hills, the one north of Pensford, on the Bristol road, the other between Pensford and Keynsham, Somersetshire; *Mr. Swayne.*" *Withering's British Plants,* ed. 3, pub. 1796. A mistake. *Vicia bithynica* is the plant found there.)

LEGUMINOSÆ.

233. L. pratensis, *L.*
Native; very common in hedges, meadows, and pastures throughout the district. VII. VIII.

234. L. sylvestris, *L.*
Native; chiefly in hedges, frequent.
G. Hambrook. Henbury. Berwick. *Swete, Fl.,* p. 25. Hedgebanks near Compton Greenfield. Very abundant on and about the railway embankment near Powderhouse Wood, Shirehampton. Brains Hill, Kingswood. Great Quarry, Clifton.
S. Banwell. Clevedon. Nailsea. Portishead. Yatton.
VII. VIII.

235. L. macrorrhizus, *Wimm.*
Native; in woods and bushy places, common.
G. Clifton and Durdham Downs. Cook's-Folly Wood. Thornbury. Sea Mills. Wick Rocks.
S. Barrow Gurney. Cheddar. Ebbor. Hutton. Leigh Wood. Portishead. King's Wood, Yatton.
Var. β. *tenuifolius.*
Well marked on Clifton and Durdham Downs, and in Cook's-Folly Wood. Intermediate variations occur also.
V.—VII.

(*L. latifolius, L.* Valueless book records have been founded on the occurrence of this plant in Stapleton Quarries, where it was stated to have been found many years ago by Mr. Anderson. See *Hooker, Br. Fl.,* and *Swete, Fl.,* pp. 25 and 99. An alien casual, originating from some garden, should not have been noticed; moreover, in this instance, it is quite probable that the specimen was merely a broad-leaved form of *L. sylvestris.*)

ROSACEÆ.

ORNITHOPUS, *L.*

236. O. perpusillus, *L.* *Bird's foot.*

Native; on dry banks, rare.

G. Brandon Hill. *Herb. Dr. H. O. Stephens.* This station is mentioned by Withering, and also in a list of plants published in *Shiercliff's Bristol and Hotwell Guide for* 1789. Clifton Down. *Miss M. Atwood, Swete, Fl.,* p. 25. Perhaps now extinct in both these localities. Crew's Hole. Kingsweston. Plentiful in the cutting at Mangotsfield Station.

S. Brislington. Court Hill, Clevedon. *Mr. W. E. Green.* Uphill. V.—VII.

HIPPOCREPIS, *L.*

237. H. comosa, *L.*

Native; in dry rocky places, chiefly on limestone; locally plentiful.

G. St Vincent's Rocks. Durdham Down, and underneath, on rocks by the river-side. Stinchcombe Hill. Above Wotton-under-Edge, abundant. Wick Rocks.

S. Cheddar Cliffs. Ebbor. Dry banks about South Stoke and Wellow. Worle Hill. Barrow Hill, near Buckland Dinham. V.—VIII.

ONOBRYCHIS, *Gaert.*

238. O. sativa, *Lam.* *Saintfoin.*

Native; in dry places, borders of fields, and on railway embankments. Usually an escape from cultivation. Rather common. VI. VII.

ROSACEÆ.

PRUNUS, *L.*

239. P. spinosa, *L.* *Blackthorn.*

Native; in hedges and woods, very common. III.—V.

240. **P. insititia,** *L.* *Bullace.*
   Native; in hedges and woods, frequent.
   G. Ashley. Bitton.
   S. Bishport. Clevedon. St. Anne's Wood. Wells. Yatton. IV. V.

241. **P. domestica,** *L.* *Wild Plum.*
   Denizen. It has become naturalized here and there, in the vicinity of houses and orchards. IV. V.

242. **P. Padus,** *L.* *Bird Cherry.*
   Native; in woods and thickets, rare.
   G. Stapleton.
   S. Brockley Combe. Leigh Wood. *Dr. H. O. Stephens.* Clevedon. *Mr. W. E. Green.*

243. **P. Avium,** *L.* *Wild Cherry.*
   Native; in woods and hedgerows, rather common.
   G. Westbury. Abundant in woods about Wotton-under-Edge.
   S. Leigh Wood, plentiful; some grand old trees overlook the Avon opposite Sea Mills. Ripe cherries gathered here at the end of June, 1881, were equal in flavour to much of the cultivated fruit. Portbury Woods. St. Anne's Wood. Walton-in-Gordano. V. VI.

   (*P. Cerasus,* *L.* As far as we know, this shrub has never been noticed in the neighbourhood of Bristol.)

SPIRÆA, *L.*

244. **S. Ulmaria,** *L.* *Meadow-Sweet.*
   Native; in damp meadows, and by water, everywhere.
   VI.—VIII.

245. **S. Filipendula,** *L.*
   Native; in dry pastures and bushy places, on limestone Locally common.

ROSACEÆ.

G. Clifton and Durdham Downs, plentiful. Also on the railway by the river-side under the Downs. Kingswood Hill. *Dr. A. C. Hassé!*

S. Abundant on the slopes of the Mendip Hills, as at Cheddar and Axbridge. Loxton. Walton-in-Gordano. Woodspring. Abundant on the hills at Kewstoke and Worle. VI. VII.

POTERIUM, *L.*

246. **P. Sanguisorba,** *L.* *Lesser Burnet.*

Native; in dry and hilly pastures, very common.

VI.—VIII.

247. **P. muricatum,** *Spach.* *a.* **P. platylophium,** *Jord.*

Alien or colonist.

G. It grows abundantly on the railway embankment between Sea Mills and Shirehampton, and also on railway embankments near the Boiling Well. First record, "Sea Mills, August 1, 1868," *Rev. W. W. Spicer.*

VI.—VIII.

AGRIMONIA, *L.*

248. **A. Eupatoria,** *L.* *Agrimony.*

Native; by roadsides and on hedgebanks, common.

VI. VII.

ALCHEMILLA, *L.*

249. **A. vulgaris,** *L.*

Native; in damp hilly pastures. It is to be found frequently on the slopes of the Mendip Hills, but elsewhere it is rare.

G. Near Patchway.

S. Leigh Wood, a very small patch not far from the Suspension Bridge. Damp, wooded slopes in the upper part of the Cheddar gorge. Pasture under Dundry Hill. Wells. Winscombe. VI.—VIII.

250. **A. arvensis,** *L.*
> Native; in pastures and cultivated fields, very common.
> Very abundant on Clifton and Durdham Downs, but the largest specimens grow on arable land.　　VI.—VIII.

POTENTILLA, *L.*

251. **P. anserina,** *L.*
> Native; in damp waste places and by roadsides, very common.　　VI. VII.

252. **P. argentea,** *L.*
> Native? In one spot near Downend, G. *Dr. A. C. Hassé.*　　VI. VII.

253. **P. verna,** *L.*
> Native; on dry banks and rocks, rare.
> G.　Plentiful on St. Vincent's Rocks, and on Clifton and Durdham Downs.
> S.　Brean Down.　Leigh Down.　Cheddar.　Penthill. *Miss Livett.*　　IV. V.

254. **P. reptans,** *L.*
> Native; on dry banks and by roadsides, common. VI.—IX.

255. **P. Tormentilla,** *Nestl.* *Tormentilla.*
> Native; on heaths, peat moors, and banks, and in woods, common.
> With double flowers on Blackdown, S. Very remarkable for its large, woody, rootstock.　　VI.—VIII.

256. **P. procumbens,** *Sibth.*
> Native; in the same situations as *P. Tormentilla*, from which we have only lately been able to separate it. Our recorded stations are therefore few at present, but it is probable that the plant is not uncommon in this district.　　VI.—VIII.

257. **P. fragariastrum,** *Ehrh.* *Barren Strawberry.*
> Native; on old stone walls and banks, common. III.—V.

COMARUM, *L.*

258. C. palustre, *L.*

Native; in marshes and peat ditches, rare.

S. Specimens from Leigh Woods, and from Ashton Manor Woods, gathered by Miss Atwood, are authenticated by Swete, *Fl. Brist.*, p. 27. The plant is now believed to be absent from those localities, and perhaps is not to be seen nearer Bristol than on the peat at Shapwick, near the extreme southern limit of the district. VII.

FRAGARIA, *L.*

259. F. vesca, *L.* *Strawberry.*

Native; abundant in woods and thickets, and on old walls. Specimens from Brandon Hill are in the Stephens' Herbarium. V. VI.

(*Fragaria elatior*, Ehrh. Straggling colonies of garden strawberries exist in several places; notably near the railway under Durdham Down, at Kingswood, Yatton, and near Clevedon. We are not certain that any of these are true *elatior*, and it seems probable that they all have escaped from cultivation in comparatively recent times.)

RUBUS, *L.*

The arrangement of the bramble-forms at present known to us in the district has been undertaken with much hesitation. It is only by using abundant leisure with enthusiastic diligence that a botanist can become familiar with this genus; and it is perhaps not a matter for surprise that the few who luckily are endowed with the essentials should prefer to employ them in other directions. That we have not in our own ranks a bramble expert can therefore be no rare misfortune, much as we regret it. To the ever-ready kindness of Mr. T. R. Archer Briggs we owe the identification of most of our specimens of Rubus and Rosa, as well as many other valuable notes. We have adopted some of the records in Swete's Flora, as the author states that his specimens were named by Mr. Edwin Lees. It will, however, be evident that our scanty notes do not justice to the bramble strength of the district. Further investigation will reveal other species, and other habitats for those here mentioned.

260. **R. Idæus,** *L. Raspberry.*
>Native ; in most of the woods about Bristol.
>G. Glen Frome, Stapleton. Shirehampton.
>S. Abbots' Leigh. Bourton. Castle and Court Hills, Clevedon. Leigh Wood. Meare, *Rev. R. P. Murray.* Worlebury Wood.   VI.

261. **R. affinis,** *W. & N.*
>G. Stapleton, *Herb. Dr. H. O. Stephens.* Conham, and Clifton Down. *Swete, Fl.*
>S. Winscombe. *Mr. W. E. Green!*   VII. VIII.

262. **R. Lindleianus,** *Lees.*
>G. Brandon Hill, and Stapleton. *Swete, Fl.* p. 28. Yate Common !
>S. Leigh Wood, *Herb. Dr. H. O. Stephens*, labelled "*R. nitidus, Bab. in lit.*" Strawberry Hill, Clevedon !
>   VII.—IX.

263. **R. rhamnifolius,** *W. & N.*
>G. Stapleton, *Herb. Dr. H. O. Stephens*, labelled *R. cordifolius, W. & N.* We have gathered by the river side under Cook's Folly the bramble mentioned by Mr. Briggs under *R. Lindleianus* in the Flora of Plymouth as very common about Plymouth, and probably an undescribed species.

264. **R. imbricatus,** *Hort.*
>G. Stapleton ! "Precisely as seen around Plymouth." *Briggs in lit.*

265. **R. discolor,** *W. & N.*
   The most common of all the species, though not usually to be seen in woods. We have a peculiar variety from Crew's Hole, G., with large leaves having the terminal leaflet nearly round, and often quite blunt. VII.—IX.

266. **R. thyrsoideus,** *Wimm.*
   S. Hedges at Ken! and a hedge in Walton by Clevedon, beyond Lady's Bay! *Mr. W. E. Green.*

267. **R. leucostachys,** *Sm.*
   G. Crew's Hole! Yate Common!
   S. Very abundant in Leigh Woods. Norton's Wood, Clevedon! "Common between Radstock and Frome." *Rev. R. P. Murray.*
   A bramble gathered under Cook's Folly, G., is said by Mr. Briggs to be "between this and *villicaulis* just as at Plymouth." VII. VIII.

268. **R. Salteri,** *Bab.*; β. **R. calvatus,** *Blox.*
   G. Yate Common!

269. **R. carpinifolius,** *W. & N.*
   Stapleton, G., and Brislington, S. *Herb. Dr. H. O. Stephens.*

270. **R. villicaulis,** *W. & N.*
   G. Stapleton. *Swete, Fl.,* p. 28.
   S. Strawberry Hill and Norton's Wood, Clevedon. Wells. *Miss Livett!*

271. **R. mucronulatus,** *Bor.*
   G. Stapleton!
   S. Norton's Wood and Norton's Lane, Clevedon. *Mr. W. E. Green.*

272. **R. macrophyllus,** *Weihe.*
   α. *R. umbrosus, Arrh.*
   Plentiful in Bourton Combe, S.!

β. *macrophyllus*, or γ. *Schlechtendalii, W. & N.*
  Abbots' Leigh, S.!
δ. *amplificatus, Lees.*
  St. Vincent's Rocks, G. *Swete, Fl.*

273. **R. Bloxamii,** *Lees.*
  Leigh Wood, S.! *Fide Mr. J. G. Baker.*

274. **R. Hystrix,** *Weihe.*
  "Wood at Stapleton, *Bab. in lit.*" Herb. Dr. H. O. Stephens.

275. **R. rudis,** *Weihe.*
  G. Pennant quarries, Stapleton. Herb. Dr. H. O. Stephens.
  S. Abbots' Leigh! Clevedon! *Mr. W. F. Green.* St. Anne's Wood. *Swete, Fl.* Weston-super-Mare.

276. **R. Radula,** *Weihe.*
  G. Plentiful on Clifton Down!
  S. Norton's Lane, Clevedon! *Mr. W. E. Green.*

277. **R. Koehleri,** *Weihe.*
  G. Stapleton!
  γ. *R. pallidus, Weihe.*
  G. Yate Common!
  S. Near Gurney Slade. *Rev. R. P. Murray.*

278. **R. fusco-ater,** *Weihe.*
  G. Stapleton. *Mr. G. H. K. Thwaites, in Swete, Fl.* p. 28.

279. **R. diversifolius,** *Lindl.*
  G. Crew's Hole!
  S. Wells. *Miss Livett!*

280. **R. Lejeunii,** *Weihe.*
  G. Crew's Hole!

281. **R. corylifolius,** *Sm.*
  G. Filton Meads! St Vincent's Rocks.

S. Gypsy Lane, Ken! Walton-by-Clevedon! Leigh Wood.

282. **R. tuberculatus**, *Bab.*
S. Gypsy Lane, Ken! Milton!

283. **R. cœsius**, *L.* *Dewberry.*
Frequent in hedges near Bristol and elsewhere. VI. VII.

GEUM, *L.*

284. **G. urbanum**, *L.* *Avens.*
Native. In hedges, woods, and bushy places, very common. VI.—VIII.

285. **G. intermedium**, *Ehrh.*
Native.
S. Asham Wood, with *G. urbanum*, and *G. rivale*. Dr. H. F. Parsons.

286. **G. rivale**, *L.*
" This formerly grew in some plenty in damp meadows about Nailsea. I know not if it has now disappeared." *Mr. T. B. Flower.* Long Ashton, S. *Swete, Fl.*, p. 29. We have not been able to ascertain if this plant still exists in the localities named. Asham Wood, between Nunney and Downhead, S. *Dr. H. F. Parsons.* Ebbor, *Mr. J. G. Baker.* Gurney-Slade, *Rev. R. P. Murray.*

ROSA, *L.*

In this genus we have followed the arrangement of Mr. J. G. Baker in his Monograph of the British Roses, *Linn. Journ.*, xi. 197. See note under Rubus.

287. **R. spinosissima**, *L.* *Burnet Rose.*
" I have seen this on sandy banks about Kewstoke, and at Clevedon, S." *Mr. T. B. Flower.* Weston-super-Mare, *Herb. Dr. H. O. Stephens*, no date. Perhaps now extinct. Within the last three years we have several times carefully examined the localities, but did

not find the rose. There are two very old bushes in the strip of shrubbery which surrounds the "Observatory" at Clifton.

288. R. tomentosa, *Sm.*
Native; in hedges and on bushy hills, not common.
G. Trooper's Hill, Crew's Hole. *Herb. Dr. H. O. Stephens.* Nibley Knoll.
S. Stockwood Lane. *Herb. Dr. H. O. Stephens.* Wells. *Miss Livett;* who sent specimens of several varying forms of this species.

Var. *scabriuscula, Sm.*
G. Crew's Hole.
S. Bank of Avon opposite Sea Mills. Walton Hill, Clevedon. Wells. *Miss Livett.* VI. VII.

289. R. rubiginosa, *L. Sweetbriar.*
Native; very rare.
S. Walton Hill, Clevedon! Whatley Combe. *Dr. H. F. Parsons.*
All Swete's stations for this rose belong to *R. micrantha.*
VI. VII.

290. R. micrantha, *Sm.*
Native; in hedges and thickets, common.
G. Aust. Black Rock Gully. Kingswood. Stapleton.
S. Bank of Avon under Leigh Woods. Bourton. Brean Down. Leigh Woods. Very plentiful on the high ground beyond Walton Castle, Clevedon, where nearly all the roses belong to this species. Stockwood. Frequent about Wells. *Miss Livett!*

Var. *Briggsii, Baker.*
Near the coast at St. Thomas' Head, Somerset. This, the naked peduncled variety of *R. micrantha* is of the greatest interest. It was first discovered in this country near Plymouth, by Mr. Briggs many years ago; and up to

last summer no botanist had found it elsewhere in Britain. We had much pleasure, therefore, in gathering it by the Bristol Channel on June 26, 1881.

Var. *hystrix, Leman.*

" St. Vincent's Rocks, G., *Dr. St. Brody* " *Baker's Mon.*, p. 222. We have searched for this in vain. VII. VIII.

291. R. inodora, *Fr.*

" Woods at Brean Down, S. *(Woods!)* " *Baker's Mon.*, p 224. It is very probable that the southern slopes of Brean Down were wooded up to a comparatively recent date. At the present time a few stumps and some low bushes alone remain, and we fear *Rosa inodora* is no longer among them. It has been reported from Castle Hill, Clevedon, but doubtless in error for *R. micrantha*, a specimen of which stands for this rose in the Stephens' Herbarium.

292. R. canina, *L. Dog Rose.*

Var. *lutetiana, Leman.* Very common. It is, we think, the commonest form in the district.

Var. *dumalis, Bechst.* Very common. Abundant on Clifton and Durdham Downs.

Var. *biserrata, Mérat.*

Very rare? Walton Hill, Clevedon. S.

Var. *urbica, Leman.*

Common.

Var. *arvatica, Baker.* Rare.

S. Bedminster Meads, near Lock's Mills. Bourton. Knowle.

Var. *obtusifolia, Desv.*

Rare. Bedminster Meads. S. *Fide Mr. J. G. Baker.*

Var. *tomentella, Leman.*

Rare.

G. Charfield. Charlton. Nibley Knoll.

Var. *verticillacantha, Mérat.*
Frequent.
G. Roadside at Aust. Hedges by the field-path between Thornbury and Aust.
S. Bedminster. Kewstoke. Weston-super-Mare.
The Aust stations belong to *R. aspernata, Déséglise*, which has the calyx-tube and sepals densely setose on the back.
Var. *collina, Jacq. R. Kosinciana, Déséglise.*
Very rare. Crox Top. S. *Rev. W. H. Painter!*
Var. *Reuteri, Godet. R. crepiniana, Déségl. M. S. S.*
Rare.
G. Black Rock Gully, Durdham Down. *Mr. T. B. Flower, fide Mr. J. G. Baker.*
S. Crox Top. *Rev. W. H. Painter!*
Var. *subcristata, Baker.*
Knowle, S. *Rev. W. H. Painter!*

293. R. stylosa, *Desv.* **R. systyla,** *Bast. E. B.*, 1895.
Native; in hedges and thickets, and on ditchbanks in the marshlands. Common. Many of the more luxuriant plants, especially in wet places, have the column of styles but little or not at all protruded, and in this way approach closely to *R. collina Jacq.* The most characteristic or typical specimens are to be had in dry situations, as for instance, on St. Vincent's Rocks.
G. Aust. Horfield. St. Vincent's Rocks.
S. Bedminster. Bourton. Cheddar. Portbury. Wedmore. Wells. Winscombe. Very abundant in the lowlands from Yatton to Clevedon and Weston-super-Mare; in some places forming quite half of the rose flora. VI. VII.

294. R. arvensis, *Huds.*
Native; in hedges and thickets. Common nearly everywhere in the wooded and enclosed portions of the

district. It occurs in the most extraordinary profusion and luxuriance near Nibley, G., almost to the exclusion of all other roses. On the Somerset bank of the Avon opposite Sea Mills, we find bushes with unripened fruits persistent until the next summer. VI. VII.

β. *R. bibracteata, Bast.* (as interpreted by Mr. Baker.) Wells, S. *Miss Livett.*

CRATÆGUS, *L.*

295. C. Oxyacantha, *L. Hawthorn.*

β. *C. monogyna, Jacq.*

Native; very common. It is doubtful if *C. Oxyacantha, Jacq.* grows in the district. We have not seen a specimen, although it has been reported to us. Intermediate states, however, occur frequently. For instance, trees on Pur Down and elsewhere have glabrous pedicels, and a bush on Leigh Down is quite glabrous; with triangular-acuminate, spreading, reflexed sepals, and glossy leaves. This bush was the very last to bloom in 1881, in fact specimens were cut from it on June 23rd. That season will be long remembered for the luxuriant flowering of the Hawthorn, whose snowy wreaths, then in full perfection, dotted our Downs with indescribable beauty. V. VI.

(*Mespilus germanica, L.* A tree, apparently wild, has been seen on the cliff at Clevedon by *Mrs. Lainson* and *Mr. W. E. Green.*)

PYRUS, *L.*

296. P. communis, *L. Wild Pear.*

Denizen; rare.

G. Shirehampton. Stapleton. *Herb. Dr. H. O. Stephens.*

S. A tree (30 feet) by the brook at the bottom of Bishport Wood; no fruit in 1881. A tree (20 feet) on the bank of a stream running through meadow-land near Woodspring Priory; full of fruit in 1881. IV. V.

297. P. Malus, *L.* *Crab Apple.*
Native; in hedges and woods, common. There are some fine trees towards Dundry; and in a wood by Stoke Park.
V.

298. P. Aucuparia, *L.* *Mountain Ash.*
Native; in woods, rather rare.
G. Wick Rocks.
S. Clevedon. Leigh Woods, chiefly on rocks near the Avon. Worlebury Wood. Yatton. V. VI.

299. P. Aria, *Sm.* *White Beam.*
Native; in woods and on limestone rocks, locally common.
G. St. Vincent's Rocks and Durdham Down. Woods above Wotton-under-Edge.
S. Bourton Combe. Brean Down. Clevedon. Cheddar. Leigh Woods. Sidcot. Yatton. On exposed rocks near Winscombe, and elsewhere in the Mendips, where it is sometimes seen in hedges.

In successive years there is a very considerable difference in the amount of blossom borne by the White Beams, and thus their appearance at the period of flowering alters greatly. In 1877 the trees on the summit of Nightingale Valley flowered splendidly. In the three following seasons there was scarcely a corymb to be seen, and, indeed, in one of those years it was only with great difficulty that an herbarium specimen could be found. But in 1881, when every tree flowered most abundantly, *Pyrus Aria* excelled them all, and shone forth once more in maximum beauty, the silvery foliage of the older trees being almost hidden by masses of inflorescence.

A variety or hybrid with lobed or pinnatifid leaves (placed under *P. scandica, Bab.,* in *English Botany*) grows somewhere in Leigh Woods, and has been gathered on several occasions; but the station of the tree is not now known. It was first recorded, in *Swete, Fl.,* pp. 30 and 99, as *P. intermedia, Ehrh.,* by Miss Atwood, from whom probably Dr. Boswell-Syme had his specimens, and was gathered also a few years ago by Mr. W. E. Green. His specimen was exhibited at the Bristol meeting of the British Association, and was then lost. Mr. Green has failed to find his way to the tree a second time, and repeated searches by other botanists have not sufficed to rediscover it. Swete's additional mention of " β. *pinnatifida, Ehrh.,* Leigh Woods, S., frequent," must be an error. V.

300. P. torminalis, *Sm*.

Native; in woods, very rare.

G. Oldbury Court Wood. *Mr. W. E. Green.* Formerly near Cook's Folly Wood (not on St. Vincent's Rocks), now extinct. *Mr. T. B. Flower.* In the Stephens' Herbarium there is a flowering specimen labelled "Wood at Conham, near the old Spelter Works." No date. This is probably the authority for the record in *Swete, Fl.,* p. 30.

S. Early in June, 1881, we discovered at least a dozen small trees growing on exposed rocks near the river under Leigh Woods. These had not flowered. Their leaves differ in shape from those figured in English Botany, being much narrower across from tip to tip of the basal lobes.

LYTHRACEÆ.
LYTHRUM, *L.*

301. L. Salicaria, *L.* *Purple Loosestrife.*
Native; in wet places. Very rare in the northern division.
G. Banks of the Frome, near Stapleton.
S. Bank of Avon under Leigh Wood. Clevedon. Paulton. Wells. Winscombe. Frequent throughout the marshlands from the Mendips to the Channel.
VII. VIII.

TAMARISCACEÆ.
TAMARIX, *L.*

302. T. anglica, *Webb.*
Alien. To be seen in many places on the Channel shore, but rarely except where planted. VII. VIII.

ONAGRACEÆ.
EPILOBIUM, *L.*

303. E. angustifolium, *L.*, *a.* **E. macrocarpum,** *Steph.*
Native; in damp and shady places, plentiful about Bristol, especially by the Avon under Leigh Wood, S. Also in great abundance on the peat towards the southern limit of the district. VII.

304. E. hirsutum, *L.* *Great Willow Herb.*
Native; in wet ditches: common. VII. VIII.

305. E. parviflorum, *Schreb.*
Native; in damp places: very common. VII. VIII.

306. E. montanum, *L.*
Native; on walls, banks, and in waste places: very common. VI. VII.

307. E. lanceolatum, *S. & M.*
Native. Very rare.

ONAGRACEÆ.

G. On rocks near Frome Glen. *Mr. G. H. K. Thwaites!* Conham. *Herb. Dr. H. O. Stephens.* VII. VIII.

308. E. roseum, *Schreb.*
Native; frequently met with at the east of Bristol.
G. Conham. Crew's Hole. Hanham. Frome Glen, Stapleton.
S. St. Anne's Wood. *Mr. G. H. K. Thwaites, Swete, Fl. Mr. W. E. Green.* VII. VIII.

309. E. tetragonum, *L.*
Native; in damp places, frequent.
G. Ashley. Horfield. Stapleton.
S. Abbots' Leigh. Draycot. Leigh Wood. Weston-super-Mare. Yatton. VII. VIII.

310. E. obscurum, *Schreb.*
Native; in wet places, and on ditch banks, common.
VII. VIII.

311. E. palustre, *L.*
Native; in wet places, frequent.
G. Sea Mills. Shirehampton.
S. Abbots' Leigh. Ashcot. Leigh Woods. VII. VIII.

ŒNOTHERA, *L.*

312. Œ. biennis, *L.* *Evening Primrose.*
Alien. Introduced from America. Locally plentiful in some sandy waste places on the coast.
G. Under Black Rock; first noticed by *Mr. H. Charbonnier,* 1867.
S. By the riverside under Leigh Wood. Kewstoke. *Rev. W. H. Painter.* Abundant on the sands and by the roadside between Brean Down and Burnham, where Œ. *odorata* was *not* seen, although carefully searched for in 1880 and 1881. VII. VIII.

313. Œ. odorata, *Jacq.*
Alien. Very rare.
S. Sandhills between Weston-super-Mare and Uphill.
We looked closely for this plant on several occasions in August, 1880, and saw only three specimens in all. It has a place in some of the neighbouring gardens, which have probably been supplied from the sands, as the plant certainly grew there before the gardens were made. We have never seen it west of the Axe.
VII. VIII.

CIRCÆA, *L.*
314. C. lutetiana, *L.* *Enchanter's Nightshade.*
Native; in woods and shady places, common. VI.—VIII.

HALORAGACEÆ.
MYRIOPHYLLUM, *L.*
315. M. verticillatum, *L.*
Native; in ponds and ditches, very rare.
G. Shirehampton. *Swete, Fl.,* p. 31.
S. Yatton. *Miss Winter.* VII. VIII.

316. M. spicatum, *L.*
Native; in ponds and ditches, frequent.
G. Pond in St. Philip's Marsh. *Herb. Dr. H. O. Stephens.* Shirehampton. *Rev. W. W. Spicer.*
S. Clevedon. Ditches about Weston Junction, Yatton, and elsewhere in the marsh lands. VI. VII.

HIPPURIS, *L.*
317. H. vulgaris, *L.* *Mare's-tail.*
Native; in marsh ditches, locally common.
S. Ken. Portbury. Yatton. Plentiful in ditches below Cheddar and Draycot. VI. VII.

CUCURBITACEÆ.
BRYONIA, *L.*

318. B. dioica, *L.* *Red Bryony.*
Native; in hedges and thickets, common.
G. Abundant in hedges about Stoke Park, Sea Mills, and Shirehampton. Combe Glen.
S. Bedminster. Clevedon. Englishcombe. Portishead.
V.—VIII.

PORTULACEÆ.
MONTIA, *L.*

319. M. fontana, *L.*
Native; in water and in boggy places, rather rare.
G. Brandon Hill. *Herb. Dr. H. O. Stephens.* No longer there. In a boggy spot close to Mangotsfield Junction.
S. Plentiful by the stream between Failand Farm and the Tan-pits. Plentiful in boggy streams on Black Down.
IV.—VII.

CRASSULACEÆ.
SEDUM, *L.*

320. S. Telephium, *L.*
Native at one or two stations; an escape in others.
G. St. Vincent's Rocks. Wick Rocks.
S. Portbury. Easton, *Miss Livett.* VII. VIII.

321. S. Fabaria, *Koch.* **S. purpureum,** *Tausch.*
G. Common about Kingswood. *Dr. A. C. Hassé.* Mr. Flower informs us that his record for this plant in *Swete, Fl.,* p. 33, is an error.
S. Great Elm. *Dr. H. F. Parsons.* VII. VIII.

322. S. album, *L.*

Native; on rocks and walls. Rather frequent, and probably planted at some of the stations.

G. Almondsbury. Frenchay. Penpole Point in abundance. Wick Rocks. Kingswood.

S. Bourton. Nailsea. Ken. Rowberrow. Worle. On rocks in Asham Wood, apparently native; on walls at Great Elm; and at Holwell, near Nunney. *Dr. H. F. Parsons.* VII. VIII.

323. S. dasyphyllum, *L.*

Native? In numerous localities, but always on walls.

G. "St. Vincent's Rocks and walls about Clifton." *Shiercliff's Bristol and Hotwell Guide*, pub. 1789. Clifton Hill. *Rev. W. W. Spicer*, June 10, 1868. Probably now extinct. "Walls at Clifton." *Herb. Dr. H. O. Stephens.* Hanham. Glen Frome, Stapleton!

S. Abbot's Leigh. Near Cadbury Camp. Bedminster. *Swete, Fl.,* p. 33. Clapton. Clevedon. Cranmore. *Miss Livett.* Nailsea, plentiful. *Miss Winter.* Tickenham. *Mr. W. F. Green.* Plentiful on a wall at Buckland Dinham.

324. S. acre, *L.* *Stonecrop.*

Native; on rocks and walls nearly everywhere. VI. VII.

(*S. sexangulare, L.,* has been planted at Wick Rocks.)

325. S. reflexum, *L.*

Native or denizen. In many places, chiefly or solely on old stone walls.

G. Almondsbury. Charfield. Thornbury. Sea Mills. Shirehampton.

S. Cheddar. Cleeve. Stanton Drew. Wells. Weston-super-Mare. Winscombe. Yatton. VII. VIII.

326. S. rupestre, *L. ?*
Native; on rocks, rare.
Var. a., *majus.*
S. Cheddar. Cleeve. Walton-in-Gordano. Wick. Planted on walls in many places.
Var. β., *minus.*
St. Vincent's Rocks, G. Also on the opposite side of the Avon, under Leigh Wood. VI.—VIII.

SEMPERVIVUM, *L.*

327. S. tectorum, *L.* *Common House-leek.*
Alien; on roofs and walls, always planted. VII.

COTYLEDON, *L.*

328. C. Umbilicus, *L.* *Navelwort.*
Native; on rocks and walls. Very common about Bristol, especially at Abbots' Leigh, Almondsbury, and Stapleton, but decreasingly frequent to the southward. VI.—VIII.

RIBESIACEÆ.
RIBES, *L.*

329. R. Grossularia, *L.* *Gooseberry.*
Denizen; in hedges and bushy places, rather common. Plentiful about Abbots' Leigh. A number of fine bushes grow at an old limekiln at Failand, and in a lane leading thence into the Clevedon road. It grows luxuriantly in pollard willows on the banks of the Chew at Pensford, where the floods have induced many plants in like manner to assume an epiphytic habit. IV. V.

330. R. nigrum, *L.* *Black Currant.*
Denizen; in woods and wet places, rare.

G. Bank of Avon at Keynsham. *Herb. Dr. H. O. Stephens.* Westbury.

S. Hedgebank at Failand. Leigh Woods. Worlebury Wood. IV. V.

331. **R. rubrum,** *L. Red Currant.*

Denizen; in hedges and woods, and on the banks of rivers; frequent.

G. Plentiful by the river side at Tortworth.

S. In many places in woods about Abbots' Leigh. Portbury. On the banks of the Chew near Pensford. Hedges about Wrington and Langford.

SAXIFRAGACEÆ.

SAXIFRAGA, *L.*

332. **S. hypnoides,** *L.*

Native. Its mat-like tangles mantle some moist and shady ledges on the Cheddar Cliffs; but it is not certainly known to grow elsewhere in the Mendips.

V.—VII.

333. **S. tridactylites,** *L.*

Native; on walls, dry banks, and rocks. Common.

IV.—VII.

334. **S. granulata,** *L.*

Native; in dry pastures; very rare.

S. Near Marksbury. *Mr. T. B. Flower.* Also reported to grow at Cheddar. V.

CHRYSOSPLENIUM, *L.*

335. **C. alternifolium,** *L.*

Native; on the swampy margins of streams in Somersetshire; local. It is said to have been found near Bristol (towards Pill) by Dr. Rogers. Abundant on the eastern border of the district near Mells and Great Elm. Frequent in damp places about Wells. *Miss Livett.* Between Wrington and Langford. IV. V.

336. **C. oppositifolium,** *L.*
Native. Not uncommon on damp banks and in shaded swamps.
G. Bitton. Between Stapleton and Filton.
S. Leigh Wood, second valley. In several places between Abbots' Leigh and Failand. Under Dundry Hill. Wells. III.—V.

UMBELLIFERÆ.

HYDROCOTYLE, *L.*

337. **H. vulgaris,** *L.* *Pennywort.*
Native; in marshes and boggy places; frequent.
G. Boggy spot close to Mangotsfield Junction. Yate Common.
S. Marsh on Burnham Sands. By the stream between Sandy Lane and Failand Farm. Uphill Drove. Walton Drove. Yatton. V.—VIII.

SANICULA, *L.*

338. **S. europæa,** *L.* *Sanicle.*
Native; common in woods and shady places nearly everywhere. VI. VII.

ERYNGIUM, *L.*

339. **E. maritimum,** *L.* *Eryngo. Sea Holly.*
Native; only on the shore of the Bristol Channel in two or three places. Chiefly on Brean sands. VII. VIII.

340. **E. campestre,** *L.*
Possibly not native; in one spot only, the precise whereabouts of which is unknown to us.

"Has been known to grow for many years at Weston-super-Mare." *Mr. T. B. Flower.* "Weston-super-Mare, Somerset." *Syme's F. B. Rev. R. P. Murray* has seen it growing there very sparingly, and in danger of being built over. See also "The Flora of Weston," by *G. St. Brody.*

CICUTA, L.

341. C. virosa, L.

Burnham, S., many years ago, and at Easton in 1880. *Miss M. W. Mayow.* We are aware that the occurrence of this plant in North Somerset is very doubtfully regarded; and we have not seen specimens. Still, believing that there is little likelihood of mistake in these records, we venture to publish them, and trust that future discovery may render them solid ground for the inclusion of the plant in the Bristol Flora.

APIUM, L.

342. A. graveolens, L. *Celery.*

Native; in marshes and ditches, particularly near tidal waters. Both banks of the Avon, from Crew's Hole downwards; but more abundant below Bristol. Burnham. Clevedon. VI.—VIII.

343. A. nodiflorum, R. *Helosciadium, Koch.*

Native; in marshes, ditches, and streams. Very common, and generally distributed.

β. *A. repens,* R.

S. Abbots' Leigh, *Rev. W. H. Painter.* Brislington.

VII. VIII.

344. A. inundatum, R.

Native; very rare and local. We have found it only in ditches on the peat below Wedmore, S. VII. VIII.

UMBELLIFERÆ.

PETROSELINUM, *Hoffm.*

345. P. sativum, *Hoffm.* *Parsley.*
Alien; on rocks, ruins, and old walls in many places.
G. Abundant on St. Vincent's Rocks. Syston, *Dr. Hassé.*
S. Portishead Point. In several places around Wells. Yatton. Weston-super-Mare. VI.—VIII.

346. P. segetum, *Koch.*
Native; in damp fields. Rather rare, or possibly it has been overlooked.
G. Ashley. Boiling Well, and Sea Mills. *Herb. Dr. H. O. Stephens.*
S. St. Anne's Wood. Burnham, *Miss Winter.* Easton. Weston-super-Mare, *Miss Livett.* VIII. IX.

SISON, *L.*

347. S. Amomum, *L.*
Native; common, and generally distributed. VIII. IX.

TRINIA, *Hoffm.*

348. T. vulgaris, *DC.* *Pimpinella dioica, Sm.*
Native; on limestone, locally plentiful. Our area includes nearly all the British stations. Occasionally we find a monœcious specimen.
G. St. Vincent's Rocks. Black Rock Gully.
S. Rocks at Hutton. Rocks by the Channel at Sand Point. Sidcot. Winscombe. Uphill. Worle Hill. V. VI.

ÆGOPODIUM, *L.*

349. Æ. Podagraria, *L.* *Gout-weed.*
Native? rather common. We have never seen this plant growing far from habitations. Its usual position is on hedgebanks bordering orchards and gardens.
G. Boyd Mill. Stapleton.

UMBELLIFERÆ.

S. Abbots' Leigh. Almondsbury. Brislington. Bedminster. Clevedon. Dundry. Failand. Englishcombe. Pensford. Wells. VI. VII.

CARUM, L.

350. C. flexuosum, *Fr.* *Bunium, Linn. Pignut.*
Native; in pastures and grassy places. Very common.
V. VI.

PIMPINELLA, L.

351. P. Saxifraga, *L.*
Native; on downs and in dry pastures. Very common, and very variable. The tallest and stoutest specimens we have ever seen (they were 2 ft. high) grew among loose stones on the top of Worle Hill, S.; one of the most barren and unproductive spots imaginable. (*P. magna* is not known in the district.) VII.—IX.

SIUM, L.

352. S. latifolium, *L.*
Native; in ditches, rather rare and local.
G. Shirehampton marshes.
S. Burnham. Ditches in the Cheddar Valley, near Cheddar and Winscombe. Ditches on peat below Wedmore. VII. VIII.

353. S. angustifolium, *L.*
Native; in ditches throughout the marshlands, from Portbury and Yatton, to Weston-super-Mare and Wells. Locally plentiful. Great Elm. *Dr. H. F. Parsons.*

BUPLEURUM, L.

354. B. tenuissimum, *L.*
Native. Very rare, and local; growing only on the banks of the estuaries in very few places.

G. Shirehampton, from the Powder House westward.
S. By the Channel near Woodspring.

(*B. rotundifolium* was gathered near Ham Green, S., many years ago, by Mr. T. B. Flower, who says the habitat has long since been destroyed.)

ŒNANTHE, *L.*

355. Œ. fistulosa, *L.*
Native; very abundant in ditches throughout the marshlands, from Portishead and Clevedon to the southern limit of the district. VII.—IX.

356. Œ. pimpinelloides, *L.*
Native; very rare with us, though said to be frequent in some other parts of Somerset.
S. Burnham, and Wells, *Miss Livett* and *Miss Mayow*. Bishport, *Mr. J. Foster*, *Swete, Fl.* 37. Uphill, *W. Christy* in *New Bot. Guide*. The plant gathered by *Mr. Flower* at the "riverside under Cook's Folly, G.," was *Œ. Lachenalii*. VI. VII.

357. Œ. Lachenalii, *Gmel.*
Native; in marshes, chiefly near salt water, frequent on the coast.
G. Bank of Avon at Sea Mills, sparingly. Syston Common.
S. Bank of Avon opposite Sea Mills. Plentiful on the marshy portion of Burnham Sands. Weston-super-Mare. VII.—IX.

358. Œ. silaifolia, *Bieb.?*
Native; in marshes, very rare.
G. Shirehampton. Marshy ground at New Passage, July, 1879.
S. Yatton. *Miss Winter*. VI. VII.

UMBELLIFERÆ.

359. **Œ. crocata,** *L.*
Native; on ditchbanks and in streams, common.
It grows near Bristol in many ditches between Long Ashton and Dundry, at the Abbots' Pond, and at Stapleton Mill. VI. VII.

360. **Œ. Phellandrium,** *Lam.*
Native; abundant in marsh ditches throughout the Cheddar Valley.
S. Axbridge. Berrow. Brent. Draycot. Easton. Wedmore. Weston Junction. Yatton. VII.—IX.

ÆTHUSA, *L.*

361. **Æ. Cynapium,** *L.* *Fool's Parsley.*
Native; a common weed on cultivated ground. VII. VIII.

FÆNICULUM, *Hoffm.*

362. **F. vulgare,** *Gaertn.* *Fennel.*
Native, or denizen; frequent.
G. Plentiful on ledges of St. Vincent's Rocks, where it has been known for more than a century. Bank of Avon under Durdham Down. Patchway.
S. Clevedon. Brean Down. Rodney Stoke. Wedmore. Yatton. VII. VIII.

SILAUS, *Besser.*

363. **S. pratensis,** *Bess.*
Native; common in meadows and pastures.
G. Charlton. Filton. Horfield. Patchway. Sea Mills.
S. Axbridge. Meadows around Dundry Hill. Failand. Easton. Winscombe. Woodspring. Yatton.
It grows in abundance at all these localities. VI.—VIII.

CRITHMUM, *L.*

364. C. maritimum, *L.* *Samphire.*

Native; in many places on the coast; both on rocks and on sandy beaches.

S. Brean Down. Burnham. Clevedon. Kewstoke sands. Sand Point. Portishead. Rocks to the north of Weston-super-Mare. Walton-in-Gordano. VI.—VIII.

ANGELICA, *L.*

365. A. sylvestris, *L.*

Native; in damp and shady places, very common.

One of the largest of our Umbellifers, attaining the height of from 8 to 10 feet in favourable situations, as in Berwick Wood, G. A specimen from Keynsham, S., preserved in the Bristol Museum, is 10 ft. 2 in. high.

VII. VIII.

PASTINACA, *L.*

366. P. sativa, *L.* *Parsnep.*

Native in many places; but in others derived from cultivation.

G. Chipping Sodbury. Filton. Henbury. Shirehampton. St. Vincent's Rocks.

S. Brean Down, and on the shore from thence towards Burnham, in profusion. Ashton. Clevedon. Draycot. Milton. Penhill. Worle. Wedmore. Yatton. VI.—VIII.

HERACLEUM, *L.*

367. H. Sphondylium, *L.* *Cow-parsnep. Hog-weed.*

Native; very common in hedges, fields, and pastures everywhere. The form, with very narrow leaf segments, was gathered at Sandford, S.   VI.—X.

UMBELLIFERÆ.

DAUCUS, *L.*

368. D. Carota, *L.*   *Carrot.*
   Native; in dry places, very common.   VI. VIII.

CAUCALIS, *Hoffm.*

369. C. daucoides, *L.*
   Colonist. A cornfield weed. Very rare.
   S. Burnham. *Miss M. W. Mayow.*   VI.

TORILIS, *Adans.*

370. T. Anthriscus, *Gaert.*
   Native; in bushy places and by roadsides. Very common.
                                                VII. VIII.

371. T. infesta, *Spr.*
   Colonist; in cornfields; rather rare.
   G. Avonmouth. Horfield. Kingswood. Montpelier.
   S. Near Buckland Dinham. Winscombe.   VII. VIII.

372. T. nodosa, *Gaert.*
   Native; in dry sheltered places. Frequent.
   G. Brandon Hill. St. Vincent's Rocks. Stapleton. Shirehampton.
   S. Anchor Head, Weston-super-Mare. Brean Down. Cheddar. Clevedon. Abbots' Leigh. Knowle. Rownham. Easton. Woodspring. Worle.   V.—VII.

SCANDIX, *L.*

373. S. Pecten-Veneris, *L.*
   Colonist; on cultivated land. Common.   VI.—VIII.

CHÆROPHYLLUM, *L.*

374. C. sylvestre, *L.*
   Native; in pastures, hedgebanks, and damp shady places.
   Very common everywhere.   IV.—VI.

   (*C. sativum, Lam.* Casual at Knowle, S. *Rev. W. H. Painter.*)

375. **C. Anthriscus,** *Lam.* *A. vulgaris, Pers.*
Native; on banks and under walls. Rare.
G. Mangotsfield Village. St. Philip's Marsh, *Herb. Dr. H. O. Stephens.*
S. Burnham, *Miss Winter.* Berrow. Bank by the roadside at Brean. Upper Knowle. Field adjacent to Kewstoke sands, in plenty for a few yards, July, 1881.

376. **C. temulum,** *L.*
Native; by roadsides. Common. VI. VII.

CONIUM, *L.*

377. **C. maculatum,** *L.* *Hemlock.*
Native; in hedges and damp waste places. Common.
G. Bank of Avon above and below Bristol. Berkeley. St. Philip's Marsh, abundant. Thornbury. Tortworth. Sea Mills, in plenty.
S. Ashton. Bishport. Bank of Avon opposite Sea Mills. South Stoke. Yatton. Wells. St. Anne's Wood. Very fine plants may be seen here in the marshy ground by the stream. VI. VII.

SMYRNIUM, *L.*

378. **S. Olusatrum,** *L.* *Alexanders.*
Denizen; near buildings. Rather rare.
G. Abundant on St. Vincent's Rocks.
S. Abundant on the beach at Clevedon. Pamborough. Uphill. Roadside in Worle Village.

HEDERACEÆ.
HEDERA, *L.*

379. **H. Helix,** *L.* *Ivy.*
Native; very common everywhere. X. XI.

CORNACEÆ.
CORNUS, *L.*

380. **C. sanguinea,** *L.* *Dog-wood.*
   Native; in most woods and hedges. Plentiful in Leigh Wood; and on Clifton and Durdham Downs. VI.

FLORA OF THE BRISTOL COAL-FIELD.

ADDITIONS TO PARTS I. AND II.

Some discoveries have been made, and much additional information received, since the publication of Part II. The more important facts are given below.

Fumaria pallidiflora, *Jord.* *a.* **Jordani.**
 On a hedge-bank between Axbridge and Cheddar. June, 1882. First record for this species.

Cardamine impatiens, L. has now another station in Gloucestershire, having been found on the border of a wood near Tortworth.

Sisymbrium Sophia, L. Berrow, S. June, 1880. *Rev. R. P. Murray.*

Draba muralis, L. We learn that this plant grows in abundance in East Somerset; at Mells, Chelwood, Stone Easton, and Horrington.

Lepidium latifolium, L. Is plentiful on a high bank by the road side at Berrow, S. No doubt an alien here.

Sagina maritima, Don. We thought this was confined to the coast, but *Rev. R. P. Murray* has gathered it on Black Down.

Rubus discolor, *W. & N.* *var.* **leucocarpus.**
 In an old hedge at the foot of the Mendips near Axbridge, S. An amber-fruited blackberry. This most interesting plant was discovered by Mr. Read, and has been described by the Editor in Journ. of Bot., Nov., 1882. It may be noted that prior to this discovery a white-fruited bramble had not been noticed in the kingdom during nearly two centuries.

The following aliens (with others) have been found on old colliery *débris* near Kingswood, G. An account of this remarkable colony is given in the Transactions of our Society:—

Delphinium Ajacis.
Farsetia incana ?
Erysimum orientale.
Satureia hortensis.
Dianthus prolifer.
Silene dichotoma.
Trifolium supinum.
Medicago sativa.
Bupleurum rotundifolium.
Glaucium phœnicium.
Camelina sativa.
Gilia capitata.
Gypsophila muralis.
Saponaria Vaccaria.
Silene noctiflora.
Melilotus alba.
Medicago falcata.

We are glad to be able to announce that renewed search has shewn that several plants which it was feared had become extinct upon Brandon Hill are still in existence. Not only *Scleranthus annuus*, but also *Montia fontana*, *Ornithopus perpusillus*, and *Trifolium subterraneum*, have been seen at this spot during the past year.

March, 1883.

FLORA
OF THE
BRISTOL COAL-FIELD.

EDITED (FOR THE BRISTOL NATURALISTS' SOCIETY) BY

JAMES WALTER WHITE,

Hon. Secretary of the Botanical Section.

"*Rerum cognoscere causas*"—VIRGIL.

PART III.
COROLLIFLORÆ.

BRISTOL:
JAMES FAWN & SON.

PRINTED BY E. AUSTIN & SON, CHRONICLE OFFICE, CLIFTON.

MDCCCLXXXIII.

PHANEROGAMIA.

Class 1. *DICOTYLEDONES.*
Div. 3. *COROLLIFLORÆ.*

LORANTHACEÆ.
VISCUM, L.

381. V. album, *L. Mistletoe.*

Native. Rather common, especially in orchards in North Somerset. Parasitic upon Apple, Ash, Aspen, Elm, Hawthorn, Pear, Poplar, and Whitebeam.   III. IV.

CAPRIFOLIACEÆ.
ADOXA, L.

382. A. Moschatellina, *L. Moschatel.*

Native; on damp or shady hedge-banks and in woods. Common.

G. Stoke Bishop. Valley of the Trym. Almondsbury.

S. Very abundant in St. Anne's Wood, Brislington. Hedge-banks about Abbot's Leigh. Chewton Mendip. Clevedon. Farrington Gourney. Stone Easton. Yatton. Wells.

When young and moist with dew it has a faint musky smell, which gave rise to its original name. The fruit is scarce, and difficult to find on account of the plant being in most instances completely overgrown and hidden under ranker vegetation before its drupes ripen.

IV. V.

SAMBUCUS, *L.*

383. S. Ebulus, *L. Dwarf Elder. Danewort.*
Denizen; in hedges, very rare.
   G. "Hedges on the north side of Troopers' Hill." *Herb. Dr. H. O. Stephens.* Netham, near Crew's Hole. *Swete, Fl.*, p. 40, and *Mr. W. E. Green*, 1880.
   S. Vobster, near Radstock.   VIII.

384. S. nigra, *L. Common Elder.*
Native; in hedges and woods, very common.   VI.

VIBURNUM, *L.*

385. V. Lantana, *L. Wayfaring Tree.*
Native; in hedges and thickets, common.   V.

386. V. Opulus, *L. Common Guelder Rose.*
Native; in hedges in damp situations, and in moist woods, common.
   G. On both banks of the Frome at Stapleton, abundant. Woods near Wotton-under-Edge. Shirehampton. Westbury.
   S. Leigh Wood and bank of Avon. Frequent in hedges between Chew Magna and Dundry; and about the "Wild Country." Long Ashton. Max Mills. Radstock. Wells. Weston-in-Gordano. Yatton.   VI. VII.

LONICERA, *L.*

387. L. Periclymenum, *L. Honeysuckle.*
Native; in copses, and hedge-rows. Very common.
                                                 VI.—VIII.

RUBIACEÆ.

SHERARDIA, *L.*

388. S. arvensis, *L.*
Native; on dry banks upon the Downs, and elsewhere; and as a weed on cultivated land. Very common.
                                                 V.—VII.

ASPERULA, *L.*

389. A. cynanchica, *L..*

Native; on dry hills and in pastures upon limestone, rare and local.

S. Clevedon Very luxuriant upon Worlebury Hill near Weston-super-Mare. Hills near Sidcot. On Mendips above Draycot.   VI. VII.

390. A. odorata, *L.* *Sweet Woodruff.*

Native; in damp woods, rather generally distributed.

G. Woods near Wotton-under-Edge.

S. Bishport. Churchill. Congresbury. Leigh Wood. Coppices under Macs Knoll. Portbury. Portishead. Wells. Weston-in-Gordano. Yatton.

Withering remarks that some old authors spell the name " Woodderowffe "; and that the repetition of the double letters affords great amusement to children learning to spell.   V. VI.

GALIUM, *L.*

391. G. cruciatum, *With.* *Crosswort.*

Native. Abundant in many places on the Somerset side of the district, but scarce on the Gloucester side, and almost absent from the near vicinity of Bristol.

G. Near Filton. Shirehampton.

S. By the river-side under Leigh Wood. Brean. Chew Magna. Clevedon. Congresbury. Sparingly in Sandy Lane near the Tan-pits. On both banks of the Chew between Pensford and Stanton Drew. Abundant on hedge-banks at Brockley and Claverham. Frequent about Bath. Abundant at Great Elm and Buckland Dinham. Saltford. Wells. Winscombe.   V. VI.

392. G. tricorne, *With.*

Colonist; in dry cornfields, rare.

G. Cornfields at Charlton, 1881. Kingswood, 1880. Horfield, *Herb. Dr. H. O. Stephens.* " Cornfields at Pucklechurch," *Withering.*

S. Weston-in-Gordano. VI.—VIII.

393. **G. Aparine,** L. *Goose-grass.* " *Clivers.*"
Native; in hedges, bushy places, and elsewhere. A very common weed. VI.—VIII.

394. **G. verum,** L.
Native; in dry, open pastures. Abundant on the Downs near Bristol, and common throughout the district.
VII.—IX.

395. **G. Mollugo,** L.
Native; in hedges and thickets, very common. The variety β. *G. insubricum* (Gaud.) has been gathered at Abbot's Leigh. VII. VIII.

396. **G. saxatile,** L.
Native; on heaths and dry moory tracts. Very common on the Downs and in similar situations about Bristol.
VI. VIII.

397. **G. sylvestre,** *Poll. G. pusillum,* Sm.
Native; on the Cheddar Cliffs, where it is plentiful. It was said to grow on " St. Vincent's Rocks near Clifton Turnpike " in Shiercliff's Guide for 1789; but we have not seen a more recent record for that locality. VI. VII.

398. **G. uliginosum,** L.
Native; in wet places, rare.
G. Near Tortworth. In the Trym valley below Westbury.
S. Ditch banks near Long Ashton. Uphill. Wells, *Miss Livett.* VI. VII.

399. **G. palustre,** L.
Native. Very common in wet places, and generally distributed. *G. Witheringii,* Sm. differing only by having

rough edges to the leaves, is found in Shirehampton marshes; and in hedges near Stapleton.   VI. VII.

RUBIA, *L.*

400. **R. peregrina,** *L. Madder.*
Native; in woods and rocky thickets, frequent.
G. Plentiful about St. Vincent's Rocks, and Clifton Down. "Habitat *in rupe* S. Vincentii, *prope* Bristolium." *Huds. Fl. Anglica,* 1778.
S. Leigh Wood. "Wood opposite St. Vincent's Rocks, Bristol"; *Withering*, 1796. Bourton. Clevedon. Congresbury. Portishead. Walton-in-Gordano. Wells. In the wood at Weston-super-Mare. Yatton. VI.—VIII.

VALERIANACEÆ.

CENTRANTHUS, *DC.*

401. **C. ruber,** *DC. Red Valerian.*
Alien. Very well established in many places about Clifton and Bristol; chiefly on old walls, as at Cornwallis Crescent.
G. Abundant at Stapleton and Frenchay.
S. Churchill. Clevedon; very abundant. Wells. Weston-super-Mare. Yatton.   VI.—IX.

VALERIANA, *L.*

402. **V. officinalis,** *L.*
Native; in damp shady places, ditches and marshes, common.
G. Plentiful about Bristol. Charfield. Frenchay. Stapleton. Tortworth.
S. In abundance near the Avon under Leigh Wood. Bedminster. Bishport. Clevedon. Nailsea. Wedmore. Wells. Winscombe.   VI. VII.

DIPSACACEÆ.

403. V. dioica, *L.*
Native; in marshes and boggy meadows, frequent.
G. Marsh at the " Boiling Well." Hallen.
S. Barrow Gurney. Bedminster. Leigh Wood. Pensford. Walton-in-Gordano. Wells. Boggy fields near Winscombe.
" The male plant is always smaller and less robust, having a more transient function to perform than the other."
V. VI.

VALERIANELLA, *Moench.*

404. V. olitoria, *Moench. Lamb's Lettuce. Corn-Salad.*
Native; on earthy banks and cultivated land. Common.
V. VI.

405. V. Auricula, *DC.*
Native; very rare. We have not seen this plant growing in our district; but there is an undoubted specimen in the Stephens' Herbarium from " Eastwood, Brislington ": no date. It will surely be found again.

406. V. dentata, *Dietr.*
Colonist; on hedge-banks and in cornfields, frequent.
G. In plenty under a hedge by the towing path near Sea Mills. Horfield. Netham, *Swete Fl.* 42. Henbury.
S. Cornfields near Abbot's Leigh, and Failand. Uphill.
VI. VII.

DIPSACACEÆ.
DIPSACUS, *L.*

407. D. sylvestris, *L. Wild Teasel.*
Native; on banks and by roadsides. Very common.
VIII. IX.

(D. Fullonum, L. Cultivated or Clothiers' Teasel.
Established in several places, but is not wild.
G. Near Aust. Horfield.

S. Near Dundry. By Worle Hill, 1854. *Herb. Jenyns.)*

408. D. pilosus, *L. Shepherd's Rod. Small Teasel.*
Native; in damp shady places, rather rare.
G. By the river Frome at Stapleton, sparingly in two or three places. Combe Dingle, *Mr. W. E. Green.* Tortworth. Henbury Combe, *Herb. Powell.*
S. One large patch and two small ones by the railway under Leigh Wood. Clevedon. Croscombe. Stanton Drew, *Rev. W. H. Painter.* VIII.

KNAUTIA, *Coult.*

409. K. arvensis, *Coult. Field Scabious.*
Native. Very common in dry places and on arable land throughout the cultivated portions of the district. We have seen proliferous plants near the Black Rock quarry, G. VII.—IX.

SCABIOSA, *L.*

410. S. succisa, *L. Devil's Bit Scabious.*
Native; in damp meadows and rough pastures, common.
G. Clifton and Durdham Downs. Very abundant in the peaty meadows known as Filton Meads. Mangotsfield. Wick. Yate.
S. Plentiful by the Avon below Leigh Wood. In pastures about Bishport and Dundry. Bedminster. Clevedon. Wells. Winscombe. Yatton. VII.—IX.

411. S. Columbaria, *L.*
Native. Frequent on dry hills and limestone rocks.
G. St. Vincent's Rocks and bank of Avon. Hills above Wotton-under-Edge.
S. Rocks under Leigh Wood. Brean Down. Cheddar; and here sparingly with white flowers. Clevedon. On Mendip above Draycot. Sidcot. Uphill. Wells. Weston-super-Mare. Yatton. VII. VIII.

COMPOSITÆ.
EUPATORIUM, *L.*

412. E. cannabinum, *L.*   *Hemp Agrimony.*

Native; on the banks of streams, and in other wet places. Common, and generally distributed.   VIII. IX.

PETASITES, *Gaert.*

413. P. vulgaris, *Desf.*   *Butterbur.*

Native; by the sides of streams, and in swampy ground, frequent.

G. Bitton. Charfield. Banks of the Avon near Conham. Wick.

S. By the stream under Bishport wood, plentifully. Backwell Common. Banks of the Chew. Claverham. Paulton. Portbury. Radford. Wells, *Miss Livett.*   IV.

414. P. fragrans, *Presl.*

An introduced species, rapidly extending its range in the country, and now completely naturalized.

G. Several large patches on the railway embankment by the Avon near the Great Quarry. Abundant at Fishponds. In a lane near Cribbs Causeway.

S. Bourton. In Talbot Lane, close to Brislington. Clevedon. In several places on the outskirts of Wells.

I. II.

TUSSILAGO, *L.*

415. T. Farfara, *L.*   *Coltsfoot.*

Native. Common everywhere on poor soil. It is the first plant to vegetate on limestone rubble, and is therefore always seen in abundance about the quarries near Clifton.   III. IV.

ASTER, *L.*

416. A. Tripolium, *L.*   *Starwort.*

Native; on mud banks by the tidal waters, plentiful. The handsome blue or lilac rayed flowers are but rarely seen, as our plants are nearly all of the discoid variety. "Shore of the Avon, a little above the Hotwell, Bristol, between the gravel walk and the river. Var. 2. All the florets tubular. About Bristol, frequent. RAY." *Withering*, iii., 727. 1796. VIII. IX.

ERIGERON, *L.*

417. E. acris, *L. Fleabane.*

Native; on old walls, and in dry sandy places, rather common.

G. St. Vincent's Rocks; and bank of Avon below Clifton. On walls at Stoke Bishop. Wick.

S. Berrow. Buckland Dinham. Brislington. Burnham. Leigh Down; and bank of Avon under Leigh Wood. Wells. Weston-super-Mare. Yatton. VII. VIII.

(*E. canadensis*, *L.* cannot be considered a Bristol plant. Although found in the neighbourhood at intervals from the time of Withering, it seems only to have occurred casually; and we believe it has not been met with during the last forty years.)

BELLIS, *L.*

418. B. perennis, *L. Daisy.*

Native; in pastures everywhere.

In the Stephen's Herbarium there is a specimen of what has been called the "Hen and Chickens" daisy, bearing seven or eight small capitula on stalks about ¼in. long, which spring from the parent receptacle. It was gathered near Clevedon by *Rev. G. W. Braikenridge.*

SOLIDAGO, *L.*

419. S. Virgaurea, *L. Golden Rod.*

Native; on rocky or bushy banks in many places, common. Abundant about the Downs; on St. Vincent's Rocks; and on the opposite side of the river.

VII.—IX.

LINOSYRIS, DC.

420. L. vulgaris, Cass.

Native; only on limestone near Weston-super-Mare. Perhaps now extinct.

"Rocks near Birnbeck Island"; *St. Brody, Fl.* 156.

A specimen in the B. N. S. Herbarium labelled "Worle Hill," no date.

"Has been observed by Dr. Wollaston on the south western extremity of the Mendip Hills, Somersetshire." *With.,* ed. 7., iii., 920, 1830.

Worle Hill, S. Sept., 1846. *Herb. Powell.*

Some specimens in the Jenyn's Herbarium at Bath, gathered at Weston-super-Mare, Sept. 27, 1851. "The spot was then being built over."

Worle Hill, Somerset; *Sy. F. B.*

INULA, L.

421. I. Helenium, L. *Elecampane.*

In moist meadows and marshes, very rare. Native in Gloucestershire.

G. In a remote part of the marshes between Hallen and New Passage, where it occurs in tolerable abundance. *Mr. D. Fry.* "In a pasture ground near Wick Cliffs, *Mr. Swayne.*" *With.,* ed. 3, iii., 730.

S. Brislington, 1853; *Herb. Stephens.* Brook side, Dundry; *ib.* Hay Hill, one mile south of Wells, in 1850; at Yarley, in 1860; also in other spots near Wells. *Miss Livett.* VII. VIII.

422. I. Conyza, DC. *Ploughman's Spikenard.*

Native; on dry and limestone soils, usually in shady situations; sometimes in sheltered sunny ones. Frequent.

G. St. Vincent's Rocks, and bank of Avon below Clifton. Crew's Hole. Stinchcombe Hill. About Wotton-under-Edge.

S. Brean Down. Bourton. Cheddar. Clevedon. Leigh Wood. Between Abbot's Leigh and Failand. Wells. Yatton ; *Miss Winter.*   VII.—IX.

PULICARIA, *Gaert.*

423. **P. dysenterica,** *Gaert.*
Native; in ditches and moist places by roadsides, very common.   VIII. IX.

FILAGO, *L.*

424. **F. germanica,** *L. Cudweed.*
Native; in cultivated fields, and dry places, frequent.
G. Horfield. Charlton. Sea Mills. Stapleton.
S. Brean. Clevedon. Congresbury. Walton-in-Gordano. Wells.
This is the *Herba impia* of old authors, so called because the stem bearing at first a solitary terminal cluster of flowers, produces from beneath it branches which overtop it and bear similar clusters, as if the offspring were undutifully exalting themselves above the parent. The name *Cudweed* arose from a supposed power in this herb to promote rumination in cattle.   VII. VIII.

425. **F. apiculata,** *G. F. Sm. F. lutescens,* Jord.
" On Pennant at Stapleton." *Herb. Stephens.*
We have not looked out for this species; and possibly it has been passed over for *F. germanica.*

426. **F. minima,** *Fr.*
Native; on barren sandy ground, very rare.
G. Near Hanham Mill; *Herb. Stephens.* Conham; *Mr. G. H. K. Thwaites,* in *Swete, Fl.* 48.
S. Brean Down; *St. Brody, Fl. Weston.* This station has not been verified.

GNAPHALIUM, L.

427. G. uliginosum, L.
Native; in wet sandy places, frequent.
G. Near Avonmouth. Dursley. Troopers' Hill.
S. Failand. Portbury. Stockwood. The Old Park near Abbot's Leigh. Yatton. Weston-super-Mare. VII. VIII.

428. G. sylvaticum, L.
Native; very rare.
S. In a bog at Downhead Common. *Dr. H. F. Parsons.*

(*Antennaria dioica*, Gaert. " Grows on rocks on the south side of Brean Down." *St. Brody, Fl. Weston*, 141. Unconfirmed.)

ACHILLEA, L.

429. A. Ptarmica, L. *Sneezewort.*
Native; in wet peaty meadows, rare.
G. Filton Meads. Between Horfield and Filton, *Herb. Stephens; and Mr. G. H. K. Thwaites* in *Swete, Fl.* 51. Yate Common. Henbury. Sept., 1834. *Herb. Powell.*
S. Bedminster, *Mr. T. B. Flower.* Clevedon, *Mrs. Lainson.* VII. VIII.

430. A. Millefolium, L. *Yarrow. Millefoil.*
Native; in pastures and waste ground, very common.
VI.—VIII.

(*A. nobilis.* Some dozens of plants on a small heap of old colliery *débris* near Kingswood, G. 1879 and subsequently.)

ANTHEMIS, L.

(*A. tinctoria*, L. Grows sparingly near Kingswood with *Achillea nobilis* and other aliens. This species has been found here and there in England, but not frequently, during the last two centuries.)

COMPOSITÆ.

431. A. Cotula, *L.*
Colonist; in cultivated fields and waste places, frequent.
S. Bishport. Pensford. Wells. Whitchurch. Yatton.
VII.—IX.

432. A. nobilis, *L.* *Chamomile.*
Native?; on commons and pastures, very rare.
G. On waste ground about Bristol] as a casual. In Tyndall's Park, 1881.
S. Wells, *Miss Livett.* Yatton, *Miss Winter.*

MATRICARIA, *L.*

433. M. Parthenium, *L.* *Feverfew.*
Denizen; on old walls, and in waste ground about villages, frequent.
G. Common about Stapleton. Conham. Hanham.
S. Bedminster. Clutton. Long Ashton. Nailsea. Temple Cloud. Wells. Winscombe. Yatton.
An aromatic bitter and tonic; anciently esteemed against hysteria, and as a febrifuge. VII. VIII.

434. M. inodora, *L.*
Native; in cultivated ground and waste places, very common. A maritime form grows on the shore of the Bristol Channel. VII. VIII.

435. M. Chamomilla, *L.*
Native; in cultivated fields, common. Florets of the ray sometimes absent. VI. VII.

CHRYSANTHEMUM, *L.*

436. C. Leucanthemum, *L.* *Ox-eye Daisy.*
Native; in meadows and pastures nearly everywhere, and in all sorts of situations. VI. VIII.

437. C. segetum, *L.* *Corn-Marigold.*
Colonist; in cornfields and waste places, rare.

G. Ashley, *Mr. W. E. Green*. Occasionally in cornfields at Horfield, *Swete, Fl.,* 50. Shirehampton, *Swete, ib.* Sparingly about the quarries at Stapleton.

S. Flax Bourton, *Swete, ib.* Cultivated land near Weston-super-Mare.   VI.—VIII.

ARTEMISIA, *L.*

438. A. Absinthium, *L. Wormwood.*

Native?; on dry banks and waste ground, rare.

S. Kewstoke; *Rev. W. H. Painter.* Tickenham; *Mr. W. E. Green.* One or two plants on the hill above Tickenham, between Clevedon and Cadbury Camp; *Mr. D. Fry.* Grows in great profusion with *Nepeta Cataria* on the hill at Weston-in-Gordano; *Mr. D. Fry.*   VII. VIII.

439. A. vulgaris, *L. Mugwort.*

Native; on hedge-banks, and borders of fields. Rather scarce near Bristol; but frequent elsewhere.

G. Roadsides at Stapleton.

S. Berrow. Clevedon. Ken. Uphill. Walton-in-Gordano.   VIII.

440. A. maritima, *L.*

Native. Occurs plentifully in many places on the shore of the Bristol Channel.

G. By the Severn near Berkeley. Avonmouth marshes near the Butts.

S. Clevedon. Kingston Seymour. Woodspring. Anchor Head, Weston-super-Mare. Under Brean Down. Burnham.

We have not seen the variety β. *A. Gallica,* Willd.

    VIII. IX.

TANACETUM, *L.*

441. T. vulgare, *L. Tansy.*

Native, or denizen. Common by waysides and on riverbanks.

G. Abundant by the Avon from Keynsham downwards. "This herb flourishes luxuriantly on the banks of the Avon near Hanham and Keynsham, where Mr. F. Russell observed boys gathering a boatload of it to convey to Bristol for the purpose of making wine." *With. ed.* 7, pub. 1830. Tortworth.

S. Bank of Avon. Clevedon. Portishead. Wells. Yatton.

The peculiar strong scent of this plant is well known. It has served to give flavour to a kind of rich pudding formerly to be seen at Corporation feasts, but now become obsolete in England. VIII.

(*Doronicum Pardalianches*, L. *Leopard's-bane*. Lane in Bourton, leading to the Combe; *Miss Winter*. Glen Frome, Stapleton. Alien. Introduced.)

SENECIO, *L.*

442. S. vulgaris, *L.* *Groundsel.*
Native; a common weed everywhere. I.—XII.

443. S. sylvaticus, *L.*
Native; on dry banks, frequent.
G. Crew's Hole. Hanham. Stoke Lane. Yate Common. Mangotsfield.
S. Clevedon. Leigh Woods. Near Edington.
VII. VIII.

444. S. viscosus, *L.*
Perhaps casual only with us; on waste ground, rare.
Reported by two observers from Clevedon. *Mrs. Lainson* sends a specimen gathered some years ago on Court Hill, on the side of the valley opposite to Bella Vista. The spot has since been disturbed by quarrying. On the Portishead Railway; *Rev. W. Painter.*

445. S. erucifolius, *L.*
Native; chiefly on ditch-banks in the lowlands, frequent.

G. Bank of Avon. Avonmouth. St. Philip's Marsh.

S. Berrow. Clevedon. Portbury. Portishead. Common to the south of Wells; *Miss Livett.* Weston-super-Mare, where it often lacks the ray. VII. VIII.

446. **S. Jacobæa,** *L. Common Ragwort.*

Native; in waste places and by roadsides. Very common and generally distributed. Plants wanting the ray were seen at Worle, S., July 1880. VII.—IX.

447. **S. aquaticus,** *Huds.*

Native; in marshy places, frequent.

G. By the river between Charfield and Tortworth. Filton Meads. Valley of the Trym below Westbury. Henbury.

S. Ditches under Brent Knoll. Clevedon. Nailsea Moor. Pensford. Portbury. Ditches south of Wedmore. Wells. Whitchurch. Winscombe. VII. VIII.

448. **S. saracenicus,** *L.*

Alien. Established in Somerset for a century at least.

S. "Between Wells and Glastonbury; near Shepton Mallet; and other places in Somersetshire." *With. ed.* 3, iii. 726. 1796. "A large patch in a stream running by the road from Wells to Shepton Mallet, near the village of Croscombe. It has been known there for very many years" *Miss Livett.* VIII.

BIDENS, *L.*

449. **B. tripartita,** *L.*

Native; in wet or marshy places, frequent.

G. Crew's Hole; Bank of Frome, Stapleton; *Herb. Stephens.* St. Philip's Marsh. Yate.

S. Burnham. Clevedon. Nailsea Moor. Paulton. Portbury. Wells. VII. VIII.

450. B. cernua, *L.*

Native; in watery places, frequent on the moors.

G. Stapleton; and Hanham; *Mr. T. B. Flower.* We do not know that either this or *B. tripartita* has been found recently in these localities.

S.⁑ Marsh ditches near Draycot, Burnham, Tickenham, Wedmore, Wells, and Yatton; abundant in some of them.   VII. VIII.

CARLINA, *L.*

451. C. vulgaris, *L.*

Native; scattered over downs, hilly pastures, and heaths, common.

Acauline plants are frequent on the Mendips. " Dying, it does not soon decay, for the leaves and even flowers which are of the nature of an Everlasting, battered and bleached, stand many a wintry storm." *Sir J. E. Smith.*
  VII.—IX.

ARCTIUM, *L.*

452. A. majus, Schk. *Greater Burdock.*

Native; by roadsides and in waste places. Common, but not so abundant as the next species.   VIII.

453. A. minus, Schk. *Lesser Burdock.*

Native; in waste places, very common.   VIII.

454. A. intermedium, Lange.

Native; in waste places.

This is apparently common enough, but we have constantly found great difficulty in distinguishing it from *A. minus*, and cannot therefore indicate its distribution. We are decidedly inclined to agree with Mr. Watson in considering it to be a variety of *A. minus*.

SERRATULA, *L.*

455. S. tinctoria, *L.*

Native; in bushy places on limestone, and in peaty meadows, frequent.

G. Wooded slopes on Durdham Down near the Gully, in plenty. Filton Meads. Crew's Hole; *Dr. H. O. Stephens.* Blaize Castle Woods.

S. Bank of Avon under Leigh Wood. Hutton. Milton. Sandford. Woods near Wells. Weston-in-Gordano. Worlebury Hill. Yatton. VIII.

CENTAUREA, *L.*

456. C. nigra, *L.*

Native; in meadows and pastures, very common.

C. decipiens, Thuill., has been observed on St. Vincent's Rocks; at Nailsea; and near Clevedon. VI.—IX.

457. C. Cyanus, *L.* *Corn Blue-bottle.*

Colonist; in cornfields, and on the borders of cultivated land, rare.

G. Horfield; St. Vincent's Rocks; *Swete, Fl.* 47. Sparingly at Kingswood.

S. Cornfield between Abbot's Leigh and Failand. Rarely at Wells; *Miss Livett.* Yatton; *Miss Winter.*

VI.—VIII.

458. C. scabiosa, *L.* *Great Knap-weed.*

Native; on the borders of fields, and in dry waste places, very common. The variety with white flowers is constant on St. Vincent's Rocks; and on the Dial Hill, Clevedon. VII.—IX.

(*C. paniculata,* L. and *C. melitensis,* L. Aliens on old colliery *débris* near Kingswood, G.)

ONOPORDUM, *L.*

459. O. Acanthium, *L.* *Cotton Thistle.*
Alien or casual. Very rare. We have not seen an example.
S. Sand hills at Berrow; *Miss Livett,* and *New Botanists' Guide.* " Rare at Weston-super-Mare. Grows in waste places near Sand Point." *St. Brody, Fl. Weston.*

CARDUUS, *L.*

460. C. nutans, *L.* *Musk Thistle.*
Native, in waste places, particularly on limestone, rather common.
G. Clifton and Durdham Downs. Kingswood. Stinchcombe hill.
S. Leigh Down; some plants here with white flowers, July, 1880. Brean. Cheddar. Dolbery Camp. Clevedon. Loxton. Walton-by-Clevedon. Wells. Weston-super-Mare. Yatton.   VI.—VIII.

461. C. crispus, *L.* including *C. acanthoides,* L.
Native; on banks, and by roadsides, common about Bristol.   VI.—VIII.

462. C. tenuiflorus, *Curt.*
Native; in submaritime habitats. Locally common by the Avon below Bristol, and on the shore of the Bristol Channel.   VI.—VIII.

463. C. lanceolatus, *L.* *Spear Thistle.*
Native; very common everywhere.   VII. VIII.

464. C. eriophorus, *L.* *Woolly-headed Thistle.*
Native; in dry pastures on limestone, frequent in Somerset. A strikingly handsome plant when well grown.
S. Buckland Dinham. Between Bishport and Dundry. Between Clutton and Stowey. Combe Hay. Hutton. Lansdown. Loxton. Plentifully at Ebbor, near Wells; *Miss Livett.* Weston-in-Gordano. South Stoke. Stockwood. Worlebury Hill. Yandy Lane.   VIII.

COMPOSITÆ.

465. C. arvensis, *Curt.* *Creeping Thistle.*
   Native; in cultivated fields and waste places. Very common and generally distributed. A most troublesome weed. VII. VIII.

466. C. palustris, *L.* *Marsh Thistle.*
   Native; in meadows and marshes; sometimes also on high, dry ground. Very common. VII VIII.

467. C. pratensis, *Huds.*
   Native; only in peaty meadows, locally plentiful.
   G. Filton Meads. Patchway. Yate Common. Alveston.
   S. Fields near the reservoirs at Barrow Gurney. Winscombe. Wells. Yatton. VI.—VII.

468. C. acaulis, *L.*
   Native; in dry limestone pastures, rather common on the Downs near Bristol.
   C. dubius, Willd., and *C. Gibsoni,* are caulescent states of this plant; sometimes found in similar situations. See *Swete, Fl.* 46. These may in some cases be hybrids between this species and *C. arvensis.* VII.—IX.

SILYBUM, *Gaert.*

469. S. Marianum, *Gaert.*
   Alien; in waste ground, and dry pastures, rare.
   G. Horfield. *Mr. W. F. Green.* Some magnificent plants on a seabank by the Channel, between New Passage and Avonmouth, 1880.
   S. Permanent on Brean Down. Banks of the Axe; *Mr. T. F. Perkins.* Yatton; *Miss Winter.* VI. VII.

LAPSANA, *L.*

470. L. communis, *L.*
   Native; in cultivated and waste ground. Very common.
   VII. VIII.

CICHORIUM, L.
471. C. Intybus, L. *Chicory.*
Native; in fields and waste places, rather scarce about Bristol except towards the South.
G. Hanham. Henbury.
S. Bishport. Keynsham. Knowle. Portbury. Portishead. Milton. Walton-by-Clevedon. Weston-in-Gordano. Sparingly near Wells. Whitchurch. Yatton.   VII. VIII.

HYPOCHŒRIS, L.
472. H. radicata, L.
Native; in fields and waste places. Very common.   VII.

THRINCIA, Roth.
473. T. hirta, DC.
Native; on stony banks, and in dry places, frequent.
G. Clifton and Durdham Downs, and underneath by the Avon. Crew's Hole.
S. Burnham. Clevedon. Wells. Weston-super-Mare.
VII. VIII.

LEONTODON, L.
474. L. hispidum, L.
Native; in dry places, as on St. Vincent's Rocks, rather common.   VI.—VIII.

475. L. autumnale, L.
Native; in dry pastures, very common everywhere.
VII.—IX.

TRAGOPOGON, L.
476. T. minor, Fries. *Goatsbeard.*
Native; in pastures, common.   VI. VII.

477. T. pratensis, L.
Native; in meadows and pastures, not so frequent as the preceding.

G. Horfield. Patchway. Fishponds. Sea Mills.
S. Clevedon. Stockwood. Tickenham. Uphill. Wells. Whitchurch. Yatton.

Prof. Babington is almost alone in considering this plant to be specifically distinct from the last. It is hardly possible to draw a satisfactory line between them, as they differ only by the relative length of florets and phyllaries; and although when growing this character is easily determined, in herbarium specimens the relative length depends partly on the age of the head when pressed, and partly on the degree of pressure used in drying the plants. VI. VII.

478. T. porrifolius, *L.* *Salsify.*

Possibly native with us, though introduced in many of its stations in this country. It was first recorded as a Bristol plant by Mr. Sowerby, who towards the end of the last century gathered the specimen figured in *English Botany* " in the meadows below St. Vincent's Rocks, Bristol." Dr. Dyer also appears to have gathered it in 1805, and it is included by Mr. Rootsey in a list of Bristol plants, publ. 1828. Swete in 1854 considered the habitat to be then lost. *Fl.* 43. However, many years later, and after the construction of the Avonmouth Railway, which must have thoroughly disturbed the soil, the plant reappeared in a spot under Cook's Folly, which without doubt corresponds with Sowerby's station. It would have been the nearest bit of meadow land below St. Vincent's Rocks. We first saw it there in 1878, and have found it every season since, but only in small quantity.

One is tempted to ask if this can be an instance of the well-attested and marvellous property possessed by many seeds of retaining their vitality under conditions adverse to germination, until eventually they become exposed to air and sunlight. We certainly think it highly improbable that this *Tragopogon* has been re-introduced at the very spot where it originally grew, especially as it has not been found anywhere else in the Bristol district.

PICRIS, *L.*

479. P. hieracioides, *L.*

Native; on dry rocky banks on limestone, locally common.

G. St. Vincent's Rocks, and slopes under the Downs. Kingsweston.

S. Buckland Dinham. Plentiful about the Cheddar Cliffs. Clevedon. Wells. Whitchurch. Yatton.

VII.—IX.

HELMINTHIA, *Juss.*

480. H. echioides, *Gaert. Ox-tongue.*

Native; in waste places in the lowlands, chiefly in submaritime situations.

G. Bank of Avon below Bristol. Conham. Syston. Abundant by the Severn near Berkeley. Shirehampton.

S. Clevedon. Plentiful about Portbury, Portishead, and Weston-super-Mare. Highbridge. South Brent. Whitchurch. Yatton.

VII.—IX.

LACTUCA, *L.*

(*L. saligna,* L. A single specimen at Weston-super-Mare, 1868. *Dr. H. O. Stephens.*)

481. L. virosa, *L. Acrid Lettuce.*

"Pathway leading to Giant's Hole, St. Vincent's Rocks." *Swete, Fl.* 44. "I have gathered this plant in the path leading to the Giant's Hole, St. Vincent's Rocks; but the station has long since been destroyed. I have not seen it since the summer of 1853." *Mr. T. B. Flower,* Feb. 1883.

It would not be surprising if this Lettuce were indigenous on St. Vincent's Rocks; and no one can say that it is not still existing on one or more of the ledges overlooking the Avon. Or can it,—together with the many other herbs, medicinal and culinary, which abound upon the rocks,—trace its descent to the herb-garden of the legendary anchorite whose hermitage was in the cave called "Giant's Hole' ?

482. **L. muralis,** *DC.*
Native; on rocky banks and old walls, frequent.
G. St. Vincent's Rocks, and bank of Avon. Old walls about Clifton and Redland.
S. Rocks and walls about Leigh Wood, Abbot's Leigh, and bank of Avon. Clapton. Clevedon. Croscombe and Emborrow near Wells. Yatton. VII.

TARAXACUM, *Juss.*

483. **T. officinale,** *Wigg. Dandelion.*
Native; in waste or cultivated ground everywhere. Universally distributed. III.—X.

SONCHUS, *L.*

484. **S. oleraceus,** *L. Sowthistle.*
Native; in borders of fields and waste places, very common.
V.—IX.

485. **S. asper,** *Hoffm. Sowthistle.*
Native; with the last, and as common. V.—IX.

486. **S. arvensis,** *L. Corn Sowthistle.*
Native; in cornfields and damp waste ground, common.
VIII. IX.

(*S. palustris,* L. Bank of Avon at Crew's Hole, and Conham; *Dr. Stephens* in *Swete, Fl.* 44. Reported to us also from the same locality; but there is no doubt that a tall and luxuriant form of *S. arvensis* which occurs in marshes and on ditch-banks has been mistaken for this species. " Dr. H. O. Stephens informed me he had mistaken some other plant for *Sonchus palustris*; consequently it must be expunged from the Bristol Flora." *Mr. T. B. Flower*, Feb. 1883.)

CREPIS, *L.*

487. C. taraxacifolia, *Thuil.*
Colonist; in cultivated land, and waste spots, rare.
G. In a cultivated field at Filton; 1882. Kingswood; *Dr. Hassé.*
S. Dial Hill, Clevedon; *Mr. W. E. Green. Mrs. Lainson. Mr. D. Fry.* VI. VII.

(*C. setosa*, Hall. Casual in fields at Westbury-on-Trym: *Mr. W. E. Green.*)

488. C. virens, *L.*
Native; in dry waste places, very common. VI.—IX.

HIERACIUM, *L.*

489. H. Pilosella, *L.*
Native; in dry exposed sunny places, nearly everywhere.
V.—VIII.

(*H. aurantiacum*, L. Alien on old walls. Near Richmond Hill, Clifton; and at Clevedon, Yatton, and Milton. A plant long known in gardens, and until recently retaining the old name recorded in Gerarde of "Grim the Collier," in allusion to the smutty effect of the black glandular hairs which invest the stalks and calyx.)

490. H. murorum, *L.*
Native; on the Cheddar Cliffs.
Although this is named *H. murorum* by Dr. Boswell, and Mr. Backhouse; it is likewise the *H. cæsium* of Fries, Babington, and others: clearly indicating that there can

be next to nothing to separate these so-called species. The two are said to differ in colour of styles and thickness of leaves; but good botanists aver that the former character is variable in the same plant from year to year.

V. VI.

491. H. vulgatum, *Fr.*

Native; on walls and banks in and about Bristol and Clifton, common.

H. maculatum, Sm., is a variety or sub-species differing slightly from *H. vulgatum* in its leaves and inflorescence.

VII.—IX.

(*H. gothicum*, Fr. Leigh woods and St. Vincent's Rocks. *Swete Fl.* 45. We cannot find that this has been gathered since Swete's time. Perhaps Dr. Stephens' plants were misnamed.)

492. H. tridentatum, *Fr.*

Native. Very rare.

G. Crew's Hole, and Redland; *Herb. Stephens.*
S. Cheddar; *Rev. R. P. Murray.*

493. H. umbellatum, *L.*

Native. Very rare.

G. Sparingly on Yate Common, Aug. 1882.

It is not uncommon on the peat moors just south of the district.

494. H. boreale, *Fr.*

Native; on rocky banks and old walls, rare.

G. Glen Frome; bank between Crew's Hole and Hanham; *Swete, Fl.* 45. On several old walls at Stoke Bishop. Stapleton; *Herb. Stephens.*

S. Plentiful about the Portishead Railway, under Leigh Wood.

VIII. IX.

(*Rudbeckia laciniata*, L. Casual. A native of North America, from the Gulf of Mexico to Canada. About a dozen stems growing up through a low thorn hedge by the roadside near Portbury, S., Aug. 18, 1880. See *Journ. of Bot.*, April, 1811.)

(*Grindelia squarrosa*. Casual. Sparingly on old colliery débris near Kingswood, G.

CAMPANULACEÆ.
CAMPANULA, L.

495. C. glomerata, *L.*   *Clustered Bell flower.*
Native; in dry hilly pastures, rare.
G. Hills above Wotton-under-Edge. With white flowers at Wick Rocks; *Dr. Stephens.*
S. Charlcombe. Cheddar. Lansdown, on the brow of the hill going up from Kelston; and also on the slopes above North Stoke, where it is more abundant and luxuriant; *Mr. D. Fry.*   VII. VIII.

496. C. latifolia, *L.*
Native? A few plants are still in Glen Frome, Stapleton, from whence there is a specimen in the Stephens Herbarium dated 1843. In 1878, after much search, we found the place, and the plant growing sparingly in a stony part of the wood near the river.

497. C. Trachelium, *L.*   *Nettle-leaved Bell flower.*
Native; in hedges and bushy places, chiefly on limestone, locally common.
G. Stinchcombe Hill. Wotton-under-Edge. Blaize Castle Woods; *Herb. Powell.*
S. Bourton Combe. Cheddar Cliffs. With pure white flowers at Congresbury, where the ordinary form also grows. Draycot. Sparingly in hedges at Failand.

Bank of Avon under Leigh Wood; *Dr. Rogers* in *Swete, Fl.* 51; still there in small quantity, 1879. Portbury. Tickenham. Loxton, in abundance. Frequent in hedges about Wells. Weston-in-Gordano. Yatton.

VII. VIII.

(*C. rapunculoïdes*, L. Bank of Avon, near St. Anne's Wood; *Mr. J. Foster* in *Swete, Fl.* 100. Hedge at Sand, S.; *Mr. T. F. Perkins*. Escapes from gardens.)
(*C. persicifolia*, L. Near coppice wood at Hutton; *St. Brody, Fl. Weston*, 117. An escape.)

498. C. rotundifolia, *L. Hare-bell.*

Native; in dry pastures, common on the Downs. It is very rarely found with white flowers; but we saw some on Mendip above Draycot in August, 1881. VII. VIII.

499. C. patula, *L.*

Native; very rare.

G. Wood on the Downend side of Glen Frome; Oldbury Court Woods; *Mr. G. H. K. Thwaites*, in *Swete, Fl.* 51. Stapleton; *Herb. Stephens*. These records probably refer to the same spot.

S. West Harptree; *Herb. Stephens*.

Mr. T. B. Flower says that both he and Mr. Thwaites used to gather this plant in Glen Frome, and he believes it to be there still. We have not been fortunate enough to find the spot.

SPECULARIA, *Heist.*

500. S. hybrida, *A. DC.*

Colonist; in cultivated fields, very rare.

G. Lawrence Weston; *Miss Powell, Swete, Fl.* 52.

S. Near Clevedon!; *Miss Winter, Mr. D. Fry, Mr. W. E. Green*, and *Herb. Powell*. Weston-super-Mare, *St. Brody*. VII. VIII.

ERICACEÆ.

(*Andromeda polifolia*, L., has been included in a published list of Mendip plants, but in error. No specimen exists. We have seen it from the peat of Shapwick Moor, just south of the district.)

CALLUNA, L.
501. **C. vulgaris**, *Salisb.* *Ling.*
Native; on heaths, and commons, very common.
We have frequently noticed it with white flowers on Yate Common, G.   VI.—VIII.

ERICA, L.
502. **E. Tetralix**, *L.*
Native; on damp and boggy heaths and commons. Rather rare, and local.
G. Durdham Down; Stapleton; *Swete, Fl.* 52. Durdham Down, June 10, 1868; *Rev. W. W. Spicer.* Formerly on Durdham Down; *Mr. T. B. Flower.*
S. Plentiful on Black Down, where the white flowered variety is rather frequent. Bog on Mendip near Priddy. Near Wells. Leigh Wood. *Mr. T. B. Flower.*
We cannot now find this heath on Durdham Down, or in Leigh Wood. Building operations and other encroachments must have long since destroyed it in the immediate neighbourhood of Bristol.   VII. VIII.

503. **E. cinerea**, *L.*
Native; on dry commons and heaths, common.
We have seen it with white flowers on Black Down, S.
     VII. VIII.

(*E. vagans*, L. Planted on Court Hill, Clevedon; with Cotoneaster, &c.)

VACCINIUM, *L.*

504. V. Myrtillus, *L.* Bilberry.

Native; on moors and heaths, rare and local.

G. Oldbury Court Woods; *Mr. G. H. K. Thwaites, Swete, Fl.* 52. "Hills about Stapleton"; *Dr. Stephens.*

S. Leigh Wood; *Mr. Thwaites, ib.* Court Hill, Clevedon; *Mrs. Lainson.* Abundant on Black Down.

(*V. Vitis-idæa*, L. Leigh Wood, S. *Bot. Guide.* Unconfirmed.)

PYROLA, *L.*

505. P. media, *Sw.*

"Woodmancote, near Dursley, G. July, 1846"; *Herb. Stephens.*

506. P. minor, *L.*

Woodmancote, with the last; *Herb. Stephens.*

MONOTROPA, *L.*

507. M. Hypopitys, *L.*

Native; under beech trees, very rare.

S. Leigh Wood; *Shiercliff's List*, 1789. *Dr. Stephens.* In Brockley Combe, nearly every summer. VII. VIII.

AQUIFOLIACEÆ.

ILEX, *L.*

508. I. Aquifolium, *L.* Holly.

Native; in woods, hedges, and combes, very common.

VI.—VIII.

OLEACEÆ.

LIGUSTRUM, *L.*

509. L. vulgare, *L.* Privet.

Native; in hedges and thickets, rather common. VI. VII.

FRAXINUS, L.

510. **F. excelsior,** L. *Ash.*
Native; in woods and hedges, very common.   IV. V.

APOCYNACEÆ.

VINCA, L.

511. **V. major,** L. *Greater Periwinkle.*
Alien; sometimes naturalized, frequent.
G.   Blaize Castle.   Horfield.
S.   Hedges at Stockwood.   Portbury.   Woodspring. Yatton.   IV. V.

512. **V. minor,** L. *Lesser Periwinkle.*
Alien, or denizen. Frequently with the last, and both are often escapes from gardens.
G.   Blaize Castle.   Horfield.
S.   Bishport.   Clevedon.   Congresbury.   Hedges about Goblin Combe. Walton-in-Gordano. In a wood near Wells. Yatton.   V. VI.

GENTIANACEÆ.

CHLORA, L.

513. **C. perfoliata,** L.
Native; frequent on the limestone, and wherever the Bee Orchis grows there will be *Chlora*.
G.   St. Vincent's Rocks, and bank of Avon under the Downs. Henbury.
S.   Clevedon.   Congresbury.   Great Elm.   Easton. Walton-in-Gordano. Leigh Wood, and bank of Avon.
    VII.—IX.

GENTIANACEÆ.

ERYTHRÆA, *Renealm.*

514. **E. pulchella,** *Fries.*
Native; on sandy ground near the channel, locally plentiful.
S. In many places between Weston-super-Mare and Burnham.   VII.—IX.

515. **E. Centaurium,** *Pers. Centaury.*
Native; in dry pastures, such as the Downs near Bristol, common.   VII. VIII.

GENTIANA, *L.*

516. **G. Amarella,** *L.*
Native; in dry pastures on limestone, frequent.
G. Clifton Down near the Avon. Pur Down. Wick Rocks. Stinchcombe Hill, some plants with white flowers.
S. Plentiful on Leigh Down, where it was known to Withering. Barrow Hill, near Buckland Dinham. Castle Hill, Clevedon. Uphill. Above Ebbor Gorge near Wells.   VIII. IX.

(*G. campestris*, L.. *Swete, Fl.* 53. This is an error. Miss Attwood informed Mr. Flower that she had mistaken *G. Amarella* for this species. We believe that to the present time all the reports of the occurrence of this plant in the Bristol district are erroneous.)

MENYANTHES, *L.*

517. **M. trifoliata,** *L.. Buck Bean.*
Native; in swamps and boggy pools, rare.
S. Sparingly in Leigh Wood, near the Keeper's Lodge: the only station near Bristol. In tolerable abundance in Max bog near Winscombe. In bogs on Mendip. The late *Rev. G. W. Braikenridge* mentions this in his

list as occurring at Tickenham; we have never found it there. Reported also to grow formerly in a boggy spot between Portishead and Clevedon. V. VII.

CONVOLVULACEÆ.
CONVOLVULUS, L.

518. C. arvensis, L.
Native; in fields and on dry hedge-banks, very common.
VI. VIII.

519. C. sepium, L.
Native; in hedges and thickets, and on cultivated land, common. VII. VIII.

520. C. Soldanella, L.
Native; on the sandy shore of the Bristol Channel.
S. On the sands north and south of Weston-super-Mare; abundant on Brean Sands. VII. VIII.

CUSCUTA, L.

521. C. europæa, L. *Greater Dodder.*
Very rare. On clover in a field at Pill. Sept., 1881.

BORAGINACEÆ.

(Echinospermum Lappula, Lehm., has grown for some years on old colliery *débris* near Kingswood, G.)

("The *Asperugo procumbens,* L., grows at Frenchay, also near the Cherry Orchard below Westbury; and I have occasionally found a little at Redland." *Mr. Rootsey* to *Mr. T. B. Flower,* June 9, 1851. We think it has not been found since.)

CYNOGLOSSUM, L.

522. C. officinale, L. *Hound's-tongue.*
Native; in barren waste ground, frequent.

BORAGINACEÆ.

G. Mangotsfield. New Passage. Stapleton.

S. Beggar's Bush Lane. Bishport. Brislington. Most abundant on the sands between Brean and Burnham. Near Cadbury Camp. Churchill. Clevedon. Leigh Down. Walton Down. Kewstoke, near Weston-super-Mare. VI. VII.

BORAGO, L.

523. **B. officinalis,** *L.* *Borage.*

Alien; in waste places. Rare, and grows sparingly wherever it occurs.

G. St. Vincent's Rocks. Stapleton, and Westbury: *Swete, Fl.* 65.

S. Ashton. Bedminster. Clevedon. Easton. Weston-super-Mare. Wookey. VI. VII.

ANCHUSA, L.

(*A. officinalis,* L. In the herbarium of the late Miss Powell there is a specimen gathered at Clevedon in July, 1839, by Miss E. Braikenridge.)

524. **A. sempervirens,** *L.*

Denizen, or alien; in waste spots and on hedge-banks, rare.

G. By the roadside near houses at Combe Glen, and in hedges bordering fields close by; noticed here first in 1868. Frenchay; *Herb. Stephens.* Between Hambrook and Mangotsfield; *Herb. Powell.*

S. Near Clevedon. Occasionally by roadsides about Wells; *Miss Livett.* V.—VII.

LYCOPSIS, L.

525. **L. arvensis,** *L.*

Native, or denizen; on cultivated and waste ground, frequent.

G. Downend. Stapleton, and Westbury; *Swete, Fl.* 65.

S. Near Brean Down. Burnham. Sparingly on Kewstoke Sands. Cornfield near Abbot's Leigh. Brislington; *Herb. Stephens.* Wells. VI. VII.

SYMPHYTUM, *L.*
526. **S. officinale,** *L. Comfrey.*
Native; in damp fields, and on ditch-banks, common.
V. VI.
(S. orientale and other species are occasionally found, but are not native.)

ECHIUM, *L.*
527. **E. vulgare,** *L.*
Native; in dry places, frequent.
G. Dursley. Horfield. Kingswood. Sea Mills. Stapleton. Wick Rocks. Hills above Wotton-under-Edge.
S. About Bath, in several places. Burnham. Clevedon. Congresbury. Hutton. Walton-by-Clevedon. Weston-in-Gordano. Wrington. VI. VII.

LITHOSPERMUM, *L.*
528. **L. officinale,** *L.*
Native; in shady and stony places, frequent.
G. Bank of Avon near the Black Rock, and lower down the river. Damory Bridge. Bushy places about Combe Down, and in the Trym Valley. Horfield. Stapleton. Lawrence Weston.
S. Bank of Avon under Leigh Wood. Brockley Combe. Near Cadbury Camp. Churchill. Congresbury. Clevedon. Tickenham. Walton Down. Weston-in-Gordano. Weston-super-Mare. Wells. VI. VIII.

529. **L. purpureo-cæruleum,** *L.*
Native; in woods and thickets on limestone, local.
S. In many places at Congresbury, and in King's Wood, near Yatton. Hutton. Sandford Hill. South Brent.

BORAGINACEÆ.

Wood on Mendip near Wells. Weston-in-Gordano. Cleeve Wood; *Herb. Stephens.* Wood between Cheddar and Axbridge, June 1, 1831; *Herb. Bristol Museum.*

V. VI.

530. L. arvense, *L.*
Colonist; in cornfields, rare.
G. Bitton. Montpelier. Westbury. Lawrence Weston; *Herb. Powell.*
S. Chew Magna. Easton. Uphill. Winscombe.

V.—VII.

MYOSOTIS, *L.*

531. M. palustris, *With.* Forget-me-not.
Native; in wet places, frequent. VI.—VIII.

532. M. repens, *Don.*
Native; in wet places, rather common.
G. Glen Frome. Valley of the Trym. Filton Meads.
S. Clevedon. Nailsea Moor, and about Yatton. Ditches near Long Ashton, and Bourton. Bedminster Meads.

VI.—VIII.

533. M. cæspitosa, *Schultz.*
Native; in damp woods and meadows, rather common.
G. Berkeley. Charlton. Mangotsfield. Patchway. Shirehampton. Lawrence Weston. Stoke Bishop.
S. Bedminster. Burnham. Portbury. Wells. Yatton.

VI.—VIII.

(*M. sylvatica*, Ehrh. "Frequent in woods and shady places." *Swete, Fl.* 64. We think this must be an error; as we have not found the plant anywhere near Bristol.)

534. M. arvensis, *Lehm.*
Native; in cultivated and waste land, very common.
The var. *umbrosa* occurs frequently. VI.—VIII.

535. **M. collina,** *Hoffm.*
   Native; on dry turfy or rocky banks, and on walls, common.
   G. St. Vincent's Rocks, and rocks under Durdham Down near the quarries. Almondsbury Hill, and very luxuriant on old shaded walls in the village. Brandon Hill. Combe Down. Penpole Point. Siston. Stapleton. Charlton.
   S. Brean Down. Burnham. Cheddar. Clevedon. Cleeve Toot. Portishead. Stone Easton. Wells. IV. V.
536. **M. versicolor,** *Reich.*
   Native; in dry places, frequent.
   G. Berkeley. Dursley. With flowers at first white at Damory Bridge. Mangotsfield. Westbury-on-Trym.
   S. Ebbor and Pen Hill, near Wells. Bedminster Down. Abbot's Leigh. Portishead. Wraxall. Yatton. V.—VII.

SOLANACEÆ.

SOLANUM, L.

537. **S. nigrum,** *L.* *Black Nightshade.*
   Native; in cultivated ground and waste places, frequent.
   G. Almondsbury. Downend. Durdham Down. Hanham. Sea Mills. Stapleton. Stoke Bishop.
   S. Berrow. Brean. Brislington. Clevedon. Kewstoke. Knowle. In many places on the peat at the southern limit of the district. VII.—IX.
538. **S. Dulcamara,** *L.* *Woody Nightshade.*
   Native; in hedges and thickets, common. VI. VII.

ATROPA, L.

539. **A. Belladonna,** *L.* *Deadly Nightshade.*
   Native, or denizen, very rare.

G. It was formerly abundant about Stinchcombe Hill; and customarily gathered there in quantity for pharmaceutical purposes. As recently as 1868, 83¼ pounds of the fresh herb were forwarded in one consignment to a chemist's laboratory in Clifton; yet in July, 1880, when the Botanical Section B. N. S. made an excursion to the spot, the joint search of the party during an afternoon resulted in the discovery of only three plants. Frequent on the wooded hills near Wotton-under-Edge, on the eastern limit of the district. Casually on the railway embankment near Stapleton Road Station.

This is perhaps the most dangerous British plant. The fruit is tempting in appearance, sweetish, and without any remarkable or repulsive flavour, so that children and others have often eaten it, and even a single berry is said to have proved fatal. VI.—VIII.

HYOSCYAMUS, *L.*

540. **H. niger,** *L. Henbane.*

Native; in waste places, preferring submaritime situations; permanent in one or two spots near the Bristol Channel; elsewhere its occurrence and recurrence are rare and uncertain.

G. On a beach between Avonmouth and New Passage. Shirehampton; two plants, July, 1880.

S. Brean Down and shore of Bridgwater Bay. Portishead. Walton Hill, Clevedon. One plant on waste ground at Weston-super-Mare, July, 1880. Three or four plants in 1881 on a shingly beach near the Rifle Butts at Clevedon; none in 1882, though searched for repeatedly; *Mr. D. Fry.* Occasionally about Wells; *Miss Livett.* VI.—VIII.

LYCIUM, *L.*

541. L. barbarum, *L.*

Alien; quite naturalized in hedges and waste places.

G. In plenty by the Severn at Berkeley.

S. Abundant about Kewstoke, Milton, and Brean.

VI.—VIII.

DATURA, *L.*

542. D. Stramonium, *L.* *Thorn-apple.*

Casual; on waste ground, rare.

G. Pilning. Redland. Shirehampton. "Dunghills;" *Herb. Stephens.* VI. VII.

OROBANCHACEÆ.

OROBANCHE, *L.*

543. O. Rapum, *Thuill.*

Native; parasitical on furze, very rare.

G. On furze bushes near Cook's Folly; *Mr. T. B. Flower.*

S. On furze at Easton. *Miss Livett.*

544. O. caryophyllacea, *Sm.* *Clove-scented Broomrape.*

There are specimens of this rare species in the herbarium of the late Miss Powell, gathered by her in a bean field near Charlton, Sept. 4, 1845. The notes attached to them do not say upon what herb these plants were growing. There is no doubt they were correctly named.

545. O. elatior, *Sutt.*

St. Vincent's Rocks; *Swete, Fl. 59.*

In a field near Clevedon Beach, Aug., 1834; *Herb. Powell.*

546. O. Hederæ, *Duby.*

Native; parasitical on ivy, frequent.

G. Plentiful on St. Vincent's Rocks. Steep bank below Sea Mills.

S. Brean Down. Clevedon. Yatton. VI. VII.

547. O. minor, *Sutt.*

Native; parasitical upon herbaceous plants, frequent.

G. On *Geranium rotundifolium* at Stapleton. Penpole, St. Vincent's Rocks, and Westbury; *Swete, Fl.* 59.

S. Brislington. On clover at Ebbor; *Miss Livett.* Walton by Clevedon, in profusion; *Mr. D. Fry.* Portishead. Yatton.

Upon *Trifolium repens* on Brean Sands. Upon *Ononis arvensis* at Brean Down. VI. VII.

LATHRÆA, L.

548. L. squamaria, *L. Toothwort.*

Native; in woods and thickets, frequent.

S. Leigh Wood; constant in several places. In plenty under a hedge west of Failand Farm, April, 1881. Norton's Wood near Clevedon. Sidcot. Near Wells. Plentiful in King's Wood, Yatton; *Miss Winter.*

"The name Toothwort is derived from the resemblance of the scaly roots of this plant to the human front teeth; for which reason it *must* be good for the tooth-ache 'as wise philosophers have judged.'" *Sir J. E. Smith.*

IV. V.

SCROPHULARIACEÆ.

VERBASCUM, L.

549. V. Thapsus, *L. Mullein.*

Native; on banks and walls, and in dry pastures, frequent.

G. Stoke Bishop. St. Vincent's Rocks. Sea Mills. Stapleton.

S. Abbot's Leigh. Brislington. Failand. Brockley and Goblin Combes. Clevedon. Weston-in-Gordano. Wells. Yatton. VII. VIII.

550. V. nigrum, *L.* *Dark Mullein.*
Native; on banks and roadsides, rare.
G. Under Stinchcombe Hill. Near Wotton-under-Edge. Woodmancote, near Dursley. Durdham Down, 1849; Stapleton; *Swete, Fl. 55.*
S. Waste ground by Church Road, Weston-super-Mare, 1879; not seen there since.
" By what figure of speech this beautiful plant can be called *black*, not having a particle of that colour about it, we will not determine. All the old botanists, however, have so denominated it; and if they had any meaning, it can only have been that it was not white." *Sir J. E. Smith.* VII. VIII.

(*V. Lychnitis*, L. was recorded from Banwell, and Milton, S. many years ago. We have no recent information about it.)

551. V. Blattaria, *L.*
Alien or casual with us, very rare.
G. "Apparently wild near Potter's Cottage at Combe, near Henbury, July, 1840." *Herb. Powell.*
S. Bishport; *Swete, Fl. 55.* On some rough land between Uphill road and the railway, Aug., 1881. On a railway embankment near Winscombe. On walls near Wells, and Yatton. VIII.

552. V. virgatum, *With.*
Alien or casual. Very rare.
G. Filton; *Herb. Bristol Museum.* On an old wall near Granby Hill, Clifton! Kingswood! On a wall between Horfield and Westbury; *Dr. Stephens.*
S. With *V. Blattaria* near Uphill, and also at Winscombe. VIII.

SCROPHULARIACEÆ.

DIGITALIS, *L.*

553. **D. purpurea,** *L. Foxglove.*
 Native. Very common in woods and hedges upon sandstone.
 The white-flowered plant has been sown on the cutting at Mangotsfield Station; and is found occasionally at Brislington, and on Walton Down, where the ordinary form grows in immense profusion. VI. VII.

ANTIRRHINUM, *L.*

554. **A. majus,** *L. Snapdragon.*
 Alien; on rocks and old walls, perfectly established in several places.
 G. On St. Vincent's Rocks, and frequent on walls about Clifton and Bristol.
 S. On rocks at Brean Down. Old walls in many places.
 VII.—IX.

LINARIA, *Mill.*

555. **L. Cymbalaria,** *Mill. Ivy-leaved Toadflax.*
 Denizen; chiefly on walls, very common. The beautiful white flowered variety grows near Westbury, G., and at Brislington, S. V.—IX.

556. **L. Elatine,** *Mill.*
 Native; on arable land, frequent.
 G. Almondsbury. Charlton. Hallen. Horfield. Thornbury. Fishponds. Yate.
 S. Clevedon. Easton. Cornfields east of Yandy Lane. Walton by Clevedon. Whitchurch. Knowle. Kingston Seymour. VII.—IX.

557. **L. spuria,** *Mill.*
 Colonist; on arable land, frequent.
 G. Between Charlton and Patchway. Chipping Sodbury. Bridge Yate. Wick. Westbury-on-Trym.

SCROPHULARIACEÆ.   131

S. Walton and Weston-in-Gordano. Milton. Lawrence Weston. Weston-super-Mare.   VII.—IX.

558. **L. minor,** *Desf.*
Colonist; by roadsides, and on railway ballast, frequent.
G. Constant on the Avonmouth Railway. Conham. Henbury; *Herb. Powell.* Wick.
S. Bourton. Cheddar. Clevedon. Hutton. On the railway under Leigh Wood. Yatton. Wells.
     VI.—VIII.

(*L. Pelisseriana, Mill,* has been gathered on an old wall at Brislington, S.)

559. **L. purpurea,** *Mill.*
Alien. Naturalized on old walls in many places about Bristol and Clifton. It has also been noticed in and near Wells; and at Winscombe, S.   VII. VIII.

560. **L. vulgaris,** *Mill.* *Yellow Toad-flax.*
Native; on hedge-banks and dry waste ground, common.
     VII.—IX.

SCROPHULARIA, *L.*

561. **S. nodosa,** *L.*
Native; in damp shady places, common.   VII. VIII.

562. **S. aquatica,** *L.*
Native; in wet places, common.   VII. VIII.

MELAMPYRUM, *L.*

563. **M. pratense,** *L.* *Cow-wheat.*
Native; in woods and on shaded banks, frequent.
G. Clifton Down; sparingly above the road from the fountain to the riverside; and abundantly on the wooded slopes near the Gully. Blaize Castle. Glen Frome. Conham. Westridge Wood, near Wotton-under-Edge.
S. Brislington. Congresbury. Portishead. Shipham. Weston-in-Gordano. Yatton.   VI.—VIII.

SCROPHULARIACEÆ.

MIMULUS, *L.*

564. M. luteus, *L.*
Alien; naturalized in a few places.
S. Little Wood pool, near Cleeve; and Lipsey Lane. *Miss Winter.* For half a mile in a small stream on the Blagdon side of Black Down. We have seen it spring up on rubbish in Clifton.

PEDICULARIS, *L.*

565. P. palustris, *L.*
Native; in boggy ditches, rare.
G. Filton meads; *Swete, Fl.* 57.
S. Sparingly on the peat near Wedmore. VI. VII.

566. P. sylvatica, *L.* *Red Rattle.*
Native; in moist heathy and hilly pastures, frequent.
G. On the furzy portions of Durdham Down, and on the south side of the Gully. Near Damory Bridge. Hillsides in the Trym valley below Westbury. Mangotsfield. Yate Common.
S. Barrow Gurney. With white flowers on Black Down. Brislington. Very abundant between Sandy Lane and Failand Farm, near the Tanpits. Tickenham. Boggy hillsides near Wells. Yatton. V.—VIII.

RHINANTHUS, *L.*

567. R. Crista-galli. *L.* *Yellow Rattle.*
Native; in meadows and pastures, very abundant in many places, usually on very poor soils. We have seen pastures full of it at
G. Thornbury. Tortworth. Sodbury. Wotton-under-Edge.
S. Chew Magna, and about Dundry Hill. Clevedon. Wells. Whitchurch. VI. VII.

EUPHRASIA, L.

568. E. officinalis, *L. Eye-bright.*
Native; in dry pastures and on banks. Very common, and extremely variable in habit. VI.—VIII.

ODONTITES, *Duby.*

569. O. rubra, *Pers.*
Native; in cornfields and waste places, common.
VII. VIII.

VERONICA, L.

570. V. scutellata, *L.*
Native; in bogs and ditches, very rare.
S. Clevedon, in a wet ditch! *Mr. D. Fry.* Near Yatton. In a bog on Mendip near Priddy, on old red sandstone; altitude about 700 ft. *Dr. H. F. Parsons.*
VI.—VIII.

571. V. Anagallis, *L.*
Native; in water, frequent; and plentiful on the alluvium and peat in the southern portion of the district. We find it sometimes with flesh-coloured flowers; and rarely with the fruit converted into a sort of gall by insect agency.
G. Boiling Well. Filton. Sodbury. Warmley. Tortworth.
S. Bedminster. St. Anne's Wood, Brislington. Barrow Gurney. Clevedon. Portbury. Woodspring. Generally distributed on the moors from Yatton and Weston-super-Mare to Wells and Highbridge. VI.—VIII.

572. V. Beccabunga, *L. Brooklime.*
Native; in ditches and streams, very common. VI.—IX.

573. V. Chamædrys, *L. Germander Speedwell.*
Native; on hedge-banks, and in grassy places everywhere. Very common. V. VI.

574. V. montana, *L.*
Native; in woods, frequent.
G. Glen Frome. Woods between Patchway and Charlton. Pucklechurch. Thornbury. Cook's Folly Wood.

K

S. Bourton Combe. Woods near Congresbury. Failand. Hutton. Knowle. Leigh Wood. Under Maes Knoll. St. Anne's Wood, Brislington. Portishead. Stockwood Lane. Weston-in-Gordano. Plentiful in two woods near Wells; *Miss Livett*. IV.—VI.

575. **V. officinalis,** *L.*
Native; on dry banks and in heathy pastures. Common, especially on the Mendips. VI. VIII.

576. **V. hybrida,** *L.*
Native; on the more inaccessible ledges of St. Vincent's Rocks, still plentiful.

Although there appears to be no important character to separate *V. hybrida* from *V. spicata, L.*, yet it is generally considered that our plants and those of the Welsh coast belong to the former. This is the most handsome of our native Veronicas. It attains its southern limit in this country on St. Vincent's Rocks, where it flourishes in great luxuriance and beauty, the plants being at least as large again as those we have seen on the Great Ormshead. VII.—VIII.

577. **V. serpyllifolia,** *L.*
Native; in damp places by roadsides, very common.

578. **V. arvensis,** *L.* IV.—VII.
Native; in dry gravelly places and on cultivated land, very common. IV.—VII.

(*V. triphyllos*, L. Dr. Stephens informed Mr. Flower that Swete's record for this plant "about Stapleton Mill" was an error.)

579. **V. agrestis,** *L.*
Native. A very common weed on cultivated land. IV.—IX.

580. **V. polita,** *Fries.*
Native; on dry banks and walls, and in cultivated fields, common.

G. Almondsbury. Bitton. Charlton. Kingsweston. Horfield. Fishponds. Warmley. Westbury.
S. Bourton. Failand. Knowle. Pensford. Stockwood. Wells. Weston-super-Mare.   IV.—IX.

581. V. Buxbaumii, *Ten.*
Colonist; in cultivated fields, common, and generally distributed.
This is a comparatively recent introduction, and has increased and spread with great rapidity during the last thirty years. In Swete's time it seems to have been considered an alien casual, occurring sparingly, and thought to be probably introduced with foreign seed. Swete does not appear to have seen a specimen. *Fl. Brist.* 56. At the present time there are few arable fields in our district which are not plentifully sprinkled with this weed.   IV.—IX.

582. V. hederæfolia, *L.*
Native. A very common weed on cultivated land.
    III.—VI.

LABIATÆ.
MENTHA, *L.*

NOTE.—The examples of this genus contained in the Stephens Herbarium are stated by Dr. Stephens to have been derived from the herbarium of the late Dr. Dyer, of Bristol. They were marked "Mentha Brittanica Sole," and in all probability they came to Dr. Dyer direct from Mr. Sole.

583. M. rotundifolia, *L.*
Denizen. Very rare.
Roadside between Westbury and Horfield, several years ago, also at Chelwood; *Mr. T. B. Flower* in *lit.* Feb., 1883.
In a high meadow near Berkeley Castle; *Sole.*

In Newton Park; *Dr. Davis* in *Fl. Bathon.* Shirehampton; *Swete, Fl.* 60.

584. **M. sylvestris,** *L. Horse Mint.*
Denizen; in damp waste places, very rare. Sole found this mint "in most home closes, farmers' bartons, and such-like places."
S. Waste places about Hinton Blewitt, and between Ashton Lodge and Tadwick; *Mr. T. B. Flower.* River side in Newton Mead; *id.* A few plants in a damp spot by the roadside near Portbury; August, 1881.
Walton-in-Gordano; *Mrs. Lainson* and *Herb. Stephens.*
Weston-super-Mare; *St. Brody, Fl. Weston.* VIII. IX.

585. **M. piperita,** *Sm. Peppermint.*
Native, or denizen; perhaps now extinct. We have not seen a specimen.
Henbury Combe, Sept., 1846. *Herb. Powell.*
Near the river at Wick; *Mr. T. B. Flower.* "It grows in a swampy place near Lansdown called the Wells, that being the spring-head of Lock's Brook. It is also found by the side of the Avon in Newton Mead, and in other places about Bath." *Sole.*
Near Bath, Wells, and Glastonbury, Somerset; *Syme's E. B.*

586. **M. aquatica,** *L.*, including **M. hirsuta,** *L.*
Native; on ditch-banks and in marshes, very common.
VII. VIII.

587. **M. sativa,** *L.*
Native; in wet places, very common. VII. VIII.

588. **M. arvensis,** *L. Corn Mint.*
Native; in cultivated ground, common. VII.—IX.

LYCOPUS, *L.*

589. **L. europæus,** *L. Gipsywort.*
Native; by water, frequent.

LABIATÆ. 137

G. Glen Frome. Baptist Mills. Bank of Avon above Bristol. Henbury brook. Syston marsh. Tortworth. Yate.

S. Very fine plants in Leigh Wood near the Avon opposite Black Rock. Burnham. Cheddar. Clevedon. Easton. Ken. Paulton. Yatton. VII. VIII.

SALVIA, L.

590. **S. Verbenaca,** *L. Sage, or English Clary.*
Native; on dry banks, frequent.
G. Berkeley. Chipping Sodbury. Henbury. Tortworth. St. Vincent's Rocks. Westbury-on-Trym.
S. Clevedon. Tickenham. Uphill. Wells. Peculiarly abundant about Weston-super-Mare. Worle. Yatton.
V. VI.

(S. pratensis, L. "On Wick Cliffs, Gloucestershire. *Mr. Swayne, With.* ed. 3, II. 21. There is every reason to believe that this was an error. Mr. Flower says he found no specimen in Withering's herbarium.)

(S. sylvestris. Alien on old colliery *débris* near Kingswood, G.)

ORIGANUM, L.

591. **O. vulgare,** L. *Marjoram.*
Native; on banks, by roadsides, and in bushy waste places, frequent.
G. Berkeley. Dursley. Henbury. Tortworth. St. Vincent's Rocks and Clifton Down. Westbury-on-Trym. Wotton-under-Edge.
S. Bank of Avon below Bristol. Clevedon. Congresbury. Draycot. Great Elm. Pensford. Abundant about Wells. Loxton. Worle. VIII.

THYMUS, L.

592. **T. Serpyllum,** L. *Common Wild Thyme.*
Native; on hills and in dry heathy pastures, common.
VI.—VIII.

LABIATÆ.

593. T. Chamædrys, *Fr.*
Native; on heathy ground, very rare. Perhaps it has been overlooked in some places.
S. Leigh Wood, June, 1868; *Rev. W. W. Spicer.* Sparingly on Leigh Down, 1879.

CALAMINTHA, *Moench.*

(C. Nepeta, Clairv. We have several times been informed of the occurrence of this species in the district; but on enquiry the plants have proved to be *C. officinalis.)*

594. C. officinalis, *Moench. Common Calamint.*
Native; on dry, rocky banks, frequent.
G. Almondsbury Hill. Conham. St. Vincent's Rocks. Stapleton.
S. Plentiful on Brean Down. Cheddar. Clevedon. Draycot. Great Elm. Loxton. Stowey. Uphill. Walton-in-Gordano. Woodspring. Wells. VII.—IX.

595. C. Acinos, *Clairv. Basil.*
Native; frequent upon limestone rocks, and rarely to be seen elsewhere.
G. St. Vincent's Rocks. Cultivated ground near Kingswood. Wick Rocks.
S. Clevedon. Rocks under Leigh Wood. Loxton. Emborrow. Walton by Clevedon. Worle Hill. VII. VIII.

596. C. Clinopodium, *Benth.*
Native; in hedges and bushy places, common and very abundant. VII. VIII.

MELISSA, *L.*

597. M. officinalis, *L. Balm.*
Alien; established here and there in waste ground.
G. Bridge Yate. By the railway under St. Vincent's Rocks.
S. By the roadside at Bourton; *Mr. W. E. Green.* Clevedon. In the corner of a field at Pill. VII. VIII.

SCUTELLARIA, *L.*

598. S. galericulata, *L.* *Skull-cap.*

Native; on ditch-banks and in marshes, frequent, but not plentiful anywhere.

G. Near Dursley. Glen Frome. Thornbury.

S. Bank of Avon below Bristol. Marshy spots on the sands at Berrow. Clevedon. Easton Moor. Failand. Kingston Seymour. Nailsea Moor. Marsh near Ham Green ; *Swete, Fl.* 63. Woodspring. Yatton. VII. VIII.

599. S. minor, *L.*

Native; on the swampy margin of a pool about a mile from Abbot's Leigh, S., where about two dozen plants are to be seen yearly. The extreme rarity of this plant in the Bristol district is very remarkable. It is said to have grown on the banks of the Avon near Bath, and to have been formerly abundant on the peat moors in the extreme south; but at present the Abbot's Leigh station is the only one known to us between Bristol and the Quantocks, and for the large portion of our area in Gloucestershire we have no record at all.

PRUNELLA, *L.*

600. P. vulgaris, *L.* *Self-heal.*

Native; in pastures, very common. The white flowered plant grows in fields near Patchway, G.   VII. VIII.

NEPETA, *L.*

601. N. Cataria, *L.* *Cat Mint.*

Native or denizen, rare.

G. Almondsbury Hill, Aug., 1839; *Herb. Powell.* Among the rocks and hollows at the side of the hill at Penpole Point. Henbury; *Swete, Fl.* 63. Wick Cliffs, *Mr. Swayne, With.* ed. iii. 520.

S. A few plants between Kewstoke Sands and Sand Point, 1880, and 1881. It has been known to grow here for many years. Near Cadbury Camp. Weston-in-Gordano; *Mr. D. Fry.*

It is said that cats delight in the scent of this plant almost as much as in that of Valerian root. Whenever they meet with the *Nepeta* they entirely destroy it by chewing the young branches, and rolling themselves upon the plant as long as any smell is left.

"Mr. Miller says that cats will not meddle with it if it be raised from seed; and in support of this opinion quotes an old saying, 'If you set it, the cats will eat it; if you sow it, the cats won't know it.'" *Withering.*

602. N. Glechoma, *Benth.* *Ground-Ivy.*

Native; on nearly every hedge-bank, very common.

IV.—VI.

LAMIUM, *L.*

603. L. amplexicaule, *L.*

Native; under walls, and on cultivated land, rare.

G. In plenty at Crew's Hole, 1880, and 1881.

S. Burnham. Clevedon. Keynsham. Under walls in several places about Weston-super-Mare. Abundant in potato fields at Worle, 1880. Yatton.

A large form of this plant with much larger leaves, the upper internodes very short, and approaching in appearance to *L. intermedium*, occurs on high ground between Weston-super-Mare and Banwell.

IV.—VII.

604. L. incisum, *Willd.*

Native; in waste places, rather rare.

G. Netham; Stapleton; *Swete, Fl.* 62. Chariton. Frenchay.

S. It is tolerably abundant about Clevedon, although more unfrequent than *L. purpureum*, with which it often grows; *Mr. D. Fry.* Pill. Portishead. Tickenham. Weston-super-Mare.

IV.—VI.

LABIATÆ.

605. L. purpureum, *L.* *Red Dead-Nettle.*
Native; on waste and cultivated ground, very common.
IV.—VIII.

606. L. album, *L.* *White Dead-Nettle.*
Native; on hedge-banks and waste ground, common.
V. VI.

607. L. maculatum, *L.*
Alien. Permanently established in one or two places; a casual in others.
G. Lane at the back of Redland Court; *Herb. Stephens;* and *Mr. T. B. Flower*, who says it grew there for many years. Stoke Bishop.
S. Abundant at Chelvey; *Miss Winter*, and *Mr. W. Green.* South Stoke. Combe Hay. Brislington; *Swete, Fl. 62.* V. VI.

608. L. Galeobdolon, *Crantz.* *Archangel.*
Native; on hedge-banks, and in bushy places, common.
It is peculiarly abundant about Bristol, and well distributed in other portions of our area. V. VI.

LEONURUS, L.

609. L. Cardiaca, *L.*
Alien, or denizen, in waste places, very rare.
G. There are specimens in Miss Powell's herbarium from Lawrence Weston, and Henbury; 18 0. " Sea banks near the Clifton Gas Works," *Dr. Stephens* (marginal note in his copy of Withering). It is said to have grown formerly at Crew's Hole, and near the Hotwells; *Bot. Guide.*
S. Near Lympsham! Aug., 1881; *Mr. T. F. Perkins.*

GALEOPSIS, L.

610. G. Ladanum, *L.*
Colonist; chiefly on arable land, frequent.
G. St. Vincent's Rocks; *Herb. Stephens,* and *Shiercliff's*

Guide for 1789. Pur Down. Filton. Horfield. Thornbury.

S. Clevedon. Congresbury. Ebbor. Leigh Wood. Queen Charlton. Walton and Weston-in-Gordano. Weston-super-Mare.   VIII. IX.

611. G. Tetrahit, *L.*   *Common Hemp-Nettle.*

Native or colonist; in damp bushy places, and on cultivated ground, frequent.

G. Aust. Almondsbury. Berkeley. By the Frome near Stapleton, with white flowers. Horfield. Yate.

S. Clevedon. St. Anne's Wood, Brislington. Walton, and Weston-in-Gordano. Wedmore. Weston-super-Mare. Winscombe. Yatton.   VII.—IX.

STACHYS, *L.*

612. S. Betonica, *Benth. Betony.*

Native; in woods and hedges, preferring dry hilly places, frequent.

G. Almondsbury. Clifton and Durdham Downs. Mangotsfield. Yate Common.

S. Congresbury. Emborrow. Leigh Wood. Walton-in-Gordano. Wells. Temple Cloud.

Great virtue was formerly attributed to Betony, but it has been long disused by our physicians. However we still meet with persons gathering it for a domestic medicine.   VII. VIII.

613. S. palustris, *L.*

Native; on ditch-banks, in damp fields, and neglected arable land, common. The variety β. *S. ambigua*, Sm. is to be gathered on the banks of the Avon, and in many similar situations.   VII. VIII.

614. S. sylvatica, *L.*

Native; in woods, hedges, and waste ground, common.

    VII. VIII.

LABIATÆ.

615. S. arvensis, *L.*
Native, or colonist ; in cornfields, common.   VII.—IX.
(S. annua, L. Alien. Sparingly for some years on old colliery *débris* near Kingswood, G.)

BALLOTA, *L.*

616. B. fœtida, *Lam.*
Native ; by roadsides, and in waste ground ; common, but not very abundant.   VII. VIII.

MARRUBIUM, *L.*

617. M. vulgare, *L.*   *White Horehound.*
Denizen ; chiefly on downs near the Channel, rare.
G. Brandon Hill ; Durdham Down ; *Swete, Fl.* 63. St. Vincent's Rocks ; *Herb. Stephens.* Penpole Point ; *Mr. W. E. Green.*
S. Brean Down. Near Cadbury Camp. Dial Hill, Clevedon. On Sand Farm, by Kewstoke. Wavering Down.   VIII. IX.

TEUCRIUM, *L.*

618. T. Scorodonia, *L.*   *Wood Sage.*
Native ; in woods and shady places, very common.
   VII. VIII.
(T. Chamædrys, L. Alien. Shirehampton, 1839 ; *Miss M. Waring. Herb. Powell.* By a roadside near Tickenham, where it has grown for many years. *Dr. Davis,* and *Rev. G. W. Braikenridge.)*

AJUGA, *L.*

619. A. reptans, *L.*   *Bugle.*
Native ; in damp shady places, very common.
We have found it with white flowers at Englishcombe, in Leigh Wood, in a wood between Abbot's Leigh and Failand, and in Westridge Wood near Wotton-under-Edge.   V. VI.

VERBENACEÆ.
VERBENA.
620. V. officinalis, *L. Vervain.*

Native; on waste ground. frequent.

G. At the foot of St. Vincent's Rocks, and all along the course of the river, plentiful. Almondsbury. Alveston. Crew's Hole. Elberton. Henbury. Stoke Bishop.

S. Bank of Avon below Bristol. Cheddar. Clevedon. Draycot. Ken. Paulton. Portbury. Tickenham. Walton by Clevedon. Wells. Weston-in-Gordano. Weston-super-Mare. Yatton.   VII. VIII.

LENTIBULARIACEÆ.
PINGUICULA, *L.*
621. P. vulgaris, *L.*

Native; in a ravine on Mendip, very rare.

In a ravine near Old Down (on the road from Wells to Bath), 1875. *Miss Livett.* It is very noteworthy that this Butterwort does not occur more frequently on boggy hillsides among the Mendips, which afford many suitable localities.

UTRICULARIA, *L.*
622. U. vulgaris, *L. Bladderwort.*

Native; in ditches here and there throughout the marshlands between the Mendips and the Channel.

S. Axbridge. Walton Drove, near Clevedon. Mark. Nailsea Moor. Tickenham. Wedmore. Yatton.

    VII. VIII.

PRIMULACEÆ.
HOTTONIA, *L.*
623. H. palustris, *L. Water Violet.*

Native; in peaty ditches in the marshlands, locally plentiful.

S. Abundant in ditches below Axbridge, Cheddar, and Draycot.

A mass of *Hottonia* in full bloom bedded in bright green duckweed, and framed by the darker tints of tall rush and sedge, forms a picture of exquisite loveliness, which will dwell in the memory for ever. Its beauty is heightened by contrast with the expanse of drear moorland in which it lies hidden. V. VI.

PRIMULA, L.

624. P. vulgaris, *Huds. Primrose.*

Native; in woods and on hedge-banks, very common.

Pure white, and purple varieties have been met with in woods near Temple Cloud, S.

β. *P. variabilis*, Goup.

A caulescent variety or hybrid, sometimes miscalled "Oxlip."

G. Filton. Wood between Patchway and Charlton.

S. Churchill. Clevedon. The Wild Country. Stockwood. Maes Knoll. Walton and Weston-in-Gordano; *Mrs. Lainson.* Plentiful about Wells; *Miss Livett.* Yatton. III.—V.

625. P. veris, *L. Cowslip. Paigle.*

Native; in meadows and pastures, common. IV. V.

LYSIMACHIA, L.

626. L. vulgaris, *L.*

Native; by the sides of rivers and pools, frequent.

G. Baptist Mills, *Dr. H. O. Stephens;* perhaps now extinct. Sparingly by the Frome near Stapleton. Tortworth.

S. Bedminster Meads, *Swete, Fl.* p. 66; probably extinct. Clevedon. Between Ken and Yatton. Yatton; *Miss Winter.* Nailsea Moor. Ditch-banks south of Wedmore. Rare in the neighbourhood of Wells. VII. VIII.

PRIMULACEÆ.

627. L. Nummularia, *L. Money-wort.*

Native; in damp meadows and pastures, and on ditchbanks. Rather local, but abundant in many places..

G. Plentiful near Berkeley. Boiling Well Marsh. Hallen, near Henbury.

S. Leigh Wood. On the margin of some swampy pools near Abbot's Leigh. Berrow. Clevedon. Marshes near Draycot, Cheddar, Winscombe, and Wells. Ken. Pensford. Portbury. Peaty meadows west of Dundry Hill. Yatton. V.—VIII.

628. L. nemorum, *L.*

Native; in nearly every moist wood; common, and generally distributed. VI.—VIII.

GLAUX, *L.*

629. G. maritima, *L.*

Native; in salt marshes, and on the margins of the tidal rivers. Locally common. VI.—VIII.

ANAGALLIS, *L.*

630. A. arvensis, *L. Scarlet Pimpernel.*

Native; on cultivated land, and in waste places near the coast, common.

β. *A. cærulea,* Sm. In cornfields, rare.

G. Ashley; *Dr. H. O. Stephens.* Henbury; *Herb. Powell.* Horfield; *Swete, Fl. p. 66.*

S. Berrow. Clevedon; with mauve and white varieties. *Mr. W. E. Green. Mr. D. Fry.* In a cornfield between Abbot's Leigh and Failand; 1881. Knowle; *Swete, ib.* Wells. VI. VII.

631. A. tenella, *L. Bog Pimpernel.*

Native; in boggy meadows, and wet places. Rather rare and local.

S. Black Down. Chelvey. Under Crook's Peak. Easton. By the side of a brook not far from the tan pits at Failand. Near Winscombe. VII. VIII.

SAMOLUS, *L.*

632. S. Valerandi, *L.*

Native; in marshes and by the sides of ditches, especially near the Channel, frequent.

G. Avonmouth marshes. Berkeley. Hallen. Marshes below Lawrence Weston.

S. Abundant in a marsh on Burnham sands. Clevedon. Draycot. Easton Moor. Nailsea. Portbury. Portishead. Walton Drove. Wedmore. Ditches about Weston Junction. VII. VIII.

PLUMBAGINACEÆ.

STATICE, *L.*

633. S. Limonium, *L.* *Sea Lavender.*

Native; on the muddy shore of the Bristol Channel, rather rare. Our plant is *S. Behen*, Drejer.

G. One or two plants on the mud near Avonmouth Station, July, 1870.

S. Very sparingly on the marshy portion of Burnham Sands. In plenty near Clevedon, and on mud-flats near Woodspring Priory. VII. VIII.

ARMERIA, *Willd.*

634. A. maritima, *Willd.* *Thrift.*

Native; on the dry turfy margins of salt marshes, and by the tidal inlets: sometimes on rocks, as at Brean Down. Locally common. It does not approach Bristol nearer than the river-bank below Shirehampton. We are told that it grows on Mendip at Cheddar, and Dr. H. F. Parsons has kindly forwarded the following note :—" In a rocky field near Great Elm, on inferior oolite, where it is established in some plenty; but may have been carried thither with garden rubbish."

PLANTAGINACEÆ.
PLANTAGO, *L.*

635. **P. Coronopus,** *L.*
Native; in barren spots near the coast, common. VI. VII.

636. **P. maritima,** *L.*
Native; in salt marshes, and on banks by the tidal waters, rather common. VI.—VIII.

637. **P. lanceolata,** *L.* *Common Rib-grass.*
Native; in meadows, pastures, and waste places. Very common and generally distributed. We once gathered at Montpelier a monstrosity bearing several heads upon one scape. V.—VIII.

638. **P. media,** *L.* *Lamb's-tongue.*
Native; in dry pastures, quite common. VI.—IX.

639. **P. major,** *L.*
Native; in waste places, by roadsides, and in fields; very common everywhere. VI.—VIII.

(*P. arenaria*, W. & K., was formerly found abundantly on the sandhills near Burnham; but we think has not been seen there since 1867. It has grown for some years in fair quantity with other aliens on a small heap of old colliery *débris* near Kingswood, G.)

FLORA OF THE BRISTOL COAL-FIELD.

ADDITIONS TO PARTS I., II., AND III.

Aconitum Napellus, L. We have now seen the Aconite growing in great abundance on both banks of a brook above Edford, S. It occurs in patches of considerable size, and extends about a mile and a half up the stream under the south edge of Downside Common. In this locality the plant has all the appearance of a native; yet possibly it was introduced at a remote date, and should be classed as a denizen. See p. 11.

40.° Papaver Lecoqii, *Lamotte.*
S. Abundant on cultivated land between Stockwood and Whitchurch; where it was shewn to us by the *Rev. W. H. Painter* in July, 1883. VI. VII.

112.° Dianthus Armeria, *L.*
S. Ball Wood, Congresbury; *Mr. D. Fry.* There is a good patch on the border of the wood, on limestone; and considered to be wild there by Mr. Archer Briggs, who saw it with Mr. Fry in August, 1883. A single plant was noticed on waste land at Clevedon by Mr. Briggs at the same date. One root under a wall not far from Bourton Combe, July, 1882. VII. VIII.

Medicago minima, Lam. One plant on dredgings from the bed of the Avon, deposited in the Black Rock Quarry; July, 1883. See p. 44.

(*Vicia lutea*, L. Several plants also on dredgings in the same place as the last; August, 1883.)

260.* **Rubus plicatus,** *W. & N.*
S. Abundant on the peat moors towards the southern limit of the district. VI. VII.

271.* **R. Borreri,** *Bell-Salter.*
S. Norton's Lane, near Clevedon; August, 1883, *Mr. Archer Briggs;* and *Mr. D. Fry.*

R. Hystrix, Weihe, in North Somerset. Bishop's Wood, Wells! *Rev. R. Murray.* See p. 60.

280.* **R. glandulosus,** *Bell.*
S. Cranmore Hill; Downhead Common; and perhaps near Congresbury; *Rev. R. Murray.* These should possibly go under *R. hirtus,* W. & K., but are not typical. VII. VIII.

280.** **R. Balfourianus,** *Blox.*
S. Whitchurch. *Rev. W. H. Painter, fide Rev. W. H. Purchas.*

281.* **R. althæifolius,** *Host.*
S. Whitchurch. *Rev. W. H. Painter, fide Rev. W. H. Purchas.*

R. tuberculatus, Bab. Additional records. Knowle Quarry, and Whitchurch! *Rev. W. H. Painter.* In abundance about Ball Wood near Congresbury. See p. 61.

R. cæsius, L. ϵ. *R. pseudo-Idæus,* Lej. Near Congresbury, S. *Mr. Archer Briggs;* and *Mr. D. Fry.*

283.* **R. saxatilis,** *L.*
S. Asham Wood, S.W. of Frome; June, 1883. *Rev. R. Murray.*

Pyrus torminalis, Sm. in Gloucestershire. A small tree grows on the face of a low cliff on the Pennant near the second mill in Glen Frome, Stapleton; a situation where it could not have been planted. See p. 67.

Œnothera odorata, Jacq. west of Brean Down. On Sept. 5, 1883, we saw one plant on the sands at Berrow, S. See p. 70.

(*Antennaria margaritacea*, R. Br. Found by Mr. D. Fry, Nov., 1883, growing on the edge of a wood at Walton-by-Clevedon. Its occurrence at a spot so far removed from gardens and habitations, and where the rest of the vegetation is purely indigenous, is very remarkable.)

458.* Centaurea solstitialis, *L.* Yellow Star-thistle.

Colonist. About a dozen large plants on sand near the Lighthouses at Burnham, S., Sept. 5, 1883. The spot had apparently been levelled for cultivation at some remote season; but was entirely waste at the time of our visit.   VII.—IX.

(*C. melitensis*, L. There was another station for this alien in 1883; on dredgings in the Black Rock Quarry, G. See p. 106.)

488.* Crepis biennis, *L.*

"Colonist. In a small field near Axbridge, S.; likely to spread." June 19, 1883. *Rev. R. Murray.*

Pyrola minor, L. First record for North Somerset. This is certainly the most important among recent additions to our knowledge of the district flora. The discoverer, Mr. R. Baker, of Clevedon, gave us a fresh specimen with the following note:—"I observed it on

July 2, 1883, in a wood in the vicinity of Clifton, on the Somersetshire side of the river. The plant was distributed over an area of about twenty square yards; sparsely in places, but in others more thickly; closely matted with the wild strawberry. It had passed full bloom, and was probably in perfection about the middle of June." See p. 118.

(*Ajuga Chamæpitys*, Schreb. Casual. One plant on dredgings from the bed of the Avon deposited in the Black Rock Quarry, G. August, 1883.)

CORRECTIONS.

Part I., pp. 25 and 30. For Minories read Mineries.

Part III., p. 85. For *Sagina maritima*, Don., read *Silene maritima*, With.

Part III., p. 114, line 13 from bottom. For Cheddar; *Rev. R. P. Murray*, read Ebbor; *Mr. J. G. Baker*.

FLORA

OF THE

BRISTOL COAL-FIELD.

EDITED (FOR THE BRISTOL NATURALISTS' SOCIETY) BY

JAMES WALTER WHITE,

Hon. Secretary of the Botanical Section.

"*Rerum cognoscere causas.*"—VIRGIL.

PART IV

MONOCHLAMYDEÆ.

BRISTOL:
JAMES FAWN & SON.

PRINTED BY E. AUSTIN & SON, CHRONICLE OFFICE, CLIFTON.

MDCCCLXXXIV.

PHANEROGAMIA.

Class 1. *DICOTYLEDONES.*
Div. 4. *MONOCHLAMYDEÆ.*

CHENOPODIACEÆ.
SUÆDA, *Forsk.*

640. S. maritima, *Dum.*

Native; in all the muddy estuaries of the district. Abundant in such situations from Huntspill northward.
VII.—IX.

SALSOLA, L.

641. S. Kali, L.

Native; on the sandy shore of the Bristol Channel; locally common.

S. Kewstoke Sands. Weston-super-Mare. Brean. Burnham. VIII. IX.

CHENOPODIUM, L.

642. C. Vulvaria, *L. C. olidum,* Curt.

Native or colonist; in waste places near houses, or by the Channel. Very rare, and possibly now extinct.

S. By the Gas Works at Bath. "Waste ground, not very frequent." *Fl. Bathon.* "About Brean and Berrow." *Mr. T. B. Flower.* VIII. IX.

643. C. polyspermum, L.

Native; in cultivated and rich waste ground. Rather rare.

G. Almondsbury. Henbury; *Herb. Powell.* Garden weed at Kingsdown; *Herb. Stephens.* St. Philip's Marsh.

S. Garden weed at Knowle! *Rev. W. H. Painter.* Weston-super-Mare, and Worle; *Mr. T. B. Flower.* Yatton; *Miss Winter,* and *Mr. W. F. Green.* VIII. IX.

(*C. urbicum,* L. We fear that the following records are not sufficient ground for believing this species to be a Bristol plant. "On waste and cultivated ground, frequent." *Fl. Bathon.* "Near Bristol; *Worsley, Cat.*" *New Botanists' Guide.*)

644. C. album, *L.*

Native; in cultivated ground and waste places. A very common weed: particularly fine and abundant in fields near Brean and Berrow; S. The variety or subspecies, *C. payanum,* Reich., is the most frequent one in this district. VIII. IX.

645. C. ficifolium, *Sm.*

Native; in cultivated and waste ground, very rare. As a garden weed at Clevedon; S. *Mr. D. Fry.* "Near Bristol; *Worsley, Cat.*" *New B. G.*

646. C. murale, *L.*

Native; on waste ground and manure heaps, rare.
G. Crew's Hole; *Herb. Stephens.* "Sea banks, near the glass houses, Bristol. *Winch, add.*" *New B. G.*
S. Farmyard at Failand, in plenty; 1878. Waste ground about Weston-super-Mare; *Mr. T. B. Flower.* Yatton and Milton; *Mr. D. Fry.* VIII. IX.

647. C. hybridum, *L.*

Perhaps only a casual in the district, very rare.
G. On dredgings from the bed of the Avon deposited in the Black Rock Quarry; Sept. 26, 1883. Crew's Hole; *Herb. Stephens.* "Near Bristol. *Worsley, Cat.*" *New. B. G.*

CHENOPODIACEÆ.

648. C. rubrum, *L.*

Native; in waste places, particularly salt marshes. Locally plentiful.

G. Bank of Avon, opposite Cook's Folly; *Herb. Stephens.* Abundant in the Black Rock Quarry; Sept., 1883. St. Philip's Marsh; in great plenty.

S. In damp places on the coast near Burnham, running down insensibly into what has been called *pseudobotryodes.* Clevedon. "On dunghills and waste ground, frequent." *Fl. Bathon.*   VIII. IX.

649. C. Bonus-Henricus, *L.*

Denizen; in waste places, chiefly near villages; rather rare.

G. Black Rock Quarry; Oct., 1883. Crew's Hole; *Herb. Stephens.* Thornbury Castle; *Herb. Powell.* Tortworth.

S. Frequent at Cheddar village. Wells. Yatton. "At Swainswick, Charlcombe, Wyck, Tadwick, &c." *Fl. Bathon.*   VI.—X.

BETA, *L.*

650. B. maritima, *L.* *Sea-Beet.*

Native; on the banks of the estuaries, and on sand and shingle by the Channel. Rather common.

G. Bank of Avon as far up as the Black Rock.

S. Portishead. Clevedon. Kewstoke. Brean. Plentiful along the coast from Huntspill to Brean Down.

       VII.—IX.

SALICORNIA, *L.*

651. S. herbacea, *L.*

Native; on mudflats by tidal waters. Frequent about all the estuaries and saltwater inlets.   VIII. IX.

ATRIPLEX, L.

652. A. angustifolia, Sm.
Native; in cultivated ground and waste places, very common. VIII.—X.

653. A. erecta, Huds.
Native; in cultivated ground and waste places, common. Plentiful on the banks of Avon, and in the Black Rock Quarry, G. VIII.—X.

654. A. deltoidea, Bab.
Native; in waste places, common. Very abundant in St. Philip's Marsh, and on the banks of Avon where the ground has been disturbed. VII.—IX.

655. A. hastata, L. *A. patula,* Sm. *A. Smithii,* Syme.
Native; in cultivated ground and in waste places, and about salt marshes; common. The fleshy prostrate coast or tidal-river form is abundant on the Channel shore near Avonmouth, and at New Passage. VII.—X.

656. A. Babingtonii, Woods. *A. rosea,* Bab.
Native; in salt marshes, and on the shore of the Channel, locally common.
G. Avonmouth. New Passage.
S. Sands east and west of Weston-super-Mare. Brean. Burnham. VII.—IX.

(*A. farinosa,* Dum. *A. laciniata,* Sm. "On the sea-coast near the mouth of the Parret, Burnham, and Steart. J. C. Collins, MSS." New B. G. No recent record.)

OBIONE, Gaert.

657. O. portulacoides, Moq.
Native; on the coast, very rare.
G. Sparingly at Avonmouth, near the railway station, 1879. Shirehampton; Swete, Fl. 68.

S. "Near the mouth of the river Parret"; *Mr. T. B. Flower.* "On the sea-coast near the mouth of the Parret, Burnham, and Steart. *J. C. Collins, MSS.*" New B. G.   VIII.—X.

POLYGONACEÆ.
RUMEX, L.

658. R. maritimus, *L. Golden Dock.*
Native; in marshes towards the southern limit of the district; very rare.
S. "Wedmore, Somersetshire; June 1843. *G. H. K. Thwaites.*" *Herb. Stephens.* "Mouth of the Parret; Steart Marsh. *J. C. Collins, MSS.*" N. B. G. Frequent on the peat moors still farther south.
               VII. VIII.

659. R. conglomeratus, *Murr.*
Native; by the sides of ditches, and in damp waste places. Common and generally distributed.   VI.—VIII.

660. R. sanguineus, *L. Bloody-veined Dock.*
Native. Very rare. It has been known to grow for many years on both banks of the Avon below Bristol: on the Gloucestershire side under Durdham Down; and in Somersetshire about half a mile below the Suspension Bridge. Specimens were gathered at the latter station in 1881. Mr. Flower says he has also seen it on Brandon Hill, but not of late years. "In a wood at Kelston"; *Fl. Bathon.* Roadside at Hanham; *Mr. W. E. Green.*

β. *R. viridis,* Sibth. *R. nemorosus,* Schrad.
Native; in woods and by roadsides, frequent.

G. Clifton Zigzag; and elsewhere in shady places about St. Vincent's Rocks, and the Downs. St. Philip's Marsh. Glen Frome, Stapleton. Stoke Bishop. Westbury.

S. Frequent in Leigh Woods. Portishead. Brislington. Clevedon. Congresbury. Barrow Gurney. Whitchurch.
VI.—VIII.

661. R. pulcher, L. *Fiddle Dock.*

Native; on dry waste and turfy places, rather common, especially on limestone.

G. Plentiful on the turfy slopes of St. Vincent's Rocks opposite Sion Hill, and about the Zigzag, and on the borders of paths in that vicinity. Brandon Hill. Cotham. Bank of Avon. Fields about Horfield. Stapleton. Mangotsfield. Old Passage. Penpole Point Church lane, Henbury. Wick Cliffs.

S. Cheddar. Clevedon. Bleadon; *Mrs. Lainson.* In the old churchyard at Uphill. Walton-in-Gordano. " Common on roadsides"; *Fl. Bathon.*

The Bristol Museum possesses a " *Hortus Siccus* presented by your humble servant, Wm Paine, Botanist. Collected from ye Rivers, Woods, Fields and Gardens of ye county of Somerset. An^o 1730." In it is a specimen of " Ye Fidle Dock, from St. Vincent's Rocks, Cheder Clieves, &c."; and also a leaf of " Ye Bloody Dock."

VII.—IX.

662. R. obtusifolius, L.?

Native; by roadsides, and in damp pastures and waste ground everywhere. Very common. VII.—IX.

663. R. acutus, L. Fr. **R. pratensis,** Mert. and Koch.

Native; in meadows and pastures. Rare, but very likely passed over in some places.

S. Congresbury; Cranmore; Shipham; *Rev. R. Murray.*
"Abundant in moist places"; *Fl. Bathon.* VI.—VIII.

664. R. crispus, *L.*
Native; by roadsides and in waste places. Very common.
VI.—VIII.

665. R. Hydrolapathum, *Huds. Great Water Dock.*
Native; in ditches and on river-banks, locally common.
G. Sparingly in Frome Glen, Stapleton. Shirehampton. Tortworth. Alveston. Compton Greenfield.
S. Very plentiful by the sides of ditches in the great alluvial tract between the Mendips and the Bristol Channel; as at Axbridge, Burnham, Easton, Clevedon, and Yatton. By the riverside at Bath. In the canal at Radford. VII. VIII.

666. R. Acetosa, *L. Sorrel.*
Native; in meadows and pastures, very common. V. VI.

667. R. Acetosella, *L. Sheep's Sorrel.*
Native; on dry hills and barren pastures in many places about Bristol. Common about St. Vincent's Rocks, Brandon Hill, Leigh Down, and Trooper's Hill; and abundant in high and dry situations elsewhere.
V.—VII.

POLYGONUM, *L.*

668. P. Bistorta, *L. Bistort. Snakeweed.*
Denizen; in moist meadows and shady places, rather rare.
G. Near Frenchay.
S. Brislington. Dundry. Hedgebank in a lane near Abbotsleigh. A large patch in a meadow on Failand Farm. Hilly pasture near Chewton Mendip. Ham Wood, near Shepton Mallet; *Miss Livett.* Whitchurch; *Herb. Stephens.*
V. VI.

669. P. amphibium, *L.*

Native; in watery places, frequent.

G. Alveston. Boiling Well. In the Avon at Conham and elsewhere. Glen Frome, Stapleton.

S. Axbridge. Clevedon. Nailsea Moor. Yatton. Marsh ditches between Burnham and Brent Knoll. In a marsh near Ham Green. In ditches between Weston Junction and Weston-super-Mare. In the Avon near Bath, and in the Kennet and Avon Canal.

VII.—IX.

670. P. lapathifolium, *L.*

Native; in damp waste ground, and on manure heaps, common. VII.—IX.

671. P. Persicaria, *L.*

Native; in cultivated and waste ground, very common.

VII.—IX.

672. P. mite, *Schrank.*

Native. Very rare. At present this species has only been gathered on the peat near Edington Station, S.; where it was observed by the Rev. R. Murray.

673. P. Hydropiper, *L.*

Native; in wet places by rivers, ditches, and ponds, very common. VIII.—IX.

674. P. aviculare, *L.* *Common Knot-grass.*

Native; by roadsides and in waste ground, very common. The var. β. *P. littorale,* Link. is singularly absent from our coast. V.—IX.

675. P. Convolvulus, *L.* *Black Bind-weed.*

Native; in cultivated ground and waste places, very common.

A plant that appears to be the var. β. *pseudo-dumetorum,* Wats. is not infrequent in hedges and thickets.

VII.—IX.

676. P. dumetorum, *L.*

S. "Among bushes, on the sides of a hollow through which the Western Railroad passes, about one mile from Keynsham towards Bristol, and near a bend in the river, 1836. (C. C. Babington, Esq., specs.)" *W. A. Bromfield, mss.* We do not doubt that this is a reliable record, especially as it is corroborated by a statement in *Topographical Botany*, ed. 2, as follows :—" Som. north. Babington sp." We have not had an opportunity of searching for the plant in the locality described.

(P. Fagopyrum, L. Is frequently met with as an outcast on rubbish heaps and in waste places.)

THYMELACEÆ.
DAPHNE, *L.*

677. D. Mezereum, *L.* *Mezereon.*

Native? It has been known to grow for a great many years in Churchill Batch, S. The shady hill side is very rough and stony, and covered with dwarf coppice. About a dozen plants were seen in February, 1883, nearly all below the road towards the bottom of the Batch; but one or two were also found on the other side of the hill growing among brambles. In this situation the shrub has unquestionably the appearance of a genuine native; although many botanists will not allow the Mezereon to be an aboriginal in England. It is commonly supposed that plants found in the woods originate from the seeds of the garden shrub dropped by birds; and that is likely enough to happen in some instances. But in Churchill Batch the Mezereon bushes which grow in the cottage gardens at the bottom of the valley have been transplanted from the hill side; for we found on making enquiry of the occupiers that they had none before the boys dug up some and brought them home from the woods. Compton Martin Wood is given as a locality in Rutter's History of N. W. Somerset, 1829. Naturalized on a hedgebank near Wells, S. *Miss Livett.* II. III.

678. D. Laureola, L. *Spurge Laurel.*
Native; in woods and occasionally in hedges, frequent.
G. Woods in Almondsbury parish. Henbury. Kingsweston. Westbury. Stinchcombe Hill. Frequent in woods above Wotton-under-Edge.
S. Sparingly in Leigh Wood: about four plants are usually to be found near the bank of the Avon. Wood between Pill and Ham Green. Between Failand and Bourton. Hutton. King's Wood near Yatton. Near Woodspring Priory. Near Wells. In a wood between Cleeve and Congresbury. Scattered abundantly in Limeridge Wood, Tickenham; *Mr. D. Fry.* In hedges in the parish of Hinton Blewett. In hedges between Keynsham and Compton Dando. Abundant in a fir wood near Chewton Keynsham, and also nearer Bath. About Lansdown. Frequent in the woods; *Fl. Bathon.*

II. III.

(Thesium humifusum, DC. "Claverton Down. (Mr. John Kitley.) *Add. Fl. Bathon.*" N.B.G.)

EUPHORBIACEÆ.
EUPHORBIA, L.
(E. Peplis, L. "Sandy coast from Burnham to Brean. J. C. Collins, *mss.*" N.B.G. Unconfirmed.)

EUPHORBIACEÆ.

679. E. Helioscopia, L. *Sun Spurge.*
    Colonist. A common weed in cornfields and neglected cultivated ground.   VI.—IX.

680. E. platyphylla, L.
    Colonist; in cornfields, rare and local.
    G.   Cornfield by Filton Meads; in plenty every season since we first noticed it in 1879.
    S.   Knowle; *Swete, Fl.* 70. "In cornfields near Marshfield and Conkwell." *Fl. Bathon.* 44. Easton.

    (E. stricta, L.   Said to have been found in a cornfield and elsewhere near Bath; *Fl. Bathon.* 44. No doubt those plants were merely starved specimens of *E. platyphylla.)*

681. E. pilosa, L.   *E. epithymoides* in *Fl. Bathon.*
    Denizen; in a small wood near Prior Park, Bath; close upon the eastern border of our area. In May, 1884, we were conducted to the spot and found this local treasure scattered sparingly over the space of about two acres in rather thick coppice, and mingled with great abundance of *E. amygdaloides.* A number of plants were also found under a hedge at some distance, perhaps a quarter of a mile from the wood. We were told that its growth is greatly influenced by the state of the underwood, which is cut in the customary way every seven to ten years. Soon after the wood has been cleared the plant appears in great plenty; and then annually diminishes in quantity as the brushwood regains its stature, until in some seasons little or none is to be found.
    It is stated that this Spurge was gathered in the same place where it now grows by Lobel before 1576, and in July, 1634, by Thomas Johnson, the Editor of

"Gerards Herbal." If this be so, the plant might reasonably expect to be accorded a more honourable position in the "London Catalogue" than it now occupies among the excluded species. V. VI.

682. **E. amygdaloides**, *L.* *Wood Spurge.*
Native. A beautiful species: most abundant in woods, hedges, the shady borders of fields, and bushy places, throughout the district. III. IV.

683. **E. Paralias**, *L.* *Sea Spurge.*
Native; on the sandy shore of the Bristol Channel. In great profusion among the sandhills from Burnham to Brean, but it diminishes in frequency higher up the Channel, and perhaps finds its eastern limit at Weston-super-Mare.
We have never met with this Spurge in Gloucestershire.
VIII. IX.

684. **E. Peplus**, *L.*
Native; in gardens and cultivated ground generally. Very common. VII. VIII.

685. **E. exigua**, *L.*
Colonist; in cornfields, common. VI.—VIII.

686. **E. Lathyris**, *L.* *Caper Spurge.*
Alien; introduced from gardens in many places, and if let alone it readily establishes itself.
S. Berrow. Long Ashton. Clevedon. In fields and gardens at Bath and Claverton; *Fl. Bathon.* Apparently indigenous in Warleigh Wood; *Add. Fl. Bathon.* "Probably native near Bath"; *Syme, E.B.*

MERCURIALIS, *L.*

687. **M. perennis**, *L.*
Native; in woods and on shady banks, very common and abundant. IV. V.

688. M. annua, *L.*

Colonist; in gardens and cultivated fields, and on rubbish heaps, chiefly about towns and villages. Common.

G. Abundant about Clifton, both in gardens and waste places. Almondsbury. Charfield. Horfield. Redland. Westbury. Warmley.

S. A common weed about Bath. Knowle. Long Ashton. Clevedon. Portisbead. Very plentiful about Weston-super-Mare.

β. *M. ambigua*, L.

Crew's Hole; *Herb. Stephens.* VIII. IX.

CERATOPHYLLACEÆ.
CERATOPHYLLUM, *L.*

689. C. demersum, *L.*

Native; in ponds and ditches, locally common.

S. Abundant in rhines and ditches near Yatton, Clevedon, Kingston Seymour, and Weston-super-Mare. In plenty in the canal near Bath; *Fl. Bathon.* VI. VII.

690. C. submersum, *L.*

Native; as yet known only in one spot.

G. In a pond near Charfield. VI. VII.

CALLITRICHACEÆ.
CALLITRICHE, *L.*

691. C. verna, *L.*

Native; in ponds and streams. We have some records which may refer to this species as at present defined; but further study is needed before a positive opinion can be offered. The genus has been so split that it is hard to say now what is left to represent *verna*.

692. **C. obtusangula,** Le G.
>   Native; in water, rare.
>   G. There are specimens in the Edinburgh Herbarium collected by 'Carpenter' in Combe Valley, Westbury-on-Trym. *J. of B.*, XIII., 110.
>   S. Berrow; *Rev. R. Murray.* Rhines near Highbridge.
>   VI.—VIII.

693. **C. stagnalis,** Scop.
>   Native; on the muddy margins of ditches and ponds, common.
>   Our plant is *C. platycarpa*, Kütz.   V.—VIII.

694. **C. hamulata,** Kütz.
>   Native; in ditches and streams, local.
>   G. Tortworth.
>   S. Rhines between Axbridge and Cheddar; and in the valley about Walton Drove, near Clevedon. VI.—VIII.

URTICACEÆ.
PARIETARIA, L.

695. **P. diffusa,** Koch. *Pellitory of the Wall.*
>   Native; on churches, ruins, and old walls; also on rocks. Common in such situations.
>   G. Henbury. Kingsweston. Westbury. Stoke Bishop. Stapleton.
>   S. Bedminster. Long Ashton. Portishead. Milton. Yatton. Common about Bath. On old walls at Wells. Very abundant on old walls about Cheddar; and at Clevedon.   V.—IX.

URTICA, L.

696. **U. pilulifera,** L. *Roman Nettle.*
>   Alien; under walls and in waste places. Very rare, and may no longer exist at the localities quoted.

G. Under walls at Winterbourne; *Dr. H. O. Stephens.*
S. Said to have grown in waste ground at Kewstoke; *Dr. St. Brody.*

697. U. urens, *L. Small Nettle.*
Native or Colonist; in waste places, by roadsides and on dunghills. Not very common; far less general than the following, and more confined to the neighbourhood of habitations.
G. Occasionally on rubbish heaps at Clifton, but not permanent. Almondsbury. Chipping Sodbury. Fishponds. Ashley Hill. Shirehampton. Stapleton.
S. Bedminster. Bishport. Very plentiful at Berrow and Burnham. Easton. Yatton. Wells; *Miss Livett.* Common about Bath; *Fl. Bathon.* VI.—IX.

698. U. dioica, *L. Common Nettle.*
Native; in waste places, pastures, &c. Very common.
VI.—IX.

CANNABINACEÆ.

(*Cannabis sativa,* L., is frequently met with on rubbish heaps about Bristol, but is not permanently naturalized. We have seen it on cultivated ground at Berrow, S., growing very luxuriantly.)

HUMULUS, L.

699. H. Lupulus, *L. Hop.*
Native; in hedges and thickets, common.
G. Alveston. Charfield. Dursley. Hanham. Stapleton. Wotton-under-Edge.
S. Axbridge. Barrow Gurney. Blackford. Brislington. Common near Bath. Ken. Nailsea. Portbury. Walton-in-Gordano. Wedmore. Wells. Wookey. Uphill.
VII. VIII.

ULMACEÆ.

ULMUS, *L.*

700. U. suberosa, *Ehrh. Common Elm.*
Native or denizen; in hedgerows chiefly, common.
β. *U. glabra, Sm.* Hanham Wood; *Herb. Stephens.*

III.—V.

701. U. montana, *With. Wych Elm.*
Native; chiefly in limestone woods, frequent.
G. Conham. Stapleton. Wyck.
S. Upper Knowle. Leigh Woods. Woods about the Mendip Hills. III. IV.

AMENTIFERÆ.

SALIX, *L.*

702. S. fragilis, *L.*
Native in some places. The fertile plant is very common on the banks of ditches and streams throughout the district, but barren trees are far less abundant.
γ. *S. Russelliana,* Sm.
G. Bank of the Frome near Stapleton.
S. About Clevedon in several places. By Walton Drove, and a good deal in Walton withy-bed; *Mr. D. Fry.* Mr. Fry says that most of this plant at Clevedon is undoubtedly planted, especially where it grows in considerable quantity by the sides of the railway; but it appears to be native in some situations. III.—V.

703. S. alba, *L.*
Most likely planted wherever we have observed it.
S. Banks of the Chew. Yatton. Walton-in-Gordano. Occasionally by streams about Wells; *Miss Livett.* IV. V.

AMENTIFERÆ.

704. S. triandra, *L.*

Rarely native; being found chiefly in osier-grounds.

G. St. Philip's Marsh; *Dr. Stephens.*

S. Burnham. In osier-beds at Wells, and in hedges elsewhere in the county; *Miss Livett.* Keynsham; *Herb. Stephens.*

β. *S. Hoffmanniana*, Sm.

Claverham, S.! *Miss Winter.* IV. V.

705. S. purpurea, *L.*

Native? in marshes, not common.

S. Coppice near Wellington Terrace, Clevedon; probably planted, and perhaps now extinct. A great many barren trees grow together in one part of the withy-bed on Walton moor; *Mr. D. Fry.*

β. *S. Woolgariana*, Borr.

G. Boiling Well; *Herb. Stephens.**

S. On Nailsea Moor; *Mr. D. Fry.* III.—V.

706. S. viminalis, *L.*

Native; in wet places, frequent.

G. Alveston. Aust. Hallen. Compton Greenfield. Crew's Hole.

S. Burnham. Clevedon. Long Ashton. Stanton Drew. Yatton. Weston-super-Mare. IV. V.

707. S. Smithiana, *Willd.*

Probably native; rather rare.

---

* Several willows formerly gathered by Dr. H. O. Stephens at the Boiling Well no longer grow there. The condition of the marsh must have been considerably altered by the construction of the various lines of railroad which run through and by the spot. In particular the huge embankment of the S. Wales Railway appears to have wiped out about a quarter of the whole area, and it is very probable that the missing Salices lie buried beneath it.

S. Three or four bushes by Ashton brook, not very far from the church. Walton Drove, and Walton withy-bed; *Mr. D. Fry.* Near Wells; *Rev. R. Murray.*
β. S. *rugosa*, Leefe.
G. Boiling Well; *Herb. Stephens.* IV. V.
(S. stipularis, Sm. " Osier-beds at St. Philip's Marsh; " *Dr. H. O. Stephens.)*

708. S. acuminata, *Sm.*
Native; in wet hedges and marshes, rather common.
G. Ditch-banks at the Boiling Well, chiefly on the Baptist Mills side of the railway.
S. Frequent about Clevedon, where however the fertile plant is extremely rare. Common on the moors about Brent Knoll, Berrow and Burnham. Plentiful in Walton withy-bed; *Mr. D. Fry.* IV.

709. S. cinerea, *L.*
Native; in wet places in the lowlands, and also in woods and hedges, very common.
If we may presume to give an opinion on the many variations of this aggregate, our observations would prompt us to conclude that typical *cinerea* is most frequently met with inland, and often in comparatively dry situations; while forms approaching β. S. *aquatica,* Sm. grow in great abundance throughout the alluvial tracts near the Severn, the Channel, and elsewhere, being more common than any other willow; and that γ. *S. oleifolia* is not rare, having been gathered at the Boiling Well and at Horfield in Gloucestershire, and also at Clevedon and Clapton in Somerset. III. IV.

710. S. aurita, *L.*
Native; in damp hedges and bushy places, rather local. We have not met with it within some miles of Bristol.

S. Not uncommon about Bath; *Mr. T. B. Flower.* Near Winscombe. Cranmore. Frequent about Wells; *Miss Livett;* and *Rev. R. Murray.*   IV. V.

711. S. caprea, *L.*
Native; in woods and hedges in dry situations, common.
G. St. Vincent's Rocks and Clifton Down. Horfield. Kingsweston. Frequent about the southern spurs of the Cotswolds near Wotton-under-Edge and Dursley. Stapleton.
S. Leigh Wood. On the pennant at Clevedon. Abundant on Mendip. Stockwood. Whitchurch. Wells. Yatton.
              III. IV.

712. S. repens, *L.*
Native; in heathy and sandy places, local.
G. Yate Common.
S. In several places on Mendip. Moors south of Wells. Abundant on sand at the back of Berrow village.
Our plant is chiefly *S. fusca,* Sm.; but at Berrow, where it grows very large and strong, there appear to be several forms, among which *S. argentea,* Sm. has been identified.   III.—V.

POPULUS, *L.*

713. P. alba, *L.* *White Poplar.*
A doubtful native, generally distributed in the district. Very abundant about Berrow and Burnham, S.; where apparently it has been planted to form shelters from the wind on the exposed lowlands.   III. IV.

714. P. canescens, *Sm.* *Gray Poplar.*
Native or denizen; in moist woods, rare.
G. Henbury. Wyck.
S. Leigh Woods.   III. IV.

715. P. tremula, *L.* *Aspen.*
Native; but often planted, frequent in woods.

G. Blaize Castle Woods. Charfield. Kingsweston. Bank of the Frome near Stapleton.

S. Leigh Wood. Portishead. Not uncommon about Bath; *Fl. Bathon.* Yatton. Bishop's Wood, Wells; *Miss Livett.* III. IV.

716. P. nigra, L. *Black Poplar.*

Alien or denizen; by the banks of rivers and in damp woods, frequent.

G. Clifton Down (the " Poet's Tree "). Some very fine trees grow in Combe Glen. Bank of the Frome at Frenchay.

S. Clevedon. Portishead. Yatton. Wells. III.

(*Myrica Gale*, L., is abundant on moors south of the district; but perhaps has never been seen inside our limit).

BETULA, *L.*

717. B. alba, L. *Common Birch.*

Native: in woods, copses, and hedge-rows, common.

IV. V.

ALNUS, *Tourn.*

718. A. glutinosa, *Gaert. Alder.*

Native; on river banks and in marshes, very common.

III.

FAGUS, *L.*

719. F. sylvatica, *L. Beech.*

Native; in woods, especially on limestone, locally common.

III. IV.

CASTANEA, *Tourn.*

720. C. vulgaris, *Lam. Sweet Chesnut.*

A doubtful native, usually planted, though we sometimes see it flourishing in our aboriginal woods, where it may have been self-sown and existing for many centuries.

The fine old tree at Tortworth Park is justly celebrated. It is mentioned in a record of the time of King Stephen as being then of great age, forming one of the boundaries of the manor, and is supposed by Strutt to have been in existence in the time of Egbert, more than a thousand years ago. V.

QUERCUS, *L.*

721. **Q. Robur,** *L.* *Oak.*

Native; in woods and hedges, very common. The var. *sessiliflora* is frequent. IV. V.

CORYLUS, *L.*

722. **C. Avellana,** *L.* *Hazel.*

Native; in woods and hedges, very common.

We have seen its catkins developed at the beginning of November. XI.—II.

CARPINUS, *L.*

723. **C. Betulus,** *L.* *Hornbeam.*

Native or denizen; rather rare.

G. Clifton Down near the Gully. Hedges near Downend.
S. Leigh Wood. Hedges on Mendip about Shipham.

V.

FLORA OF THE BRISTOL COAL-FIELD.

ADDITIONS TO PARTS I., II., AND III.

Cardamine impatiens, L. in Somerset. Cheddar, sparingly among rocks in the gorge; *Miss Livett!* Near Whatley, *Dr. Parsons.* Prior Park and Lyncombe; *Add. Fl. Bathon.* See pp. 16, 85.

(*Gypsophila paniculata*, L. Casual. On the old colliery débris near Kingswood, G., so often referred to on preceding pages. Sept., 1884.)

128.* **Alsine tenuifolia,** *Wahl.*

Can take an undoubted position in the Bristol Flora. In June, 1884, Mr. H. Fisher brought us a tiny specimen from Penpole Point, G. On subsequent examination of the place the plant was found in fair quantity and well distributed on the limestone promontory, where, during so many years, it had contrived to elude observation. See p. 30.

130.* **Arenaria leptoclados,** *Guss.*

S. About Clevedon in several places. Mr. D. Fry has been able quite satisfactorily to separate this from typical *sphærocarpa.* The latter, however, is the prevailing form.

Cerastium pumilum, Curt. We have now a good series of stations for this plant in N. Somerset. It grows at Clevedon on the Court and Strawberry Hills, and elsewhere. Also on rocky waste ground on the hill at Weston-super-Mare. In abundance on the S.W. slope of Brean Down. On walls near the Mineries towards Wells; and on walls between Black Down and Cheddar. See p. 32.

Cerastium tetrandrum, Curt. Is plentiful on the sands near Burnham, S. See p. 32.

274.* Rubus rosaceus, *Weihe*.

Worle Hill, S.! *Mr. D. Fry.* Confirmed by Mr. J. G. Baker, who says that this bramble is also abundant at Wyck Rocks, G.

299.* Pyrus scandica, *Bab.* *P. latifolia*, Pers?

On p. 67 we mentioned a variety of *Pyrus Aria* which formerly had been known in Leigh Woods, but which we had been unable to rediscover; nor could we find any specimen. We could not therefore assign it a place in the Flora. However, in June, 1885, we were so fortunate as not only to see specimens gathered by Mr. T. B. Flower, but also, a few days afterwards, to come across the large tree from which they had been taken. This, the solitary representative of the species in North Somerset, grows on the rocky verge of Nightingale Valley.

301* Peplis Portula, *L.*

S. On the borders of marshy pools on Mendip, not far from the Mineries; Aug. 20, 1884.

(*Xanthium spinosum*, L. Nine or ten plants on dredgings from the bed of the Avon deposited in the Black Rock quarry; flowering in October and November, 1884.)

(*Solanum rostratum*, L. Casual. On old colliery *débris* near Kingswood, G.)

Scutellaria minor, L. Additional stations in N. Somerset. Boggy and peaty ground on Mendip, four or five miles north of Wells, scattered over a large area. Aug. 20, 1884. Sparingly in a damp wood near Abbot's Leigh, half a mile from the published locality, where, this season (1885), we have noticed an increased quantity of the plant. See p. 139.

FLORA
OF THE
BRISTOL COAL-FIELD.

EDITED (FOR THE BRISTOL NATURALISTS' SOCIETY) BY

JAMES WALTER WHITE,

Hon. Secretary of the Botanical Section.

"*Rerum cognoscere causas.*"—VIRGIL.

PART V.

DICTYOGENÆ, ET FLORIDÆ.

BRISTOL:
JAMES FAWN & SON.

PRINTED BY E. AUSTIN & SON, CHRONICLE OFFICE, CLIFTON.

MDCCCLXXXV.

PHANEROGAMIA.

Class 2. *MONOCOTYLEDONES*:
Div. 1. *DICTYOGENÆ*.

TRILLIACEÆ.
PARIS, *Linn.*

724. **P. quadrifolia,** *L. Herb Paris.*
Native; in woods, rather common. Plants bearing five, and even six leaves are often met with.
G. Berwick Wood. Bean Wood, Chipping Sodbury, *Rev. E. Johnson.* Woods between Charfield and Tortworth. Stapleton.
S. Leigh Wood, rare. Stockwood. In many woods near Bath. Maes Knoll. Norton Malreward. Plentiful in Paul Wood between Temple Cloud and Clutton; and in a wood at Rush Hill, near Farrington Gurney. East Harptree Combe. Scattered all over a small copse on Mendip, near Sidcot. King's Wood, Yatton. Portbury. Portishead. Weston-in-Gordano. Abundant in woods about Wells. Abundant in woods from Binegar to Asham. *Rev. R. Murray.* IV. V.

DIOSCOREACEÆ.
TAMUS, *Linn.*

725. **T. communis,** *L. Black Bryony.*
Native; in hedges and thickets, frequent.
G. Almondsbury. Charlton. Filton. Patchway. Stapleton. Westbury-on-Trym.

S. Abbot's Leigh. Leigh Wood. Bishport. Chew Magna. Englishcombe. Combe Hay. Long Ashton. Dundry. Upper Knowle. Portbury. Wraxall. Frequent about Clevedon, Weston-super-Mare, and Wells.
V. VI.

Div. 2. FLORIDÆ.

HYDROCHARIDACEÆ.
HYDROCHARIS, *Linn.*

726. **H. Morsus-ranæ**, *L. Frog-bit.*
Native; in peaty ditches of the lowlands, locally common.
G. Awkley, *Herb. Powell.* Shirehampton marshes.
S. Near Clevedon. Nailsea Moor. Tickenham. Yatton. Weston-super-Mare. Marsh ditches throughout the Cheddar Valley, as far as the southern limit of the district. VII. VIII.

ANACHARIS, *Rich.*

727. **A. Alsinastrum**, *Bab. Elodia canadensis*, Mich.
Now naturalized with us, as in many other parts of the country; and to be met with frequently in ponds and streams in both counties. VII. VIII.

ORCHIDACEÆ
ORCHIS, *Linn.*

728. **O. Morio**, *L. Green-winged Orchis.*
Native; in meadows and pastures. Common and widely distributed. It is often very abundant in cowslip meadows, where the blossom contrasts pleasantly with its neighbours. We have observed many spikes of pure white flowers in fields near Hallen, G., and also at Failand and Compton Martin, S., as well as all the intermediate shades, from pale rose to purple. V. VI.

ORCHIDACEÆ.

729. O. mascula, *L.* *Early purple Orchis.*
Native; abundant in woods and pastures throughout the district. White-flowered plants grow in a meadow near Henbury, G. V.

730. O. ustulata, *L.*
Native; in elevated pasture land on limestone. Very rare.
G. " On Wick Cliffs, Mr. Swayne." *Bot. Guide.*
S. " Worle Hill, near Weston-super-Mare, May 16, 1838." *Herb. Powell.* Pastures near Weston-super-Mare, *St. Brody, Fl.* Claverton Down, *Mr. T. B. Flower.* Weston-in-Gordano, *Rev. G. W. Braikenridge:* and *Mr. T. B. Flower* in 1850. V.

731. O. maculata, *L.*
Native; in damp woods and meadows, common and generally distributed. V. VI.

732. O. latifolia, *L.* *Marsh Orchis.*
Native; in marshes and moist, peaty meadows, frequent.
G. Alveston. Aust. Filton Meads. Patchway. Siston. Abundant in meadows near Thornbury. Yate.
S. Between Abbot's Leigh and the Tan-pits. Meadows under Dundry Hill. Compton Martin. Nailsea. Bogs and peaty meadows near Winscombe. Yatton. Wells.
V. VI.

733. O. incarnata, *L.*
Native; in boggy pastures, local. Like many other botanists, we were for a long time unable to feel sure of this species; but we have been led to the conclusion that, at the stations mentioned below, the plants are *incarnata* and not *latifolia.* They agree entirely with the former as regards leaf-characters, which seem to be the only tangible ones whereby the two species can be separated. Babington's remark on the time of flowering is also confirmatory of these plants being *O. incarnata.*

G. Hallen marshes. Compton Greenfield. Near Filton.
S. Boggy meadows between Dundry Hill and Barrow Gurney. Boggy spots in the lowlands near Burnham, and in the Cheddar Valley. VI.

734. O. pyramidalis, *L.*

Native; on banks, downs, and dry bushy places, chiefly on limestone; rather local, but abundant in many places.

G. Formerly frequent in the Avon gorge below Bristol; now destroyed or nearly so. Blaise Castle, and Kingsweston Hill. Railway banks near Horfield, and at Patchway. Plentiful on the hills above Wotton-under-Edge, Nibley, and Dursley. Wyck Rocks. Stapleton, 1842. *Herb. Stephens.*

S. Brean Down. Hilly pastures near Clevedon, and above Congresbury. Rocky hills about Combe Hay, and not uncommon in the vicinity of Bath. Between Buckland Dinham and Great Elm. On banks on both sides of the high road between Pensford and Whitchurch. On the high ground above Wraxall. Above Tickenham. Uphill. Abundant about Wells. Weston-in-Gordano. Worle Hill. VII.

GYMNADENIA, *R. Br.*

735. G. conopsea, *R. Br.*

Native; in boggy meadows and in hilly pastures, frequent.

G. Alveston. Filton Meads, plentiful in some seasons. Oldland. Pucklechurch. Wickwar. Near Wyck Rocks.
S. Meadows near Clevedon. Hutton. Weston-in-Gordano. Between Buckland and Great Elm. On Mendip at Tining's Farm, sparingly. Pasture N.W. of Dundry Hill. Several stations near Bath. Moors near Wells. VI. VII.

HABENARIA, *R. Br.*

736. H. viridis, *R. Br. Frog Orchis.*

Native; in meadows and hilly pastures, rather rare, and does not often occur in quantity.

G. Alveston, *Herb. Powell.* Filton Meads. Between Henbury and Patchway. Nailsworth. Pasture above Wotton-under-Edge.

S. In several fields between the Bridgwater road and Dundry Hill. Hutton. Mells. Portbury. Pastures on Mendip, near Cheddar. Near Bath; *Fl. Bathon.*

VI. VII.

737. H. bifolia, *R. Br. Lesser Butterfly Orchis.*

Native; in moist open places, rare. Nearly all the records purporting to relate to the distribution of this Orchid in the Bristol district have been found to refer to *H. chlorantha.* *Eu-bifolia* undoubtedly grows on the southern peat moor, and in several localities nearer Bristol, one of which is that happy hunting ground for botanists—Filton Meads.

738. H. chlorantha, *Bab. Greater Butterfly Orchis.*

Native; in woods and shady places, frequent.

G. Rarely on the wooded slope under Clifton Down beyond the Great Quarry. Wood near Filton. Duchess Woods, Stapleton. Woods above Wotton-under-Edge. Abundant in woods near Patchway.

S. Leigh Wood in several places, but always very sparingly; usually one plant only is to be seen on each occasion. Bishport. Buckland Dinham. Chewton Keynsham. Congresbury. Shutshelf Wood near Axbridge. Ebbor. Great Elm. Hutton. Limeridge Wood near Tickenham. Stockwood. Nightingale Valley, Weston-in-Gordano. Wells. Yatton. V. VI.

OPHRYS, *Linn.*

739. O. apifera, *Huds. Bee Orchis.*

Native; on downs, banks, and in rough pastures, and stony places; chiefly on limestone and oolite. Rather common, and in some years very plentiful. We have seen a striking variety of this species, of which only four specimens were found on the Leigh side of the Avon in July, 1885. In all the flowers on the spike, the labellum, viewed in front, instead of being broadly oval or semiglobose, presented a long triangular outline four times as long as broad, tapering from the base to the normal long reflexed point of the terminal lobe.

G. There are many old records for St. Vincent's Rocks, and for Clifton and Durdham Downs, where formerly the Bee Orchis may have been very abundant. As might be expected, it is now almost eradicated; although in most seasons half a dozen plants are still to be seen by those who know where to look. Bank of Avon below Bristol. Cromhall. Henbury. Kingsweston Down.

S. Bank of Avon about the Portishead Railway, and on the slopes under Leigh Woods. Scattered all over a rough pasture near Failand Inn. Failand Hill. Hills near Clevedon. Elevated grassy banks near Congresbury, where four or five hundred plants have been seen blooming together. Brean Down, in plenty 1885. Cheddar. Sandford. Tickenham. Yatton. Portishead. Clevedon road-side near Wraxall. Frequent about Dunkerton, Englishcombe, Combe Hay, and elsewhere towards Bath. "Abundant among the sand-hills at Burnham, *J. C. Collins.*" *New Bot. G.* Still there, 1885. Marshy sands near Berrow. Ebbor. Easton. Lyat, near Wells. Whitchurch. About Buckland Dinham and

Great Elm. *Dr. H. F. Parsons.* Uphill, in great profusion, 1885. VI. VII.

740. O. muscifera, Huds. *Fly Orchis.*
Native; in woods, on bushy banks, and occasionally on downs, rare, but well distributed.

G. Many old writers agree in stating that this Ophrys used to grow with the Bee Orchis on St. Vincent's Rocks and on Clifton Down; and that it was at one time even more plentiful than the latter. Towards the end of the last century "the high ground at the back of the Old Well House" was especially singled out as a favourite station for the Fly Orchis. It is unnecessary to dwell upon the circumstances which have long ago unfitted this locality for the growth of Orchids. But still we believe that even now, in spite of all the changes a century has effected, few summers pass in which this delicate and dainty species is not detected, either upon St. Vincent's Rocks or among the bushy slopes adjacent. Woods near Dursley; *Herb. Stephens.*

S. Leigh Wood; constant in several spots, both in deep shade and also on the open stony banks above the river. Many localities near Bath are given in the *Flora Bathoniensis*, and we ourselves have seen it, several years in succession, in and about a wood near Fortnight not far from the *Cephalanthera grandiflora*. Woods at Weston-in-Gordano, constant. "The Fly Orchis grows in Limeridge Wood near Tickenham." *Rutter's Hist. N. W. Somerset.* This statement has been confirmed several times during the last half century, and as lately as June, 1885, by Mr. D. Fry. VI.

HERMINIUM, *R. Br.*

741. H. Monorchis, *R. Br. Musk Orchis.*
Native; very rare.

S. "*H. Monorchis* grows in a field between Buckland Dinham and Great Elm (square 19 of Sanders' map), in company with *Ophrys apifera, Habenaria chlorantha, Orchis pyramidalis, Spiranthes autumnalis, Gymnadenia conopsea*, and about half a dozen common orchids"; *Dr. H. Franklin Parsons.* Pastures near Bath; *Fl. Bathon.*

SPIRANTHES, *Rich.*

742. S. autumnalis, *Rich. Lady's Tresses.*

Native; on dry calcareous downs; rarely in the lowlands. Rather common on limestone.

G. Scattered all over Clifton and Durdham Downs, and noticed to be more plentiful opposite the Zoological Gardens than elsewhere. Bitton. Wyck.

S. Leigh Down, in fair quantity. Yatton. Clevedon. Walton-in-Gordano. Worle Hill. In the lawns at Ellenborough Park, Weston-super-Mare; Aug. 1882. In several places on the Mendips. Milton Hill, Wells; *Miss Livett.* VIII. IX.

LISTERA, *R. Br.*

743. L. ovata, *R. Br. Tway-blade.*

Native; in woods and moist shady places, common throughout the district. V. VI.

NEOTTIA, *Linn.*

744. N. Nidus-avis, *Rich. Bird's-nest Orchis.*

Native; rather frequent in both counties. It is most often found in beech woods, in deep shade amid thick underwood, where plenty of rotten stumps and decaying leaf-mould form a congenial soil.

G. Berwick Wood. Duchess Woods, Stapleton. Common in woods about Tortworth. Woods about Wotton-under-Edge. Stinchcombe Hill, near Dursley.

S. Woods between Abbot's Leigh and Failand Hill. Leigh

Wood. Bourton Combe. Ebbor. Hutton. Nightingale Valley, Weston-in-Gordano. Limeridge Wood, Tickenham. Portishead. Paul Wood, between Temple Cloud and Clutton. VI.

EPIPACTIS, Rich.

745. E. latifolia, All.

Native; in woods, frequent.

G. Abundant in the woods about Dursley. Tortworth. Woods near Wotton-under-Edge.

S. Leigh Wood, rare; one or two plants are found from time to time, as in 1835 by Dr. H. O. Stephens, and at intervals since by other botanists. Ebbor. Bourton Combe. Occasionally near Wells. St. Ann's Wood, Brislington, 1840; *Mr. T. B. Flower*. Brislington, 1885; *Mr. R. Baker*. Woods near Hallatrow and Clutton, plentiful. Several localities are mentioned in *Fl. Bathon.*

VII.

746. E. palustris, Sw.

Native; in swamps, rare.

S. Abundant in marshy spots amid the sand-hills at Berrow. Formerly in a swamp near Winscombe. Near Weston-super-Mare, *Herb. Stephens;* which may refer to the Berrow station. VII. VIII.

CEPHALANTHERA, Rich.

747. C. grandiflora, Bab.

Native; in woods, rare.

G. In woods at Tortworth Park.

S. Several localities near Bath are given in the *Fl. Bathon.* and its *Additions.* In one of these (that near Fortnight) we have seen eight or ten plants in 1882 and 1883. In a wood near Clevedon; unsuspected until 1883, when three or four plants were observed. Mr. D. Fry saw seven or eight in 1884. This locality is a good deal frequented by visitors, and to specify it more exactly would expose the plant to probable destruction. Wick Grove, Brislington. *Dr. Withering. Swete, Fl.* 75. Not mentioned in Withering's 3rd edition. VI.

IRIDACEÆ.
IRIS, *Linn.*

748. I. Pseud-acorus, *L.* *Yellow Flag.*
Native; in and by water. Very abundant throughout the alluvial portions of the district. VI. VII.

749. I. fœtidissima, *L.*
Native; in woods and hedges, and occasionally on more open ground. Frequent, but mostly in small quantity.
G. In a wood on Spaniorum Hill above Compton Greenfield. Sparingly at Stoke Bishop.
S. Hedges near Bishport. Woods near Clevedon. In thickets on the coast near Woodspring Priory. Slopes on the S.W. of Brean Down, and here and there among the sand-hills towards Burnham. Easton and Wookey, *Miss Livett.* In many places near Bath. *Fl. Bathon.*
V.—VII.

AMARYLLIDACEÆ.
NARCISSUS, *Linn.*

750. N. biflorus, *Curt.*
Denizen; in fields and old orchards, rather rare.
G. "Near Stoke Bishop, May, 1839, *Miss Fisher.*" *Herb. Powell.*
S. Ashton Park, *Dr. Stephens.* Open pasture near Dundry Hill. Bourton. Meadows near the Church at Churchill, in plenty. Hutton, *Dr. Stephens.* Uphill,

Mr. T. F. *Perkins*; and Dr. St. *Brody*. Walton-in-Gordano. Winscombe. "In an old orchard at Pill. J. *Anderson, MSS.*" *New Bot. Guide, Suppl.*

751. N. Pseudo-narcissus, L. *Daffodil. Lent-Lily.*
Native; in pastures and open woods, rather common in Somerset. Where it does occur it usually grows in great abundance.

G. Wood at Henbury, *Herb. Powell*. Sparingly in pasture between Stoke Bishop and Westbury-on-Trym. Filton Meads, *Swete, Fl.*

S. Bishport. Churchill. Plentiful in a pasture on Failand Farm. Leigh Wood! *Rev. C. B. Dunn*. In thick underwood at Churchill Batch. Pensford. Yatton. At Edford in immense profusion, both in woodland and pasture; covering nearly a square mile of country. The "Daffodil Valley," near Sidcot. Here the plant is abundant on wooded slopes and grows over a considerable area. Abundant in some of the other Mendip valleys, notably near Witham, and by Stoke Lane, near Wells. III. IV.

(*N. incomparabilis, N. lobularis, N. poeticus,* and *N. aurantius?* have all been recorded on good authority from localities where they have been introduced from gardens.)

("*Leucojum æstivum*, L., grows in some quantity in one place in Almondsbury parish; but as the snowdrop and large periwinkle are its near neighbours there may once have been a cottage garden on the spot, though not in the recollection of any one living." *Rev. K. A. Deakin;* March, 1879.)

GALANTHUS, *Linn.*

752. G. nivalis, *L.* *Snowdrop.*

Denizen; perfectly naturalized in woods and on hedge-banks in many places, but very seldom in quantity.

G. Almondsbury. Formerly near Sea Mills, *Bot. Guide;* and *S. Rootsey, F.L.S.* Plentiful on a shady slope in Henbury Combe, near Blaise Castle, where it has been known very many years. Formerly in the Powder-House Wood, and woods at Stoke Bishop, *Swete, Fl.* 77.

S. In a hedgebank at Whitchurch; *Rev. W. H. Painter.* Barrow Gurney and Hutton; *Dr. H. O. Stephens.* A few plants on the wooded bank of a stream near Edford, growing with *Ribes nigrum;* March, 1884. By the brooklet below Winscombe, not far from some cottages. Uphill. Goblin Glen, near Yatton. II. III.

ALISMACEÆ.

ALISMA, *Linn.*

753. A. Plantago, *L.* *Water-Plantain.*

Native; in ditches and ponds. Common and generally distributed. The variety β. *A. lanceolata,* With., grows at Baptist Mills, G. VII. VIII.

754. A. ranunculoides, *L.*

Native; in the peaty ditches of the great alluvial tract between the Mendips and the Channel, from Tickenham and Nailsea Moor as far as the district extends to the south-west. Locally common. We have no record for Gloucestershire. VI. VII.

SAGITTARIA, *Linn.*

755. S. sagittifolia, *L.* *Arrowhead.*

Native; in ditches and rivers, rather rare and l.cal.

G. Formerly at Baptist Mills, and in Shirehampton Marshes; *Swete, Fl.* 80. In the river Frome near Stapleton. In the river Avon at Crew's Hole and Conham.

S. In the river Avon and the canal at Bath. In the canal near Radford. Nailsea Moor. Tickenham. Yatton. Marsh ditches in the Cheddar valley extending to the south of Wedmore. VII. VIII.

BUTOMUS, *Linn.*

756. **B. umbellatus,** *L. Flowering Rush.*

Native; in ditches and rivers. Rare in the north of Bristol, but quite common in the southern lowlands.

G. In the river Frome near Stapleton. In the Avon at Crew's Hole.

S. Formerly in Bedminster Meads; *Swete, Fl.* 80. In the canal near Radford. Ditches near Brean, Burnham, and Brent Knoll. Kingston Seymour. Nailsea Moor. Tickenham. Yatton. Weston-super-Mare. Pools and ditches throughout the Cheddar valley, and near Highbridge. VI. VII.

TRIGLOCHIN, *Linn.*

757. **T. maritimum,** *L.*

Native; on the muddy banks of the estuaries, and in salt marshes on the channel shore: marking the tidal limit in both counties. VII. VIII.

758. **T. palustre,** *L.*

Native; in boggy, wet meadows, and on ditchbanks, frequent.

G. Boiling Well. Hallen bog, near Henbury; *Herb. Powell.* Meadow below Cook's Folly; *Dr. H. O. Stephens.* Olveston. Littleton-on-Severn.

S. Bedminster Meads. Nailsea Moor. Moor at Walton-in-Gordano near Clevedon. Meadows under Crook's Peak. Brean. Burnham. Easton. Uphill. Yatton. Moors south of Wedmore. Frequent on the banks of the river Avon and of the canal at Bath. VI. VII.

ASPARAGACEÆ.
ASPARAGUS, *Linn.*
759. **A. officinalis**, L.

Denizen; in salt marshes and damp sandy soil near the Channel, rather rare. It is thoroughly naturalized, having been noted in one or two of the localities named nearly two centuries ago. None of our plants are the *A. prostratus*, Dum.

G. " Below Look's Folly, two miles from Bristol; *Mr. Newton.*" *Ray, Syn.* The mis-spelling " Look's " instead of " Cook's " is perpetuated by both Hudson and Withering. " In the salt marshes below Kingsweston, near Bristol." *Withering;* and *Dr. H. O. Stephens*, about 1835. Marsh near Thornbury, *B. G.* We saw a small quantity below Sea Mills in 1877 and 1880.

S. On the grassy bank of Avon opposite Cook's Folly, in several places. Uphill. Salt marsh near Berrow. " Sandbanks at Steart and Burnham, from three to five feet high when in blossom. (Mr. Clark.) *J. C. Collins, MSS.*" *New B. G. Suppl.* Still on sands near Burnham, plentiful in 1884 and 1885, and quite as luxuriant as is stated in the old record. VI.—VIII.

CONVALLARIA, *Linn.*
760. **C. majalis**, *L. Lily of the Valley.*

Native; in rocky woods, rare. It grows on wooded slopes where the soil is little else than broken limestone compacted with a little loam, from which the roots cannot be disengaged without much labour. We have visited the localities in Leigh Wood and near Wotton-under-Edge. Both these have a north-eastern aspect. With us the plant flowers very sparingly. We feel sure that in a favourable season the yield would not exceed one handful to the acre.

G. Very steep stony slope in Westridge Wood, in plenty.
S. A large patch in Leigh Wood near the Avon. King's Wood, near Yatton; *Miss Winter.* Asham Wood; *Rev. R. Murray.* Wood near Bath; *Add. Fl. Bathon.* V.

POLYGONATUM, Tourn.

761. P. officinale, *All.* *Convallaria Polygonatum*, L.

Native; in rocky woods on limestone, rare. Often associated with the Lily of the Valley. It fruits but seldom.

G. Woods above Wotton-under-Edge in several places.
S. Leigh Wood, by no means extinct, as is feared in *E. B.*, ed. 3; but not so plentiful as formerly, a good deal having been destroyed by quarrying. " Cheddar Cliffs. *W. Christy,* sp. Woods on the N. side of the Mendip Hills; woods at East Harptree, under Mendip. *B. G.*" *New B. Guide.* V.

762. P. multiflorum, *All.* Solomon's Seal.

Native; in woods on limestone, very local.

G. Wood at Dursley, *B. G.*
S. Harptree Combe. Wood at Leigh-on-Mendip. Paul Wood, near Temple Cloud, to 3 ft. 9 in. high, June, 1885; *Mr. D. Fry.* Bishop's Wood, and in one or two other woods near Wells; *Miss Livett.* Abundant in woods from Binegar to Asham; *Rev. R. Murray.* Near Bath; *Fl. Bathon.* Not known in Leigh Wood, where it is likely that *P. officinale* has been mistaken for it. VI.

LILIACEÆ.

RUSCUS, Linn.

763. R. aculeatus, *L. Butcher's Broom.*

Alien ; occasional in hedges and about gardens. Clearly not indigenous with us.   III. IV.

LILIACEÆ.

TULIPA, Linn.

764. T. sylvestris, *L.*

Doubtfully native in a field near Bath. Plentiful in a meadow by the side of the canal near Combe Hay ; now ploughed up, but still occupied by the Tulip, which, as Mr. Flower informs us, did not flower in 1885. "Bitton meadows, Gloucestershire, opposite the church ; *Rev. H. J. Ellacombe.*" *With.*, ed. 7., II., 426. An escape, long since extinct. See note by Mr. T. B. Flower in *Phytol.* III., 854.

FRITTILLARIA, Linn.

765. F. Meleagris, *L.*

Native ; in pastures, probably now extinct.

G. "In a meadow below Winterbourne Church, since ploughed ; May, 1859." Note in Dr. Stephens' copy of Withering. In meadows at Bitton, near the Paper Mills. Now extinct. *Mr. T. B. Flower ; Phytol.* I., 70.

S. Formerly abundant in a field or fields close to the village of Compton Martin, as recorded in *New B. G.* and by botanists more recently. This locality has been thoroughly searched on two occasions, in 1883 and 1884, but the result was disappointing. We fear there is little doubt that the report current in the neighbourhood is well grounded ; and that " Old Henniker," as the former proprietor of the land is irreverently called, did malevolently grub up and destroy the whole of this beautiful plant, in order that people should no longer annoy him by coming from all the country round to gather it in his fields. We have conversed with old inhabitants of the parish who have pointed out to us the exact spot where they remember to have gathered it, and who say that there were some plants with white flowers. Reported to grow also in meadows in Litton parish, but this we have not been able to inquire into.

ORNITHOGALUM, *Linn.*

766. O. umbellatum, *L.*

Denizen or alien; in meadows or orchards, and about old gardens, very rare.

S. Bishport; *Herb. Stephens.* "In a field near the caisson at Combe Hay, *Dr. Davis.*" *Fl. Bathon.* Also reported from near Combe Hay by Mr. T. B. Flower. Ditchbank at Burnham, not near a house, 1879; *Miss Winter.* Meadow at Uphill; *Dr. St. Brody.* Noted at Walton-in-Gordano by two or three observers; the place being probably the site of an old garden. "On the top of a hill, three miles on this side Bristol"; *Ray. Syn.*, 372. V.

767. O. pyrenaicum, *L.*

Native; in woods and on grassy hedgebanks. Very local, but usually abundant where it does occur.

In our district this species is confined to a narrow tract of country in North Somerset. The neighbourhood of Bath is its headquarters, and it extends from that city about eight miles to the westward, as far as Stockwood, which we believe to be its western British limit.* At

---

* We may conclude from Ray's mention of this Ornithogalum in the Bristol district that in his time it did not occur further west

this point it approaches within four miles of Bristol. The plant is found at intervals along the lanes from Stockwood to Keynsham, and more abundantly between the latter place and Bath. Here it is met with in profusion in many of the woods; and we have noticed it in plenty as far south as Dunkerton.

The young, unexpanded spikes are sometimes eaten like asparagus. They are to be had in Bath Market and in the shops of the city under the names of "Bath asparagus," " wild asparagus," or " wild grass." Our opinion, on experiment, is that the Bath substitute as " a vehicle for melted butter " is very little inferior to the cultivated esculent. VI.

GAGEA, *Salisb.*

768. G. lutea, *Ker.*

Native; in woods and bushy places, very rare and no longer to be found in some of its old stations.

G. In thickets at Granham Rocks, near Bitton; quite plentiful at one time, but now destroyed by quarrying; *Mr. T. B. Flower.* " Wyck; *Miss Worsley.*" *Bot. Guide.* Wyck; *Mr. S. Rootsey, F.L.S.* Mr. Flower tells us that formerly he found it very sparingly at Wyck, among rocks on the left bank of the stream.

S. St. Ann's Wood, Brislington; *Rev. G. W. Braikenridge.* Brislington; *Mr. S. Rootsey.* It is likely that the plant was extirpated at St. Ann's by the construction of the Great Western Railway, as none has been found there for many years. "Twerton Wood; *Mr. Aldham.*" *Add. Fl. Bathon.* Near Mells; *Rev. R. Murray.*

---

than it does now. "*Tho. Willisellus* observavit in colle quodam tribus cis *Bristoliam* milliaribus via qua inde Bathoniam itur." *Ray. Syn.*, 372.

SCILLA, *Linn.*

769. S. autumnalis, *L.*

Native; formerly on St. Vincent's Rocks, and perhaps also on Clifton Down. Ray noticed it upon the Rocks, and many other observers have recorded it from the same place. Specimens from thence are to be seen in most of the local herbaria of the last generation with dates coming up to about 1860. We doubt if it has been seen since the completion of the Clifton Suspension Bridge and its approaches. Our information goes to show that the plant grew plentifully near the Clifton pier of the bridge, and was confined within a very small compass. Swete, however (*Fl.* 78), gives also "the sward on the top of the rocks." We will yet cherish the hope that a few bulbs still remain in some little-trodden morsel of turf; but as year after year passes without a sign of their existence, the probability grows rapidly fainter.

ALLIUM, *Linn.*

770. A. vineale, *L.* *Crow-Garlic.*

Native; in pastures and on dry banks.

The flowering variety *(β. bulbiferum. Syme, E. B.)* is very rare. About twenty well-marked plants were found in August, 1883, growing in loose sandy soil upon a ledge of St. Vincent's Rocks. The form *compactum* is rather common in both counties. VII. VIII.

771. A. sphærocephalum, *L.*

Native; very rare and local.

G. In small quantity on some ledges of St. Vincent's Rocks; perhaps a dozen plants yearly. More plentiful on Durdham Down, nearly a mile away from the first station. Here as many as forty flower-heads have been seen in one season.

This species is one of the gems of the Bristol Flora. We are glad to say it runs no risk of destruction at the hands of the quarryman,—a fate which in *F. B.*, ed. 3, is stated to have already befallen it,—but the more refined weapons of the collector are hardly less deadly, and from these there is danger, unless they be used solely by scientific and unselfish hands. VIII.

772. A. oleraceum, *L.*

Native; in pastures, among rocks, and sometimes in cornfields, rare. Singularly indifferent to the nature of soil or situation: flourishing alike on limestone rocks and in the rich riverside pasture land.

G. Prope Bristolium copiose; *Huds. Fl. Angl.* Cornfields at Lawrence Weston, July, 1833; *Herb. Powell.* Stapleton; *Herb. Stephens.* A good patch in a small hollow on Durdham Down, 1882 and 1883. In plenty for half a mile on the bank of Avon near Sea Mills.

S. Ashton fields; *Miss Atwood,* and *Mr. T. B. Flower.* Very abundant in one spot near the encampment on the hill at Weston-super-Mare; but, as might be expected from the nature of the ground, the plants are smaller and less vigorous than those on the Avon bank. *Mr. D. Fry.* VII. VIII.

773. A. ursinum, *L.* *Ramsons.*

Native; very abundant in most woods, copses, &c., throughout the district. V. VI.

ENDYMION, *Dumort.*

774. E. nutans, *Dum.* *Blue-bell.*

Native; in woods and damp shady places, very common. White-flowered plants have been observed at Filton, and between Patchway and Charlton, G.; and in Somerset near Clevedon, and in a wood between Abbot's Leigh and the Tanpits. V.

MELANTHACEÆ.

COLCHICUM, *Linn.*

775. **C. autumnale,** *L.* *Meadow-Saffron.*

Native; in pastures, woods, and old hedgebanks, rather common.

G. In a pasture close to Westbury-on-Trym. Iron Acton. Tortworth. Yate.

S. Bishport Wood. Brislington. Pastures on Dundry Hill, and on the Bridgwater road under Dundry. Abundant on Failand Farm. Field near Barrow Court in plenty. Clevedon. Keynsham. Portbury. Yatton. Whitchurch. Immense quantities in meadows on Mendip, near Shipham. Shutshelf Wood, near Axbridge. Ball Wood, near Congresbury. Paul Wood, near Temple Cloud. In old lanes on Mendip above Sidcot; and on the rough stony ground at the hill-top towards Churchill. In meadows at Churchill. Frequent about Bath. Cameley. Chew Stoke. Compton Martin. Horrington Bottom; and elsewhere near Wells. Weston-in-Gordano. Wrington. Plants bearing white flowers grow at Sutton, near Chew Magna; near Whitchurch; near Hallatrow; at Chelwood—" dozens of 'em in one place"; also at Whitley Batch, near by, and in meadows at Stanton Prior.

An account of Colchicum flowering in spring (March, 1880), both on Failand Farm and in pastures on the Bridgwater road, will be found in the *Journ. of Bot.* for May, 1880. The author expressed an opinion that this would not prove to be a permanent condition of the plants, but one temporarily induced by the peculiarly early and severe cold of the previous autumn. This view has been justified by subsequent observation. In the succeeding years the onset of winter was not heralded by frost in September, and no spring-flowering Colchicum has been seen since. IX. X.

NARTHECIUM, *Huds.*

776. **N. ossifragum,** *Huds. Bog-Asphodel.*

Native; on boggy hill sides, in elevated bogs on Mendip, and in peaty marshes, rare and local.

S. About the sphagnous, boggy sources of streams on Black Down. In bogs on Mendip, near Priddy and the Mineries. Moors south of Wedmore. VI. VII.

JUNCACEÆ.

JUNCUS, *Linn.*

777. **J. maritimus,** *Sm.*

We cannot find this rush either in Gloucestershire or in Somerset at the stations recorded, and are doubtful if we do right in including the species here. The tract of salt marshes where it is stated to have been found by Mr. Collins is of large extent, and a most suitable locality for the plant. Until further search has been made we must not relinquish our claim to it.

G. Shirehampton Marshes; *Swete, Fl.* 83.

S. Mouth of the Parret, in ditches; not unfrequent near the Channel. *J. C. Collins, MSS. New B. G. Suppl.*

778. **J. effusus,** *L.*

Native; in marshes and on damp ground generally. Very common. VII.

779. **J. conglomeratus,** *L.*

Native; in wet places. Common in many parts of the district, but not so well distributed as the last species.
 VII.

780. **J. glaucus,** *Sibth.*
   Native; in wet places, common. VII.

781. **J. obtusiflorus,** *Ehrh.*
   Native; in marshes, very rare.
   G. Ashley (Boiling Well); *Mr. G. H. K. Thwaites* and *Mr. W. E. Green.*
   S. Walton Moor; *Herb. Powell.* Yatton; *Miss Winter.*

782. **J. acutiflorus,** *Ehrh.*
   Native; in peaty meadows and damp places, very common.
   VI.—VIII.

783. **J. lamprocarpus,** *Ehrh.*
   Native; on wet and peaty ground, common. VII. VIII.

784. **J. nigritellus,** *D. Don.*
   Native. It grows abundantly on the marshy sands near Berrow, S. VII. VIII.

785. **J. supinus,** *Moench.*
   Native; in bogs and on peaty moors, rare and local.
   S. Bogs on the slopes of Black Down, and about the Mineries. Boggy ravine near Wells. Moors south of Wedmore. VI.—VIII.

786. **J. squarrosus,** *L.*
   Native; on wet heaths and moors, rare and local.
   S. Bogs on Mendip at the Mineries and about Black Down. Moor near Clevedon. VI. VII.

787. **J. compressus,** *Jacq.*
   Native; rather rare? We have been favoured with several localities for this rush; but the species is so little understood that we regard them as resting on doubtful authority.
   G. Horfield; *Herb. Stephens.*

788. **J. Gerardi,** Lois.
   Native; in salt marshes and damp places near the coast. Very common in such situations.   VI.—VIII.

789. **J. bufonius,** L.   *Toad-rush.*
   Native; in wet places, common.
   The Toad-rush, although common enough in many localities, is singularly absent from a few. For instance, it is a rare plant in the vicinity of Clevedon.   VII. VIII.

LUZULA, Cand.

790. **L. sylvatica,** *Bichen.*
   Native; in woods and on shady banks. Very abundant in many places.   IV.—VI.

791. **L. pilosa,** *Willd.*
   Native; in woods, common.   V.

792. **L. campestris,** *Willd.*
   Native; in pastures and dry places, very common. IV. V.

793. **L. multiflora,** *Lej.*
   Native; in damp peaty places, frequent. Our plant is the form *congesta.*
   G.   Copse between Horfield and Stapleton; *Herb. Stephens.* Yate Common.
   S.   On Black Down. Cheddar. Downhead. Wells; *Miss Livett.* Moors south of Wedmore.   VI. VII.

TYPHACEÆ.

TYPHA, *Linn.*

794. **T. latifolia,** L.   *Reed-Mace.*
   Native; in ponds and wet swamps, rather common.
   VI. VII.

795. **T. angustifolia,** L.
   Native; very rare.
   S.   In a ditch on the peat moor south of Wedmore; *Mr.*

T. F. Perkins! Formerly in one of the locks on the canal at Combe Hay; *Add. Fl. Bathon.* " Ditches at Burnham and Wembdon; *J. C. Collins, MSS.*" *New B. G. Suppl.*

SPARGANIUM, L.

796. S. ramosum, *Huds.*

Native; in wet ditches and pools, rather common. VI. VII.

797. S. simplex, *Huds.*

Native; in ditches and streams, rare.

G. Baptist Mills; *Dr. Stephens.* Ditches near Stapleton; *Herb. Stephens.*

S. Ditches near Clevedon. Walton-in-Gordano. Nailsea Moor. Draycot. Moors south of Wedmore. In the canal at Radford. Yatton. VII.

(*S. natans*, L., is stated by Swete (*Fl.* 82) to occur in "ditches and marshes," as if common about Bristol. This is an error.)

ARACEÆ.

ACORUS, *Linn.*

798. A. Calamus, *L.* *Sweet Flag.*

Alien or denizen; naturalized in one or two places.

S. Banks of the Avon at Batheaston, and between Newton Bridge and Saltford; where it is supposed to have been introduced by the late Mr. Sole. In old turf pits at Wedmore; *Collinson's Hist. Somerset,* 1791.

ARUM, *Linn.*

799. A. maculatum, *L.* *Cuckoo-pint.* " *Lords and Ladies.*"

Native; in woods and shady places, and on hedgebanks. Very common. IV. V.

LEMNACEÆ.

LEMNA, Linn.

800. **L. trisulca,** L.

Native; on water in ditches and stagnant pools, frequent.

G. Marsh ditches about Avonmouth and Shirehampton.

S. Marsh ditches in the Cheddar valley. Clevedon. Easton. Radford. Weston-super-Mare. Yatton. Ditches south of Wedmore.

801. **L. minor,** L.

Native; very common everywhere on stagnant water.

802. **L. gibba,** L.

Native; on stagnant water, not very common.

G. Plentiful in ditches of brackish water near the Severn, between the Passages and Avonmouth. Horfield. Shirehampton. Westbury-on-Trym.

S. Claverham. Yatton. Marsh ditches in the lowlands towards the Channel.

803. **L. polyrrhiza,** L.

Native; chiefly in the peaty lowlands in the southern portion of the district, rather local.

G. Stapleton. Littleton-on-Severn.

S. Near Brent Knoll. Draycot. Portbury. Wedmore. Yatton.

POTAMOGETONACEÆ.

POTAMOGETON, Linn.

804. **P. natans,** L.

Native; in rivers and ponds, rare.

G. In the river Frome near Stapleton. Pond at Henbury.

S. The Abbots' Pond. In the Avon near Brislington. Clevedon. Yatton. VI. VII.

805. **P. polygonifolius,** *Pourr.*
Native; in ditches and slow streams, frequent.
G.   Dursley.   Berkeley.   Yate Common.
S.   In the canal at Radford.   South Brent.   Pools on Mendip near the Mineries and towards Wells.   VII.

806. **P. rufescens,** *Schrad.*
Native; in slow streams and ditches, rare.
G.   Near St. Philip's Marsh; *Dr. H. O. Stephens.*
S.   Marsh ditches near Axbridge.   VII.

807. **P. lucens,** *L.*
Native; in rivers and deepish water, frequent.
S.   Frequent in the Avon between Bath and Bristol.   In the river Brue.   In the canal near Radford.   Nailsea Moor.   VI.

808. **P. perfoliatus,** *L.*
Native; in deep water, rare.
S.   Plentiful in the canal near Bath.   In the river Avon at Brislington.   VII.

809. **P. crispus,** *L.*
Native; in ditches and ponds, common.   VI.

810. **P. pusillus,** *L.*
Native; in ditches and ponds, frequent.
G.   River Frome near Stapleton; *Mr. G. H. K. Thwaites.*
S.   River Avon near the Cotton Mills, and towards Keynsham.   In the canal by Bath; *Add. Fl. Bathon.* Yatton.   VI.

811. **P. pectinatus,** *L.*
Native; in marsh ditches, frequent.
G.   Ditches in Shirehampton Marshes.   St. Philip's Marsh.
S.   Ditches near Pill; *Mr. W. E. Green.* Kingston Seymour; *Mr. D. Fry.*   VI. VII.

812. **P. densus,** L.
   Native; in ditches and streams, common.   VI. VII.

   RUPPIA, Linn.

813. **R. rostellata,** Koch.
   Native.
   G. In a brackish pool near the Avon below Shirehampton.   V. VIII.

   ZANNICHELLIA, Linn.

814. **Z. palustris,** L.
   Native; in stagnant water, rather common.
   G. Abundant in Avonmouth Marshes. Filton Meads. Horfield.
   S. Pools at Bedminster and at Whitchurch. Stockwood. Congresbury. Portishead. Yatton.   V.—VIII.

NAIADACEÆ.

ZOSTERA, Linn.

815. **Z. nana,** Roth.
   Native; in the muddy estuaries.

816. **Z. marina,** L.
   Native; on the coast of N. Somerset.

Flora of the Bristol Coal-Field.

ADDITIONS TO PART I.

113.* **Dianthus deltoides,** *L.* *Maiden Pink.*
Native; fairly abundant in a pasture between Brislington and Keynsham, S. One plant has lilac petals; and a small patch, with pure white flowers and very pale foliage, may be *D. Glaucus*, L. First noticed by Mr. David Fry, in May, 1886. The plant is recorded for North Somerset in *Topogr. Botany*, on the authority of Dr. Thwaites, but his locality remained unknown. Very possibly Mr. Fry has rediscovered it.

Moenchia erecta, Sm. in Somerset. See page 32. Prior to May, 1886, our claim to possess this little plant rested entirely upon the specimens contained in the Stephens' Herbarium. As far as we know no one living had seen it growing in the Bristol district. We were therefore extremely glad to receive from Mr. David Fry a specimen which he had gathered on the coal-measures a short distance from Keynsham. Shortly afterwards we examined the locality, and found the plant distributed in tolerable quantity over a rather limited area. It was associated with *Trifolium subterraneum, T. filiforme, Ornithopus perpusillus, Myosotis versicolor, Aira præcox*, and, to our great satisfaction, with *Scleranthus annuus*. One of Dr. Stephens' records is thus confirmed; and on consideration of the situation and surroundings of the plant at Keynsham, we have no doubt whatever that *Moenchia* did formerly grow on Brandon Hill, the other station mentioned by him. It may indeed lurk there still, though we fear it has been trampled out of existence.

There are some interesting facts connected with the species found in association with the *Moenchia*. They are all scarce plants in the vicinity of Bristol, to be found for the most part in small quantities in a very few places, and on the same geological formation. But whether on Brandon Hill, at Clevedon, at Mangotsfield, or in the Keynsham locality, they are ever companions, sharing in fellowship the barren and scanty soil upon which alone they seem able to maintain themselves. It may be that these plants are too weak and tiny to exist among more robust vegetation, and that the force of species competition is powerful in restricting them to the spots they occupy. It certainly does not appear that dry and sterile habitats are those best suited for the growth of the plants in question. We have seen *Scleranthus annuus* flourishing most luxuriantly as a weed on cultivated land, where it was taking full advantage of depth of soil and elbow-room. But when at large in the world, and left without favour to carry on an unequal competition with the crowd of larger species, the result in our experience is that it becomes banished to spots bare of, or unsuited to, most other phanerogams.

Scleranthus annuus, L., in Somerset. On the coal-measures near Keynsham; not very plentiful. See page 33.

FLORA
OF THE
BRISTOL COAL-FIELD.

EDITED (FOR THE BRISTOL NATURALISTS' SOCIETY) BY

JAMES WALTER WHITE,

Hon. Secretary of the Botanical Section.

"*Rerum cognoscere causas.*"—VIRGIL.

PART VI.

GLUMIFERÆ, GYMNOSPERMÆ ET CRYPTO-
GAMEÆ VASCULARES.

BRISTOL:
PRINTED FOR THE SOCIETY.

1886.

PHANEROGAMIA.

Class 2. *MONOCOTYLEDONES.*
Div. 3. *GLUMIFERÆ.*

CYPERACEÆ.

CYPERUS. Linn.

817. **C. longus.** *L.*

Native at Walton-in-Gordano, S.

This rare and beautiful sedge has grown from time immemorial in a small plot of very wet marshy ground, believed to have been anciently a fish-pond, and situate behind some cottages in the upper part of the village. Sole, in a MS. dated 1782, says of it, "Abundantly in a pond at Walton-in-Gordano, near Possit, Somerset, a village belonging to Sir Abraham Elton" (Possit = Portishead). The plant continued to be plentiful until 1882, when the occupier of the land ploughed it and planted potatoes. At the end of August, 1883, we found many stems coming up by the sides of two ditches which intersect the field, and also among the crop; but in consequence of the disturbance their development was much retarded, and flowering delayed nearly two months. Since that time, owing to the drainage and cultivation, the sedge has become reduced in quantity, and the stems produced in successive seasons have failed to come to maturity, whence it is to be feared that *Cyperus longus* will soon be numbered among the lost rarities of the district. VIII. IX.

SCHŒNUS, Linn.

818. **S. nigricans**, *L.*

Native; formerly on the coast between Clevedon and Portishead, but now extinct.

"Clevedon"; *Herb. Stephens.* "By the side of a fresh-water spring which bubbles forth from amid the bosom of the rocks, was *Schœnus nigricans*, brown and muddy from the tide washing over it." *Mr. Leo H. Grindon: Phytol.* vol. i. 566. Dr. Stephens' specimen probably came from the spot described by Mr. Grindon; a place on the coast towards Portishead, where we are satisfied the plant no longer grows.

Mr. Grindon's discovery of *Schœnus*, as narrated above, forms part of a pleasantly-written account of a botanical ramble from Bristol to Clevedon, and thence to Portishead, on July 6, 1842. In this day's work, the botanist was fortunate, as besides the sedge, he records *Phleum arenarium* at Tickenham, and *Calamagrostis Epigeios* at Clevedon. All of these plants are now unknown at the places named.

(*Cladium Mariscus*, R. Br. "Wedmore and Burtle Moor, Somerset." *W. Sole, MS.* 1782. Requires confirmation.)

RHYNCHOSPORA, *Vahl.*

819. R. alba, *Vahl.*

Native; in turfy bogs, very local.

S. About the boggy sources of streams on Mendip at Blackdown. Plentiful in peat-moors on the southern border of the district. VII. VIII.

820. R. fusca, *Sm.*

Native; on peat-moors, perhaps now extinct.

S. "Burtle Moor, near Mark." *W. Sole, MS.* 1782. See also remarks by Mr. Thos. Clark in his *Catalogue of the Rarer Plants of the Turf Moors of Somerset.*

ELEOCHARIS, *R. Br.*

821. E. palustris, *R. Br.*

Native; in marshy places, ditches, and about ponds. Common. VI. VII.

822. E. multicaulis, *Sm.*

Native; in marshy places, less frequent than the last. VII.

SCIRPUS. *Linn.*

823. S. maritimus, *L.*

Native; plentiful in brackish ditches and salt marshes, by the sides of the Channel and tidal rivers, sometimes occurring two or three miles inland. VI. VII.

824. S. sylvaticus, *L.*

Native; in damp meadows, rare.

G. "Boiling Well!" Mangotsfield.

S. Abundant in a meadow under Highbury Hill, near Hallatrow. A marshy field near Wells, *Miss Livett.* "In wet places, frequent;" *Fl. Bathon.*

VII.

CYPERACEÆ.

825. S. lacustris, *L.*
Native; in deep water, rare.
G. Baptist Mills. In the river Avon here and there sparingly; at Hanham Mill dam there is a larger quantity. VI. VII.

826. S. cæspitosus, *L.*
Native; in boggy and heathy places, local.
S. Plentiful on Mendip at Blackdown and about the Mineries. On the peat-moors in the south.
VII. VIII.

(*S. fluitans*, L. "Ditches frequent." *Swete, Fl.* 84. Error.)

827. S. setaceus, *L.*
Native; in marshes and on the borders of streamlets, not common.
G. Boiling Well; *Herb. Stephens.* Stapleton; *Mr. W. E. Green.* By a little stream near Mangotsfield Station. Damp wood between Charfield and Tortworth.
S. Marshy spot close to the iron works at Ashton Gate. Clevedon. Yatton Weston-in-Gordano.
VI. VII

BLYSMUS, *Panz.*

828. B. compressus, *Panz.*
Native; probably extinct.
G. Mill dam, Stapleton; *Herb. Stephens.* Stapleton, *Mr. G. H. K. Thwaites.*
S. In Claverton Wood, *Dr. Davis. Fl. Bathon.* From a remark of Mr. Hewett Watson, it would appear that the Bath record was subsequently confirmed by Mr. R. Withers.

ERIOPHORUM, *Linn.*

829. E. vaginatum, *L.* Hare's-tail Cotton Grass.

Native; in bogs, local.

S. Plentiful in bogs on Mendip about the Mineries, and very abundant in another bog near the Miners' Arms Inn, also on Mendip. Peat-moor on the southern border of the district. V. VI.

830. E. polystachion, *L.* Common Cotton Grass.

Native; in bogs and marshes; of wider distribution than the last.

S. In all the bogs on Mendip, including the swampy springs on the slopes of Blackdown. East Harptree. Pensford. Yatton. Peat-moors in the south. V. VI.

CAREX, *Linn.*

831. C. pulicaris, *L.*

Native; in boggy and damp heathy places; also on commons among long grass.

G. Alveston. Abundant in some spots on Clifton and Durdham Downs; close to the Zoological Gardens, and on the upper slopes of the Gully.

S. On Leigh Down, near the reservoir. By the stream between the Tanpits and Failand Farm. In the fir plantation towards the upper end of Cheddar Gorge. On Blackdown, near the Mineries. King's Wood, Yatton. V. VI.

(*C. Davalliana,* Sm. "Lansdown, on the slope of a hill on which there is a clump of firs, about 1¼ mile from Bath (Mr. E. Forster);" *Fl. Bathon.* Now lost.)

832. **C. disticha,** *Huds.* *C. intermedia,* Good.
   Native; in boggy pastures, rare.
   G. Filton Meads.
   S. Near Hampton Rocks, Bath; *Mr. T. B. Flower.*
   Plentiful in some marshy pastures near Draycot Peat-moors in the south. V. VI.

833. **C. arenaria,** *L.*
   Native; abundant on the sandy shore of the Bristol Channel, particularly at Kewstoke, Weston-super-Mare, and Burnham. VI.

834. **C. divisa,** *Huds.*
   Native; in marshes, very rare.
   S. "In considerable abundance on Burtle turf-moor, near the sea-coast." *R. Withers,* 1850. Label in *Herb. Watson.* Near Kewstoke, *Mr. T. F. Perkins.*

835. **C. vulpina,** *L.*
   Native; in wet, shady places, and on ditch-banks. Common and generally distributed. VI. VII.

836. **C. muricata,** *L.*
   Native; in damp hedge-banks and the borders of pastures, rather common.
   G. Plentiful in the lane leading from Sneyd Park towards Sea Mills. In plenty near the bank of Avon above Sea Mills. Peaty pastures in Filton Meads. Pur Down. Stapleton; *Herb. Stephens.* Tortworth. Woods above Wotton-under-Edge.
   S. Bishport. Clevedon. Combe Hay. Great Elm. Sidcot. Shipham. Winterhead. Plentiful about Wells. Weston-super-Mare. VI. VII.

837. C. divulsa, *Good.*

Native; on grassy banks, rather common.

G. In several places about Coombe Dingle. In a grassy hollow (old quarrying) on Durdham Down, 1884. Plentiful about Charfield and at Damory Bridge. Abundant on some damp hedge-banks between Thornbury and Aust. Shirehampton. Wotton-under-Edge.

S. Leigh Woods. Clevedon. Churchill. Congresbury. Between Cleeve and Yatton. Great Elm. About the Taupits and on Failand Farm. Keynsham. Norton Malreward. Portishead. West Harptree. Whitchurch. Yatton. V. VI.

838. C. paniculata, *L.*

Native; in wet and boggy places, rare and local.

S. Ditch-banks near Axbridge. Bog in the valley near Winscombe. Ditch-banks south of Wedmore. Bogs on Mendip at the Mineries. In very large tussocks abundant on both banks of the canal near Radford and Camerton. VI. VII.

(*C. teretiuscula*, Good. The old records in Swete's Flora and elsewhere much need verification.)

839. C. axillaris, *Good.*

Native; very rare.

G. It grows plentifully in one spot between Charfield Station and the gates of Tortworth Park, where it was first noticed by Mr. W. B. Waterfall in 1882.

S. Cheddar, 1883; *Mr. Richards.* Several stations a little outside our district are mentioned in *Add. Fl. Bathon.* VI.

840. C. remota, *L.*

Native; in moist woods and on hedge-banks. Abundant in many places a few miles from Bristol, but is not seen very frequently close by the city.

G. Aust. Very plentiful about Berkeley, and also near Tortworth. Near the Duchess Ponds at Stapleton. Henbury. Near Filton. Littleton-on-Severn. Sodbury. Thornbury. Winterbourne.

S. Bishport. Churchill. Clevedon. Border of a field near the Tanpits under Failand Hill. Leigh Wood. Near Hallatrow. Portbury. St. Ann's Wood, Brislington. Woodborough and Winscombe. In plenty between Yatton and Clevedon. Bishop's Wood and Knowle, near Wells. Easton. Asham Wood. Whatley. Wrington.　　　　VI.

841. C. stellulata, *Good.*

Native; in bogs and swamps, frequent.

G. Near Damory Bridge. Marshy spots by Mangotsfield Common. Shirehampton; *Herb. Stephens.* Stapleton; *Swete, Fl.* 85. Yate Common.

S. Abundant on the swampy margin of the stream between the Tanpits and Failand Farm. Blackdown. Cheddar. Downhead Common. Upper Knowle. The Mineries. Boggy fields below Winscombe. Walton-in-Gordano. Wells. Yatton.
　　　　V. VI.

842. C. ovalis, *Good.*

Native; on commons and in damp pastures, frequent.

G. Formerly on Durdham Down; *Mr. G. H. K. Thwaites.* Berkeley. Mangotsfield Common. Tortworth. Yate Common. Near Stapleton; *Mr. W. E. Green.*

S. Damp places in many of the rough pastures on the Mendip Hills. By the stream below Failand Farm. Walton Drove, near Clevedon. Upper Knowle; *Rev. W. H. Painter.* Wedmore. Wrington.
VI. VII.

438. C. vulgaris, *Fries.*

Native; in marshes and wet places, frequent.

G. Marsh near Baptist Mills. Filton Meads. Charlton. Stoke Gifford. Yate Common.

S. Boggy pastures under Dundry Hill, near the reservoirs. Bedminster Meads. Blackdown, on Mendip. Clevedon. Marshy pastures in the lowlands between Cheddar and Draycot. By the stream below Failand Farm. Radford. Timsbury. Stanton Prior.
V. VI.

844. C. pallescens, *L.*

Native; in damp woods and pastures, rare.

G. Copse between Horfield and Filton; *Dr. H. O. Stephens.* Berwick Wood, near Henbury, June, 1883.

S. Sparingly in a marshy pasture under the western slope of Dundry Hill, May 30, 1880. One or two plants in an open glade in Leigh Wood; *Mr. E. Wheeler.* Peaty meadow below Winscombe; *Mr. W. E. Green.*
V. VI.

845. C. panicea, *L.*

Native; in meadows and marshes, and also on limestone hills. Common and well distributed.

G. Plentiful in Black Rock Gully, and in one or two other spots on Durdham Down (limestone). Ashley Hill. Alveston. Charlton. Filton. Horfield. Mangotsfield. Thornbury. Yate Common.

S. Among the heath and in long grass on Leigh Down (limestone). Barrow Gurney, and the meadows under the western slope of Dundry Hill. Bedminster Meads. Common about Blackdown on Mendip, and elsewhere in that district. Between the Tanpits and Failand Farm. Walton Drove, and in other places near Clevedon. Bogs on Mendip towards Wells. Woodborough. Yatton.
V. VI.

A curious variety or monstrosity of *C. panicea* was met with near Bristol some years ago. It had double perigynia, the second or upper one with its peduncle passing through the orifice in the lower one.

(*C. limosa*, L., has been recorded from the bogs on Mendip; but probably in error.)

846. C. strigosa, *Huds.*

Native; in ditches and wet places, rare.

G. Llewellyn's Wood, Westbury; *Dr. H. O. Stephens.* Lanewood and Shortwood, Pucklechurch; *Withering*, II. 97.

S. Ditch-bank by the side of a lane between Cleeve and Yatton; first reported by Miss Winter. The plant grows here plentifully in a patch some yards in extent. Bishop's Wood, Wells; *Rev. E. S. Marshall*, 1883. Banks of the brook, Nailsea; *Herb. Stephens.* Wraxall; *Dr. H. O. Stephens.* "In woods at Charlcombe and Claverton, *Dr. Davis*"; *Fl. Bathon.* V. VI.

847. C. pendula, *Huds.*

Native; in moist woods and damp, shady hedge-banks, rather common.

CYPERACEÆ. 223

. Baptist Mills. In many places between Almondsbury and Compton Greenfield. Abundant about Berkeley. Charfield. Tortworth. Plentiful in Berwick Wood, Henbury.

S. Bishport, and in several other places under Dundry Hill. St. John's Lane, Bedminster. Long Ashton. Leigh Woods. Stockwood. Whitchurch. Canal Bank, and elsewhere near Monckton Combe. Farrington Gurney. Stone Easton. Paul Wood, near Temple Cloud. Borders of streams near Wells; *Miss Livett.* Wrington. Yatton.

V. VI.

848. C. humilis, Leyss. (*C. clandestina,* Good.)

Native; on downs and limestone hills, very rare and local. It is seldom found in level turf, but prefers steep, rocky banks, and the edges of old excavations.

G. St. Vincent's Rocks and Clifton and Durdham Downs, plentiful in some spots. Not abundant above the Suspension Bridge, although it is scattered over the slopes towards the Zigzag, and more sparingly between the Zigzag and Ghyston House.

S. Limestone slopes under Leigh Wood, rather scarce. Abundant on Brean Down. IV.

849. C. digitata, *L.*

Native; in a wood and thickets on limestone, now confined to a very small area.

G. Amid the underwood on St. Vincent's Rocks; usually closely concealed in long grass beneath the bushes, and needing sharp eyes to detect it.

S. Mossy ledges and recesses in Leigh Wood, where the rock is damp and shaded. Here the plants are

850. C. præcox, *Jacq.*

Native; on downs, dry banks, and pastures, common, and generally distributed. Tall specimens are sometimes found in marshy fields, which in habit much resemble the next species. IV. V.

851. C. pilulifera, *L.*

Native; on downs, heaths, and commons, probably more frequent than our records show.

G. Clifton and Durdham Downs, growing chiefly in the furzy spots among coarse grasses. Blaise Castle Wood; *Herb. Powell.*

S. Downhead Common. Wells. V. VI.

852. C. glauca, *Scop.*

Native; in meadows and pastures, on downs and about rocks. Very common and universally distributed. V. VI.

853. C. flava, *L.*

Native; in marshes and boggy places, frequent.

It is probable that all our plants belong to var. β *C. lepidocarpa*, Tausch, as we have not yet met with any *eu-flava genuina*, Syme.

G. Wet places about Mangotsfield Common. Yate Common. Formerly on Durdham Down and at Shirehampton; *Swete, Fl. 85.*

S. On the swampy margin of the stream between the Tanpits and Failand Farm. Boggy sources of streams on Blackdown and elsewhere on the Mendip Hills. Cheddar. The Mineries. Shipham. Walton-in-Gordano. V. VI.

854. **C. extensa,** *Good.*
   Native; in salt marshes, very rare.
   S. Sandy marsh on the coast at Berrow. Weston-super-Mare; *Herb. Stephens.* VI.

855. **C. distans,** *L.*
   Native; in meadows and marshes, frequent.
   G. Abundant in the meadows by the Avon below Cook's Folly. Baptist Mills. By the Severn near Berkeley, and elsewhere in the lowlands lower down. Chipping Sodbury. Plentiful in Filton Meads.
   S. Bedminster Meads. Barrow Gurney. Chew Magna. Great Elm. Highbridge. Uphill. Walton-in-Gordano. Yatton. V. VI.

856. **C. binervis,** *Sm.*
   Native; on moors and commons, rather rare and local.
   G. Blaise Castle; *Swete, Fl.* 85. Horfield, and Boiling Well; *Herb. Stephens.* Yate Common.
   S. Downhead Common. Abundant on Blackdown, and at the Mineries on Mendip. VI. VII.

857. **C. depauperata,** *Good.*
   Native. We understand that this has only been gathered twice, and is likely to be now extinct.
   S. "Axbridge (Norman)"; *Herb. Watson.* Wood near Axbridge; *Mr. T. B. Flower*, who sent specimens to the British Museum, and states that the locality has been destroyed.

858. **C. sylvatica,** *Huds.*
   Native; in woods, common throughout the district.
   V. VI.

859. C. Pseudo-cyperus, *L.*

Native; on the margins of ponds and ditches. Frequent in the southern portion of the district; very rare in the northern.

G. Winterbourne; *Mr. T. B. Flower, Phytol.* I. 328.

S. In many places in the lowlands from Clevedon to Ken and Yatton. Very abundant by Walton Drove. Pondside, Woodborough. The Watchets, near Wells. Ditch-banks south of Wedmore towards the peat-moors, where this sedge becomes extremely common. VI. VII.

860. C. hirta, *L.*

Native; in wet pastures, frequent.

G. Alveston. Charlton. Cromhall. Baptist Mills Chipping Sodbury. Charfield. Patchway. Stapleton. Tortworth. Tytherington. Wotton-under-Edge. Yate.

S. Pastures by the stream at Bishport. Crox Top. Brean. Plentiful in peaty fields near Barrow Gurney. Failand Farm. Walton-in-Gordano. Wells. Winscombe. IV. V.

861. C. ampullacea, *Good.*

Native; in bogs and marshes, rare.

S. Clevedon; *Mr. E. Wheeler.* Bogs at the Mineries on Mendip; *Rev. R. P. Murray.* Abundant on the peat-moors in the south. VI.

862. C. paludosa, *Good.*

Native; in ditches and marshes, frequent. It is very likely to be more widely distributed than appears from our notes.

G. Marsh at Baptist Mills. By the Frome near Stapleton.

S. Clevedon. Keynsham; *Mr. D. Fry.* Flax Bourton. Monckton Combe. About Wells! *Miss Livett.* Yatton! *Miss Winter.* Common near Bath; Fl. Bathon.   V. VI.

863. C. riparia, *Curt.*

Native; in water, and by the sides of rivers and streams, frequent.

G. Alveston. Aust. Elburton. Filton. Siston. Marsh at Baptist Mills. Glen Frome. Tortworth.

S. Bank of Avon under Leigh Wood. Clevedon Portbury. Long Ashton. Brislington. By the Avon at Keynsham, and higher up the river. Marsh ditches in the Cheddar Valley.   V. VI.

GRAMINEÆ.

(*Echinochloa Crus-galli,* Beauv. This large coarse grass appeared in 1883 upon the dredgings from the bed of the Avon and from the Float, which had been deposited the year before in the Black Rock Quarry. In 1884 there were eight or nine fine plants. Like many other aliens which sprang up at the same time and place, it will perhaps continue for a short time, and then disappear.)

(*Panicum miliaceum,* L. Casual. Seven or eight plants on dredgings deposited in the Black Rock Quarry, 1883 and 1884.)

SETARIA, *Pal. de Beauv.*

864. S. viridis, *Beauv.*

Colonist. A weed in cultivated fields, gardens and waste ground, rather rare.

G. In turnip fields by the Avon, at Hanham, 1882.

Near Stapleton Mill, 1883. St. Philip's Marsh. On dredgings in the Black Rock Quarry, 1883 and 1884.

S. Bank of Avon near Rownham Ferry. On the railway near Paulton, 1881. VII. VIII.

(*S. glauca*, Beauv. Casual. Several plants on dredgings in the Black Rock Quarry, 1884.)

PHALARIS, *Linn.*

865. **P. canariensis**, *Canary-grass.*

Alien; in waste places, roadsides and occasionally in cornfields, frequent. It may always be found on the rubbish in St. Philip's Marsh, and about the floating harbours in Bristol, in company with other waifs and strays from town and trade. VII.

866. **P. arundinacea**, *L.*

Native; in and by water, common.

G. Bank of Avon as far down as Crew's Hole. Between Redland and Horfield. Berkeley. Charfield. Charlton. Ditches near Henbury. Glen Frome, Stapleton. Westbury-on-Trym.

S. Ashton Gate, near the iron works. Bank of Avon, abundant from Bath downwards. Lock's Mills, near Bedminster. Camerton. Paulton. Portbury. Portishead. Walton-in-Gordano. Croscombe and Knowle, near Wells. Winscombe. Weston-super-Mare. Marsh ditches throughout the Cheddar Valley. Brent. Burnham. VI. VII.

ANTHOXANTHUM, *Linn.*

867. **A. odoratum**, *L. Sweet-scented Vernal Grass.*

Native; in meadows and pastures. Very common, and generally distributed. V. VI.

PHLEUM, *Linn.*

868. P. arenarium, *L.*

Native; on the sands of the Channel shore between Burnham and Weston-super-Mare; also on Kewstoke sands. VI. VII.

(*P. asperum*, Jacq. "Habitat in pratis, infra King's Weston prope Bristolium;" *Huds. Fl. Anglica.* Swete gives it as having grown near Kingsweston Inn, in 1845. These were probably ballast plants, as would be also the *Trifolium resupinatum* formerly found in the same locality. They have since been searched for many times in vain.)

869. P. pratense, *L.* Timothy-grass.

Native; in meadows and pastures, everywhere common. The slightly tuberous form (*P. nodosum*, L.) is not unfrequent on dry hills. VI.

ALOPECURUS, *Linn.*

870. A. pratensis, *L.* Fox-tail Grass.

Native; in meadows and pastures, very common and abundant on all rich land. V. VI.

871. A. geniculatus, *L.*

Native; in marshes and on edges of ponds and wet ditches, common and generally distributed.
VI. VII.

872. A. bulbosus, *L.*

Native; in salt marshes, very local.

G. Pastures adjoining the Avon below Bristol, extremely abundant near Shirehampton. VI.

873. A. agrestis, *L.*

Colonist; in cultivated fields and in waste places, often on the lias clays, frequent.

G. Bank of Avon under the Downs. St. Philip's Marsh. Cornfields at Lawrence Weston.

S. Permanent and plentiful in cornfields about Bishport. Knowle. Whitchurch. Abundant in cornfields near Portishead. Worle Hill. Wells. Frequent about Bath. IV.—VII.

NARDUS, *Linn.*

874. **N. stricta,** *L.*

Native; on wet heaths and commons, rather rare.

G. Mangotsfield. Warmley. Yate Common.

S. Sparingly among the sedges on the boggy margin of the stream between the Tanpits and Failand Farm. Bogs on Blackdown. Frequent on Mendip near the Mineries. VI. VII.

MILIUM, *Linn.*

875. **M. effusum,** *L.*

Native; in woods, frequent.

G. Almondsbury. Aust. Henbury. Patchway. Between Stoke Bishop and Shirehampton. Wooded banks in Glen Frome, Stapleton.

S. Leigh Wood. Stockwood. Abundant in woods at Portishead. Clevedon. Barrow Gurney. Chew Magna. Maes Knoll. Woods around Pensford. Bishop's Wood, Wells. Wraxall. VI.

PHRAGMITES, *Trin.*

876. **P. communis,** *Trin.* Reed.

Native; in wet ditches, and by the sides of rivers and ponds. Common, especially in the extensive marshlands of the district. VII. VIII.

PSAMMA, *Pal. de Beauv.*

877. **P. arenaria**, *R. & S.* *Mat Grass.*

Native; in loose sea-sands, abundant on the coast of North Somerset. Its great importance as a means of restraining the drifting sand is recognised among the huge sand-hills towards Berrow and Burnham, where this grass is systematically planted in situations needing its binding agency. Were it not for its powerful influence in building up suitable barriers against the advance of the shore sand, impelled by the prevailing west winds, a large tract of land now under cultivation would be rendered desert and useless. VII. VIII.

CALAMAGROSTIS, *Adans.*

878. **C. epigeios**, *Roth.*

Native; in thickets and shady places, very rare.

S. Border of Bishop's Wood, Wells; *Miss Livett.* By the roadside between the Monument and Tracy Park; *Fl. Bathon.* It has been reported to grow also at Clevedon, Hutton, and elsewhere, but upon insufficient authority. VII.

AGROSTIS, *Linn.*

879. **A. canina**, *L.*

Native; on downs, heaths, and commons, frequent.

G. Clifton Down. Filton. Mangotsfield Common. Stapleton. Yate Common.

S. Backwell. Blackdown on Mendip. Upper Knowle. Dundry Hill. Leigh Down. VII. VIII.

880. **A. vulgaris**, *With.*

Native; on banks and in dry pastures, very common.
VI. VII.

881. A. alba, *L.*

Native; in marshes and damp pastures everywhere. The var. β *stolonifera* has been gathered on sea-sand at Burnham and Weston-super-Mare, and on mud in the New Cut by Bathurst Wharf. VII.

POLYPOGON, *Desf.*

882. P. monspeliensis, *Desf.*

Alien. Until a few years ago this beautiful grass was connected with the Bristol Flora solely through a communication ("Near Bristol") made by Miss Alice Worsley (afterwards Mrs. Russell) to Mr. Hewett Watson, and published in the *New Botanists' Guide*, 1835. In 1883 it was found growing luxuriantly upon the material dredged from the bed of the Avon and from the basins, which had been placed the year before in a river-side quarry. It has continued there to the present time. Although the circumstances under which it was gathered by Miss Worsley are unknown, the recurrence of this species on the bank of the river goes toward showing that it may formerly have been an inhabitant of the Avon valley.

883. P. littoralis, *Sm.*

Possibly native in St. Philip's Marsh, G., where we have known it many years.

In weighing the claim of this plant to be indigenous in a locality where the original soil is in process of conversion into bricks and pottery, and of replacement by mounds of ashes, rubbish, and refuse of all sorts, it should be borne in mind that, in its primitive condition, St. Philip's Marsh undoubtedly was a fitting station for the species under notice, which in this country grows only near the sea or in marshes washed by tidal rivers. Unhappily, our interest in the question whether *P. littoralis* truly belongs to the aboriginal Bristol Flora is overborne by the certainty that in a little while it will exist only in our herbaria.

GASTRIDIUM, *Pal. de Beauv.*

884. **G. lendigerum,** *Gaud.*

Native; scattered over a very small area on the Gloucestershire bank of the Avon, below Bristol. There is little doubt that all the published records of the occurrence of this grass on St. Vincent's Rocks, Durdham Down, and the bank of Avon, may be referred to the same small tract of limestone upon which it now grows; although its extent is less than it was formerly. Mr. T. B. Flower tells us that he used to find it behind the New Hotwell House, long since removed. That spot is situate on the river-bank, some distance from the present station for the plant. VII. VIII.

HOLCUS, *Linn.*

885. **H. lanatus,** *L.*

Native; in meadows, pastures, hedge-banks, and waste places. Very common and universally distributed. VI. VII.

886. **H. mollis,** *L.*

Native; in woods, hedge-banks, and pastures, very much less common than the preceding species.
VI. VII.

AIRA, *Linn.*

887. A. cæspitosa, *L.*

Native; in moist woods and damp hedges. Common and abundant in suitable positions.

We have observed the var. *brevifolia* in Leigh Woods.

VII.

888. A. flexuosa, *L.*

Native; on heaths, banks, and dry open spaces in woods, frequent.

G. Berkeley. Dursley. Conham, and Trooper's Hill; *Herb. Stephens.* Glen Frome. Stapleton. Mangotsfield. Sodbury. Wotton-under-Edge.

S. Lane between Abbot's Leigh and the Tanpits. Hedge-banks between Portbury and Tickenham, and on the high ground near Wraxall. Court Hill and Norton Wood, Clevedon. Blackdown on Mendip. On Lansdown, near Bath. In several places near Wells. VII.

889. A. caryophyllea, *L.*

Native; in dry places, rare.

G. Almondsbury. On the pennant at Conham.

S. Abundant on Leigh Down. Brean Down. Near Keynsham. V.

890. A. præcox, *L.*

Native; on dry, rocky, or sandy soil, chiefly on the coal measures, frequent.

G. Brandon Hill, still in plenty. On Durdham Down, sparingly. Mangotsfield Common. Conham; *Mr. W. E. Green.* Yate Common.

S. Between Brislington and Keynsham, plentiful. On the Court and Strawberry Hills, and in other spots about Clevedon, apparently confined to the pennant formation; *Mr. D. Fry.* IV. V.

TRISETUM, *Pers.*

891. T. flavescens, *Beauv.*
Native; in meadows and dry places, very common.
VII.

AVENA, *Linn.*

892. A. fatua, *L. Wild Oat.*
Colonist; on the borders of cultivated fields and among the crops, rather rare.
G. Henbury. Horfield. Fishponds.
S. Near Abbot's Leigh. Portishead. Plentiful in fields on the coast near Woodspring, 1883 and 1885. Occasionally near Wells; *Miss Livett*. Weston-super-Mare. Frequent about Bath; *Fl. Bathon.* VII.

893. A. pratensis, *L.*
Native; on limestone hills and banks, frequent.
G. In plenty on Clifton and Durdham Downs. Kingsweston Down. Stinchcombe Hill. Nibley Knoll.
S. Brean Down. Leigh Down. Common on the Mendip Hills, as at Winterhead, Shipham, and Cheddar. Hilly pastures near Bath. VI. VII.

894. A. pubescens, *L.*
Native; on downs, dry hills, and sometimes in meadows. Much more common than the last, and not so strictly confined to the carboniferous limestone strata, although showing a decided preference for that formation.
G. St. Vincent's Rocks. Clifton and Durdham Downs. Henbury. Sodbury. Wotton-under-Edge and Nibley Knoll. Wyck. Yate.
S. Leigh Down. Bedminster Down. Brean Down.

In pastures at Whitchurch. Pastures between Bedminster and Bourton, and in the railway cutting. Frequent at Clevedon. Keynsham. Wraxall. Cranmore and Milton Hill, Wells. Hilly pastures near Bath. VI.

ARRHENATHERUM, *Pal. de Beauv.*

895. **A. elatius,** *M. & K.* Oat-grass.

Native; in hedges, pastures and cultivated fields. Very common, and generally distributed.

The *var. β nodosum*, with the base of the stem enlarged into a string of bulb-like knobs, is very abundant, especially in cultivated ground. VI. VII.

TRIODIA, *R. Br.*

896. **T. decumbens,** *Beauv.*

Native; on downs, heaths, and dry hills, rare and local.

G. Clifton and Durdham Downs. Yate Common.

S. Leigh Down. Pasture near Brislington. On the Mendips above Draycot. Near Claverton, *Fl. Bathon.* Dulcote Hill, Wells. VI. VII.

KŒLERIA, *Pers.*

897. **K. cristata,** *Pers.*

Native; on downs and dry banks, rather common.

G. Very abundant nearly over the whole of Clifton and Durdham Downs, particularly near the river. St. Vincent's Rocks. Wyck Rocks.

S. Leigh Down. Brean Down. Upper Knowle Clevedon, abundantly. On the hill-side at Weston-super-Mare. Cheddar. Shipham. Winterhead.

VI. VII.

MELICA, Linn.

898. M. uniflora, Retz.

Native; in woods and shady places, common.

G. Berkeley. Dursley. Wotton-under-Edge. Tortworth. Cook's Folly Wood. Blaise Castle Wood. Sea Mills.

S. Leigh Wood. St. Ann's Wood, Brislington Bishport. Barrow Gurney. Clevedon. Congresbury. Portbury. Portishead. Weston-in-Gordano. Wells. V. VI.

MOLINIA, Schrank.

899. M. cœrulea, Moench.

Native; on wet heaths and commons, rare and local.

G. Yate Common. Specimens in the Stephens Herbarium show that it formerly grew on Durdham Down, where it is no longer to be found.

S. Abundant on the Mendip Hills, at Blackdown, and about the Mineries. VII. VIII.

POA, Linn.

900. P. annua, L.

Native; very common everywhere. III.—IX.

901. P. nemoralis, L.

Native; in woods and hedges, frequent.

G. St. Vincent's Rocks. Blaise Castle Wood. Stoke Lane, Stapleton. Copse between Horfield and Filton. Bitton. Westbury-on-Trym.

S. Leigh Woods. Brislington. Flax Bourton. Portishead. Walton-in-Gordano. Wells. VI. VII.

902. P. trivialis, L.

Native; in meadows, pastures, and waste places, very common and generally distributed. VI.

GRAMINEÆ.

903. P. pratensis, *L.*

Native; in meadows, pastures, and waste places, very common and generally distributed.

The *var. β subcœrulea* is the common grass of wall tops in the vicinity of Bristol.   VI. VII.

904. P. compressa, *L.*

Native; on dry banks and walls, chiefly by the tidal Avon, rather rare.

G.   Bank of Avon at intervals from Sea Mills to the Suspension Bridge.

S.   Bank of Avon under Leigh Wood. Bedminster. Clevedon.

The wall-top variety of *P. pratensis* is sometimes reported for this species.   VII.

GLYCERIA, *R. Br.*

905. G. aquatica, *Sm.*

Native; in ditches, rivers, and ponds. Common and abundant in the marshy lowlands of North Somerset.

G.   Bank of Avon above Bristol at Conham. Pilning. Littleton-on-Severn.

S.   Bank of Avon at St. Ann's, Brislington. Canal at Radford. Marsh ditches throughout the Cheddar Valley to Brent, Burnham, and Highbridge.   VII.

906. G. fluitans, *R. Br.*

Native; in water, very common.   VI.—VIII.

SCLEROCHLOA, *Beauv.*

907. S. maritima, *Lindl.*

Native; in salt marshes and on the muddy banks of

tidal rivers, and inlets from the Channel. Abundant in the mud on both sides of the Avon.

VI. VII.

908. **S. procumbens,** *Beauv.*

Native; on waste ground near the banks of the tidal Avon, very local.

G. St. Philip's Marsh. New Cut, by the General Hospital. Hotwells. Bank of the river under the Downs, and here and there as far as Shirehampton. Abundant on dredgings deposited in the Black Rock Quarry, 1883 and 1884.

S. Bank of the river at Rownham. VI. VII.

909. **S. distans,** *Bab.*

Native; in damp waste places by tidal water, local.

G. In many places near the Avon, from St. Philip's Marsh to Shirehampton.

S. Similarly by the New Cut, and at Rownham Ferry. Burnham. VI.—VIII.

910. **S. rigida,** *Link.*

Native; on and under old walls, and in other dry places. Very common. VI. VII.

911. **S. loliacea,** *Woods.*

Native; in one or two spots near the Bristol Channel, very rare.

S. Sparingly on the hill-side near the pier at Birnbeck, Weston-super-Mare. Burnham; *Miss. Livett.*

BRIZA, *Linn.*

912. **B. media,** *L. Quaking Grass.*

Native; in meadows and dry pastures, very common.

VI.

(*B. minor,* L. There is a specimen in the herbarium

of the Bristol Naturalists' Society, stated to have been collected on St. Vincent's Rocks by Dr. Dyer. It was doubtless a casual introduction.)

CATABROSA, *Pal de Beauv.*

913. **C. aquatica,** *Beauv.*

Native; in ponds and ditches, frequent.

G. Alveston. Berkeley. Bank of Avon above Bristol. Hallen. Henbury. Filton Meads. Pools about Horfield Common. Edges of ponds near Chipping Sodbury and Yate. Siston.

S. Meadows by Lock's Mills. Ditches at Portbury and towards Portishead. Nailsea. Yatton. Marsh ditches and ponds near Woodborough and in the Cheddar Valley. Pools on Mendip near the Mineries. Peat-moors below Wedmore. Common near Bath; *Fl. Bathon.* VI. VII.

CYNOSURUS, *Linn.*

914. **C. cristatus,** *L.* *Dog's-tail Grass.*

Native; in meadows and pastures. Very common and generally distributed. VII. VIII.

DACTYLIS, *Linn.*

915. **D. glomerata,** *L.* *Cock's-foot Grass.*

Native; in meadows and pastures. Very common and generally distributed. VI. VII.

FESTUCA, *Linn.*

916. **F. uniglumis,** *Sol.*

Native; on sea-sands, very local.

S. Abundant on dunes and among loose sand on the Channel shore above Burnham. VI.

917. **F. sciuroïdes,** *Roth.*

Native; on dry banks and waste sandy places, showing a partiality for the pennant formation. Frequent.

G. On banks about Clifton and Durdham Downs. Dry places on the bank of Avon under the Downs. Brandon Hill. On quays by Cumberland Basin Plentiful on rubble about the pennant quarries in Glen Frome. Troopers' Hill, by Crew's Hole. Mangotsfield. Pucklechurch.

S. Dry places on the bank of Avon below Bristol. On walls and dry rocky banks at Clevedon; *Mr. D. Fry.* Between Brislington and Keynsham, on coal-measures. On the hill at Weston-super-Mare.

VI. VII.

918. **F. Pseudo-Myurus,** *Soyer.*

Native; on dry waste ground, rare.

G. In plenty at the foot of the rocks under Durdham Down. On the mounds of scoriæ, Crew's Hole. On old colliery *débris* near Warmley. Stapleton; *Herb. Stephens.* Near Mount's Hill, Kingswood; *Dr. Hassé.* Sparingly on a rocky bank close to Thornbury station, June, 1884. Wyck Rocks; *Add. Fl. Bathon.*

S. About the quarries on the bank of Avon, under Leigh Wood. Stockwood; *Herb. Stephens.*

VI. VII.

919. **F. ovina,** *L.*

Native; in dry pastures, commons and banks, common.

VI.

920. **F. rubra,** *L.*

Native; on the Downs, banks, and dry pastures, common.

VI.

921. **F. oraria,** *Dum.*

Native. Mr. J. G. Baker has considered some plants gathered on the bank of Avon, in Ashton Fields, S., to be the *F. subulicola* of Leon Dufour and other botanists; *Swete, Fl.* 92. As this Festuca is generally distributed on European sea-coasts, it is highly probable that we shall also find it among the sand dunes between Burnham and Brean.

922. **F. gigantea,** *Vill.*

Native; in woods and hedges, rather common.
G. Clifton Down. Shady banks of the Frome, near Stapleton. Filton. Henbury. Copse near New Passage. Between Thornbury and Littleton-on-Severn. Tortworth. Wotton-under-Edge.
S. Thickets on Bedminster Down. St. Ann's Wood, Brislington. Between Abbot's Leigh and the Tanpits. Flax Bourton. Clapton. Congresbury. Abundant about Clevedon. Walton-in-Gordano. Wrington. Frequent near Wells. In woods and hedges near Bath, plentiful. VII.

923. **F. elatior,** *Sm.*

Native; in meadows and by the sides of ditches and streams, especially near the coast. Rather common.
G. Marsh under Ashley Hill. Bank of Avon at Hanham and Conham, and again below Bristol, plentiful. Sodbury. Stapleton. Tortworth. Pilning. The Passages.
S. Bank of Avon near Keynsham, and it grows in very large tufts on the edge of the tideway below Bristol. Ken. Yatton. Wells. Frequent on ditch-banks in the lowlands about Brent, Burnham, and Highbridge. VI. VII.

924. F. pratensis, *Huds.*

Native; in damp rich meadows, by no means common close to the city. We have observed it in Ashton Fields; in meadows above Sea Mills; at Long Ashton; Brislington; and on the slopes of Macs Knoll. At a greater distance it becomes frequent in grass-fields. The var. β *loliacea* has been noticed between Redland and Horfield, and at Henbury, in the northern division of the district. In Somerset we have it recorded from Bedminster, Bishport, Brislington, and Portishead.   VI. VII.

BROMUS, *Linn.*

925. B. erectus, *Huds.*

Native; on downs and dry banks, in pastures and by roadsides. Common.

G. Abundant on Durdham Down and the slopes of the Gully. St. Vincent's Rocks. On the railway embankment between Sea Mills and Shirehampton. Rough pastures between Horfield Common and Filton Meads. Henbury. In profusion on the slopes of Nibley Knoll, and on the other hills in the same neighbourhood. Pucklechurch. Westbury-on-Trym.

S. Leigh Down. Bedminster Down. Borders of fields near Abbotsleigh. Very abundant on roadsides between Upper Failand, Wraxall, and Tickenham. At Upper Knowle, and between Knowle and Brislington; flourishing both among the mowing grasses and also upon the old stone walls. Abundant in a hilly field at Keynsham; *Mr. D. Fry.* Near Park Farm, Clevedon; also on the coast towards Portishead. Great Elm. Wells.   VI. VII.

Var. β *villosus.* Combe Hay, near Bath; *Syme, E.B.* Easton, *Miss Livett.*

926. **B. asper,** *Murray.*
Native; in woods, thickets, and damp shady hedges. Rather common and generally distributed. VII.

927. **B. sterilis,** *Linn.*
Native; on old walls, roadsides, and dry, waste places, very common. VI.

928. **B. madritensis,** *L. a. B. diandrus,* Curtis.
Native; on banks, and rocky slopes near the Avon, below Bristol. Only upon the carboniferous limestone; very local, but fairly abundant.
G. On St. Vincent's Rocks, and scattered along the Downs and at the foot of the quarries as far as the Sea Wall.
S. Bank of Avon under Leigh Wood, exactly opposite to the Gloucestershire station. VI. VII.

SERRAFALCUS, *Parlatore.*

929. **S. secalinus,** *Bab.*
Casual; on the quays, in waste places, and as a weed on cultivated ground, rather rare.
G. St. Philip's Marsh. Bank of Avon. Sneyd Park. On dredgings deposited in the Black Rock Quarry.
S. Railway embankment near Hallatrow. Roadside at Woodborough. VI. VII.

930. **S. racemosus,** *Parl.*
Native; in meadows and pastures, common. VI.

931. **S. commutatus,** *Bab.*

Native; in dry pastures and cultivated ground, and by roadsides. Not so common as the last species.

VI. VII.

932. **S. mollis,** *Parl.*

Native; in meadows, pastures, and waste places. Very common, and generally distributed. V. VI.

933. **S. arvensis,** *Godr.*

Casual or Colonist; on cultivated ground and waste places, rather rare.

G. Bank of Avon, under the Downs. On the quays, near Prince Street. On old colliery *débris*, near Warmley. Hanham. On dredgings deposited in the Black Rock Quarry, 1883 and 1884.

S. In clover-fields at Whitchurch; *Rev. W. H. Painter.* Cornfield between Bedminster and Bishport. VII.

BRACHYPODIUM, *Pal. de Beauv.*

934. **B. sylvaticum,** *R. & S.*

Native; in woods and hedges. Very common and abundant. VII.

935. **B. pinnatum,** *Beauv.*

Native; on limestone hills, rare.

G. Abundant on Stinchcomb Hill. Gorge near Black Rock; *Herb. Stephens.* In addition to the specimens in the Stephens Herbarium, there is plenty of evidence that this grass formerly grew on rocky slopes above the Avon, towards the Sea Wall. We have searched for it frequently without success.

S. Abundant at the Fir-wood and Strawberry Hill. Clevedon. In plenty on Crook's Peak. At Charlcombe; *Fl. Bathon.* VII.

The plant occurs in large patches of a bright yellowish green colour. This brilliant tint contrasts strongly with the brownish hue of the turf around, and renders the spots conspicuous at a long distance.

TRITICUM, *Linn.*

936. T. caninum, *Huds.*

Native; in thickets and woods, rather rare.

G. Sparingly in thickets on Clifton Down. Combe Dingle. Henbury. Bitton. Stapleton. Alveston; *Herb. Powell.*

S. Brislington. King's Wood, near Yatton. Portishead. Woods at Walton-in-Gordano. Wookey Hole and Ebbor Rocks; *Mr. J. G. Baker.* Frequent near Frome; *Dr. Parsons.* VII.

937. T. repens, *L. Couch Grass.*

Native; in cultivated ground and waste places. Common and generally distributed.

The awned variety, β *barbatum,* has been remarked on ditch-banks at Portbury, at Congresbury, and elsewhere. VI.—VIII.

938. T. pungens, *Pers.*

Native; on the banks of tidal rivers, and in muddy waste places near the Channel. Locally common. The forms *littorale* and *pycnanthum* are well represented by the Avon estuary below Bristol.

VII. VIII.

939. T. acutum, *D. C. T. laxum,* Fries.

Native; specimens gathered by Miss Atwood on the banks of the river Avon were authenticated by Mr. Baker. *Swete, Fl.* 94. We cannot find it; but the plant is so generally distributed in maritime districts that we see no reason to doubt that it exists upon our extensive coast-line, although it may no longer grow where Miss Atwood detected it.   VII. VIII.

940. T. junceum, *L.*

Native; on the coast sands of North Somerset at Burnham, Brean, and Kewstoke, locally common.

VI. VII.

ELYMUS, *Linn.*

941. E. arenarius, *L.*

Native; formerly on the shore of the Bristol Channel near Burnham, and elsewhere; probably extinct.

S. "Burnham, Berrow, and Steart, *J. C. Collins' MSS.*" *New Bot. Guide.* In August, 1880, we found a small quantity in a cove on the coast near Woodspring Priory. The plant grew in a patch of about two square yards on the shingle above high-water mark. At that date the flowering-stems were, many of them, four feet or more high, and bore spikes nearly a foot long. We saw it again in 1881, but on the next visit, in 1884, there was none remaining. Cattle from an adjoining pasture had made their way down the low cliff at the back, and were seemingly answerable for the destruction, by having trampled a path over the spot.

HORDEUM, *Linn.*

942. H. pratense, *Huds.* *Meadow Barley.*

Native; in moist meadows and grass-fields, common. Extremely abundant in the lowland pastures near the Severn and Bristol Channel, forming a very considerable portion of the crop.

G. Alveston. Berkeley. Dursley. Charfield. Littleton-on-Severn. Queen Charlton. Henbury. Pucklechurch, in great abundance. Pilning. The Passages. Shirehampton.

S. Bedminster Meads. Bishport. Long Ashton. Nailsea. Wells. Yatton. Plentiful in maritime pastures towards Brean, Burnham, and Highbridge.

VII. VIII.

943. H. murinum, *L.*

Native; by roadsides, and in dry, waste places, common. VI. VII.

944. H. maritimum, *Withering.*

Native; in salt marshes and in sandy places near tidal water. Rather rare.

G. Bank of Avon, below Bristol, from Sea Mills to Avonmouth. Here and there between Avonmouth and New Passage.

S. Coast sands above Burnham. VI.

LEPTURUS, *R. Br.*

945. L. filiformis, *Trin.*

Native; in maritime pastures and on ditch-banks in salt marshes; sometimes fringing the edges of the muddy estuaries. Common in such situations.

G. New Cut, near the Hospital. Plentiful on the verge of the mud-banks near Rownham Ferry. Bank of Avon below the Suspension Bridge at intervals down to the mouth of the river. Shirehampton Marshes.

S. Bank of Avon at Rownham. In fair quantity on the mud-flats outside the sea-bank below Clevedon; *Mr. D. Fry.* Sands west of Weston-super-Mare.

Marshy sands near Berrow. Ditch-banks and salt marshes between Burnham and Highbridge, on the banks of the Brue. VII. VIII.

LOLIUM, Linn.

946. **L. perenne,** *L. Rye Grass.*
Native; in meadows and pastures, and by roadsides; very common and generally distributed.
A very curious form, assuming a stoloniferous habit, grows in sea-sand at Kewstoke, and also at Burnham. VI.

947. **L. italicum,** *A. Braun.*
Alien. Half naturalised. Introduced by cultivation, Common among mowing-grass, by roadsides, and in waste places. VI.

948. **L. temulentum,** *L.*
Casual or Colonist; in cultivated fields and waste places, rare.
G. Prince Street, Bristol. Roadside at Sneyd Park. Cornfields, Alveston; *Herb. Powell.*
S. In a barley-field near Nailsea, 1880. Roadside at Ken, 1881. In several cornfields near Bath; *Mr. T. B. Flower.* VII. VIII.

PHANEROGAMIA.

Class 3. GYMNOSPERMÆ.

CONIFERÆ.

TAXUS, *Linn.*

949. **T. baccata,** *L.* Yew.

> Native; in nearly all old woods upon the carboniferous limestone. Locally common.
>
> It is very abundant in Leigh Woods, and about the rocky combes and hills at Brockley, Cleeve, and Congresbury. There are some especially fine trees in the churchyard at West Harptree, and in the villages of Churchill and Compton Martin; but perhaps the finest and most perfect yew grows in Winscombe churchyard, where its sheltered position has preserved it from the shattering storms of centuries. A larger and more ancient tree is enclosed in the vicarage grounds. These trees may have been planted when Winscombe manor was a possession of Glastonbury Abbey.　　　III. IV.

JUNIPERUS, *Linn.*

950. **J. communis,** *L.* *Juniper.*

> Native; abundant on some hill-sides east of Bath; on the extreme border of our district. Dr. St. Brody, in his *Flora of Weston,* gives a locality near Uphill, which has not been confirmed.　　　V.

CRYPTOGAMIA.

EQUISETACEÆ.

EQUISETUM, *Linn.*

951. E. arvense, *L.*
Native; in damp fields and on banks and roadsides, very common.   IV.

952. E. maximum, *Lam.*
Native; in wet places in woods, ditches, and hedges, frequent.
G. Ashley Hill and Baptist Mills. Hedge-banks between Eastfield and Filton. Queen Charlton. Westbury-on-Trym.
S. Wet hollow in Leigh Wood near Rownham Ferry. Lane on Maes Knoll. Chew Magna. Clevedon. Kewstoke. Woodspring. Woodborough. Yatton.
We have two specimens of the fertile stem, in which the terminal cone has its upper half divided, one into five and the other into eight, erect branches.
    IV.

953. E. limosum, *L.*
Native; in stagnant water, ditches, and swamps, frequent.
G. Between Thornbury and Littleton-on-Severn. Horfield.
S. Pond near the lodge in Leigh Woods; *Herb. Stephens.* Bedminster Meads. Abundant below the reservoirs of the Bristol Water Company under Dundry Hill, 1881. Walton Drove, Clevedon. Very plentiful in marsh ditches about Draycot and else-

where in the Cheddar Valley. Yatton. In the canal by Bath; *Add. Fl. Bathon.* VI. VII.

954. E. palustre, *L.*

Native; in marshes, swamps, and ditch-banks, frequent.

G. Marsh at the Boiling Well. Filton Meads.

S. By the Abbot's Pond, near Abbot's Leigh. Bedminster Meads. Clevedon. Winscombe. Yatton. Abundant on ditch-banks between Brean and Berrow. Frequent in boggy places; *Fl. Bathon.*

VI. VII.

FILICES.

POLYPODIUM, *Linn.*

955. P. vulgare, *L. Common Polypody.*

Native; on shady banks, walls, and old trees, very common. Pinnæ occasionally bifid at the end, sometimes serrate or even (*P. cambricum,* L.) doubly pinnatifid. VIII.—X.

956. P. Phegopteris, *L. Beech Fern.*

Native; in a damp, mossy dell near Wells, S., where we saw a patch extending some yards, in 1883 and 1884. VII.—IX.

957. P. Dryopteris, *L. Oak Fern.*

S. In Leigh Wood, rare. *Shiercliff's Guide,* 1789.

Leigh Wood, sparingly, 1839. *Mr. T. B. Flower.*

In conversation Mr. Flower has explained to us that this fern formerly grew with others in a damp, boggy hollow near Rownham. We know the place very well; but the ferns are not there now.

958. **P. Robertianum,** *Hoffm.* *Limestone Polypody.*
   Native; on limestone, rare and local.
   In Leigh Wood, rare. *Shiercliff's Guide,* 1789. We understand that before the construction of the Suspension Bridge and its approaches, the high ground on the Leigh side, above Nightingale Valley, was covered with heath, sand, and loose stones; and that *P. Robertianum* grew among the latter. Plentiful at Cheddar. Brockley. Burrington. Cleeve. Ebbor Gorge; *Miss Livett.* V. VIII.

LASTRÆA, *Presl.*

959. **L. Thelypteris,** *Presl.* *Marsh Fern.*
   Native; in wet peat bogs, very local.
   S. Once seen in a boggy spot between Portishead and Clevedon; *Mr. R. V. Sherring.* Abundant on the peat-moors at the southern limit of the district. VII. VIII.

960. **L. Oreopteris,** *Presl.* *Sweet Mountain Fern.*
   Native; in woods and about heaths and commons, rather rare.
   G. Conham; *Herb. Stephens.* Henbury; *Herb. Powell.*
   S. Sparingly in Leigh Wood; *Mr. S. Rootsey; Dr. Thwaites;* and *Mr. T. B. Flower.* Ashton Manor Woods; *Miss Atwood; Swete, Fl.* 96. Portbury. Two or three plants in Norton's Wood, by Clevedon; *Mr. R. V. Sherring.* A great many in a small combe between Cleeve and Brockley. In some of the combes of Blackdown. On Mendip near Cranmore Tower, where the old red sandstone occurs; *Dr. H. F. Parsons.* VII.

961. L. Filix-mas, *Presl.* *Male Fern.*
Native; in woods and on hedge-banks, common.
VI. VII.

962. L. spinulosa, *Presl.*
Native; in wet thickets and bogs, rare.
S. Between the hummocks in boggy ground on Mendip, near the Mineries. Leigh Wood, 1881; *Rev. W. H. Painter.* Peat-moors in the extreme south. VIII. IX.

963. L. dilatata, *Presl.*
Native; in woods and thickets, rather common.
VIII. IX.

POLYSTICHUM, *Roth.*

964. P. aculeatum, *Roth.*
Native; on hedge-banks and in woods. Frequent, but no longer to be found in some of the recorded stations.
G. Blaise Castle Woods; *Herb. Powell.* Hanham and Bitton; *Mr. T. B. Flower.* Stapleton Wood; and hedges near the Zoological Gardens, Clifton; *Swete, Fl. 96.*
S. Leigh Woods; St. Anne's Wood; Kelston and Claverton; *Mr. T. B. Flower.* Dundry Hill; *Herb. Stephens.* Hallatrow. Portishead. Damp hedge-banks close to the village of Compton Martin. Lanes near Great Elm.
Var. β *Aspidium lobatum,* Sw.
G. Blaise Castle Woods; *Herb. Powell.* Shirehampton; *Mr. T. B. Flower.*
S. Sparingly in Leigh Woods; at Bourton and on Dundry Down; *Dr. Thwaites.* In several places

near Bath; *Mr. T. B. Flower.* Clevedon; *Mr. W. E. Green.* Upper end of Cheddar Gorge.

VII. VIII.

The form or variety *lobatum* is unsatisfactory, inasmuch as it graduates imperceptibly into the type, and *vice versâ*. Our account is substantially correct; all doubtful plants being referred to *aculeatum*.

965. **P. angulare,** *Newman.*

Native; on very shady hedge-banks and in woods. Not at all common near Bristol.

G. Dursley. Frenchay. Tortworth. Wotton-under-Edge. Stapleton Woods; *Swete, Fl.* 96.

S. Leigh Wood. Wood by the river Avon between Pill and Ham Green. Hedges in Upper Failand. Macs Knoll. Banwell. Churchill. Clevedon. Clapton. Great Elm. Beechen Cliff, and wood on Lansdown; *Mr. T. B. Flower.* VII. VIII.

CYSTOPTERIS, *Bernh.*

966. **C. fragilis,** *Bernh. Bladder Fern.*

Native; on rocks and walls, showing a great partiality for the carboniferous limestone.

G. A few plants on a wall at North Stoke, 1878.

S. Nightingale Valley, Leigh Woods; *Herb. Stephens.* Dr. Stephens' specimens are very fine. Recorded from the same locality by Mr. Leo. H. Grindon, and by Dr. Thwaites, about 1840. The latter botanist sent examples from Nightingale Valley to the London Botanical Society, a fact which leads us to suppose that the fern was then plentiful. At the present time we much doubt if a single plant

exists in Leigh Woods. On Dundry Hill, still plentiful. Under fir trees near Brockley, many very large plants. Burrington Combe. Cheddar Cliffs, on both sides of the gorge. In crannies of the water-worn rocks on Mendip above Draycot. Abundant on damp hedge-banks under Dolbery Camp. Of very fine growth in East Harptree Combe. On walls at Chewton Mendip; Gurney Slade; Litton and Stone Easton. Ebbor. Emborrow. Dulcote Hill, near Wells. On walls near the Mineries on Mendip. Stanton Drew. Yatton.
VII. VIII.

ATHYRIUM, *Roth.*

967. **A. Filix-fœmina,** *Roth.*   *Lady Fern.*

Native; in damp, shady places, frequent.

G.   Almondsbury. Pucklechurch. Tortworth. Wood near Stapleton.

S.   Several localities in Leigh Woods, and between Abbot's Leigh and Failand. Axbridge. Bourton Combe. Brockley Combe. Norton Wood, Clevedon. Wood between Temple Cloud and Clutton; *Mr. D. Fry.* Sidcot. Frequent near Wells. In several woods near Bath.   VI. VII.

ASPLENIUM, *Linn.*

968. **A. lanceolatum,** *Huds.*

Native; on sandstone rocks, very rare.

G.   Frome Glen, Stapleton; *Herb. Stephens.* Oldbury Court Woods, and lanes about Stapleton; *Swete, Fl.* 97.

These records relate to one and the same locality, where the plant was discovered by Mr. J. W.

Ewing, of Norwich, who sojourned in Bristol about 1830. See note by Dr. Thwaites in the *Phytologist*, I. 75. Swete (*Fl.* 97) writes that at his date its area was "not more than half a mile," implying that it occurred over a considerable space, which is to some extent confirmed by Dr. Thwaites, *loc. cit.* Undoubtedly the fern has shared the fate allotted by collectors to all good things; for the late Mr. W. W. Stoddart spoke of it ten years ago as being only obtainable with the aid of a quarryman and a rope, and other information is to the same effect.

969. **A. Adiantum-nigrum,** *L.*   *Black Spleenwort.*
Native; on walls and rocks, and occasionally on hedge-banks, frequent.
G. Henbury Combe. Almondsbury. Anst. Tortworth. Wickwar.
S. Abbot's Leigh. Failand. Clevedon. Chew Magna. On rocks at Brean Down. Cheddar Cliffs. South Stoke. Sandford. Shipham. Rarely near Wells. Walton-in-Gordano. Weston-in-Gordano. Near Yatton.   VI.—IX.

970. **A. Trichomanes,** *L.*   *Common Spleenwort.*
Native; on walls and rocks, frequent.
G. Frampton. Kingswood. Stoke Gifford. Westbury-on-Trym.
S. Rocks in Leigh Woods. Old walls at Long Ashton. Clapton. Tickenham. Walton-in-Gordano. Shipham. Stanton Drew. On Mendip above Axbridge, Draycot, and Cheddar. Old mine shaft on Dolbery Camp. In all the parishes at the back of the Mendips. Wells. Frequent about Bath.   V.—X.

971. **A. marinum,** *L.*

    Native; in the crevices of rocks on the coast of North Somerset, very rare.

    S. Between Portishead and Clevedon; *Herb. Stephens.* It grows on rocks at Walton-in-Gordano, and between there and Portishead. Sparingly on rocks at Brean Down; *Mr. T. F. Perkins,* 1881.

972. **A. Ruta-muraria,** *L.*   *Wall Rue.*

    Native; on rocks and old walls, very common. It may often be seen in the older parts of Clifton; as underneath Royal York Crescent, and on Richmond Terrace.   V.—IX

SCOLOPENDRIUM, *Sm.*

973. **S. vulgare,** *Sym.*   *Hart's-tongue.*

    Native; in damp, shady places, common. We have seen plants bearing fronds bifid, crisped, or contorted in various ways.   VII. VIII

CETERACH, *Willd.*

974. **C. officinarum,** *Willd.*   *Rustyback.*

    Native; on old walls, rocks, and banks, common. Very abundant about Bristol, and one of the prettiest ornaments of our limestone walls.

    G. In plenty at Almondsbury. Rocks at Penpole Point. Frenchay. Thornbury. Westbury-on-Trym.

    S. Limestone rocks in Leigh Woods. Old walls at Long Ashton. Flax Bourton. Banwell. Congresbury. Churchill. Clevedon. On Mendip at Cheddar and Draycot. Downside. Compton Martin. Tickenham. Stanton Drew. Stone Easton. Walls

about Pill and Ham Green. Rocks at Brean Down.
Wells. Winscombe. Yatton. Abundant in all
the parishes at the back of the Mendips. Frequent
on walls near Bath. IV.—IX.

BLECHNUM, *Linn.*

975. **B. boreale,** *Sw.* *Hard Fern.*

Native; in woods and on commons, rather rare.
Nearly absent from the neighbourhood of Bristol,
and, in common with all other ferns, much reduced
in quantity by the ravages of itinerant street
hawkers, who bring the roots into Bristol for sale.

G. Wyck. Yate Common.

S. Still plentiful in some of the preserved portions
of Leigh Wood. Formerly in St. Anne's Wood,
Brislington. Blackdown. Sparingly in Cleeve
Combe. Norton Wood, Clevedon. Sparingly near
Wells. Near Yatton. VII. VIII.

PTERIS, *Linn.*

976. **P. aquilina,** *L.* *Brakes or Bracken.*

Native; in woods, and on heaths and commons. Very
common, except in the alluvial lowlands.
VII. VIII.

(*Adiantum Capillus-Veneris*, L. We have come across
several accounts of the capture of maiden-hair
ferns in various localities in the vicinity of Bristol
and we give them for what they are worth.

" Under a bridge at Compton Dando, S., where it has
been known some years."

" At the mouth of an old well near Clevedon";
quoted in *Cyb. Brit.*, vol. iii.

"Three plants, growing in the air-shaft of a stone quarry some thirty feet below the ground, at Combe Down, near Bath," 1853. *E. J. Lowe; Phytol.* iv. 1100.

"In the year 1851 I found a plant or two of it on moist rocks in the neighbourhood of Cheddar, in an out-of-the-way situation, and left the roots uninjured." *W. H. Hawker; Phytol.* v. 82.)

(*Hymenophyllum tunbridgense*, Sm. In a shady lane near Shepton Mallet; *Sole, MS.* 1782. Not confirmed.)

OSMUNDA, *Linn.*

977. **O. regalis**, *L. Royal or Flowering Fern.*
Native; in peat bogs and swamps, very rare.
S. An old publication (*West of Engl. Journ. of Science and Literature*) states that it formerly grew in Leigh Woods. Formerly in a wet copse on Walton Moor; now extinct. On the Burtle turf moor, north of the railway, July, 1881. At one time it extended north as far as Wedmore; but is now chiefly confined to the southern turf moors outside the district. VII. VIII.

BOTRYCHIUM, *Sw.*

978. **B. lunaria**, *Sw. Moon Wort.*
Native; on downs and hilly pastures, rare.
G. Kingsweston Hill; *Miss Powell, Swete, Fl.* 98. Penpole Point; *Mr. W. W. Stoddart.*
S. Clevedon; *Mr. E. Green.* By Walton Castle, Clevedon; *Mr. T. B. Flower.* Callow Hill, near Sidcot; *Herb. Stephens.* On the hills about Wins-

combe. One plant in a field on Tining's Farm, near Cheddar, with *Vicia Orobus;* June 27, 1883. Between Claverton and Bath; *Add. Fl. Bathon.* Pen Hill, near Wells. V.—VII.

OPHIOGLOSSUM, *Linn.*

979. **O. vulgatum**, *L. Adder's Tongue.*

Native; in damp pastures, and on grassy roadsides, common.

G. In fields under Ashley Hill, and near the Duchess Ponds, Stapleton. Filton Meads. Haw Wood, and Blaise Castle Wood; *Herb. Powell.* Frome Glen; *Swete, Fl.*, 98. Very abundant in meadows between Henbury and Compton Greenfield, 1886. Stoke Gifford. Thornbury.

S. Roman encampment, Leigh Wood. Grassy bank by the side of a road near the Abbot's Pond. Brislington. Failand. Abundant in fields between the Bridgewater road and Dundry Hill. On the hill at Kewstoke. Fields at Breach Hill, near Chew Stoke; and at Compton Martin. Orchards at Winscombe. Pastures near Wells. Yatton. Frequent about Bath; *Fl. Bathon.* V. VI

LYCOPODIACEÆ.

LYCOPODIUM, *Linn.*

980. **L. clavatum,** *L.* *Common Club Moss.*
   Native. Among long grass in open ground, on a hill near Clevedon. Stated in the *Phytologist* to have been abundant towards the beginning of the century. In fair quantity, 1885.

981. **L. Selago,** *L.* *Fir Club Moss.*
   Native; with the last species, very sparingly. Discovered by Mr. Mason in 1884. The plant is fairly common in the west of the county.

CHARACEÆ.

CHARA, *Linn.*

982. **C. flexilis,** *L.*
   S. In the canal at Bath; *Fl. Bathon.*

983. **C. fœtida,** *A. Br.*
   G. Syston; *Dr. Hassé.* Eastfield.

984. **C. hispida,** *L.*
   S. Walton-in-Gordano; *Kew Herbarium.* In th canal at Bath; *Fl. Bathon.*

985. **C. aspera,** *W.*
   S. Ditches near Portbury. Clevedon. Yatton.

986. **C. vulgaris,** *L.* var. *longibracteata.*
   S. Pool between Bedminster and Whitchurch, 1882.

The Characeæ have not received a fair measure of attention.